FOREWORD

ACKNOWLEDGEMENTS

The series of books published by *Equipment for Disabled People* provides authoritative information on the range of equipment available for people with special needs. It comprises thirteen titles each one dealing with a specific area of disability, and all the equipment included has been assessed by professional staff with the help of disabled people.

The books are of interest to disabled people, their helpers and to those professionally concerned with their care. They give guidance on the selection of equipment and advice on overcoming problems but it is recommended that in most cases people seek professional help before making a final selection. The exclusion of a particular item does not necessarily imply that it is unsatisfactory, just that space has limited the number of similar examples of one type of equipment.

Once a piece of equipment has been selected potential purchasers are advised to check for any design changes, its availability and the current price with the manufacturer, because although these facts are correct when the book goes to press, they can change without warning.

The books are revised in rotation and new titles are added occasionally. Publication of a new edition is announced in professional journals, newsletters of voluntary organisations and through the extensive mailing list maintained by *Equipment for Disabled People*.

We are indebted to all the disabled people who cooperated with us in the evaluation of the equipment.

We acknowledge with thanks the help given by the Nursing Staff of Mary Marlborough Lodge, Nuffield Orthopaedic Centre and of Ritchie Russell House, Churchill Hospital, Oxford, together with the Community Occupational Therapy Department at the Slade Hospital, Oxford, and all the contributions from the following: Mrs S Martin and Ms A Finbow, Mary Marlborough Lodge; Ms J Leydon and Ms D Gilliland, Ritchie Russell House; Mrs M Gunn and Ms A Corbett, Churchill Hospital; Ms A Summers, Department of Neuroscience and Rehabilitation, Radcliffe Infirmary, Oxford; Ms M Smith, Stoke Mandeville Hospital, Aylesbury and Mr J Abbey, Department of Planning and Property Services, Oxford.

We also acknowledge with thanks information from the Disabled Living Foundation used in selecting the items of equipment for inclusion in the book.

SECOND EDITION   1990

HOISTS AND LIFTS

Author/Compiler: A.K. Wilson BSc

Editors: G.M. Cochrane MA, FRCP
A.K. Wilson BSc

Researcher: R.H. Houghton BSc Eng, PGDip

Equipment for Disabled People

Mary Marlborough Lodge
Nuffield Orthopaedic Centre
Oxford OX3 7LD

Orders for titles in this series, shown on the back cover,
and for binders to hold the books, should be sent to:
Equipment for Disabled People
Mary Marlborough Lodge
Nuffield Orthopaedic Centre
Headington
Oxford OX3 7LD
Telephone: Oxford (0865) 750103

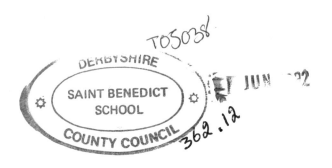
Disclaimer
The Oxfordshire Health Authority and the Department of
Health do not warrant the adequacy or efficiency of any of
the equipment featured in this publication.
  Prices were approximate at the time of going to press.
Addresses are given at the back of the book and purchasers
should check prices and availability before ordering.

Published by the Oxfordshire Health Authority,
Nuffield Orthopaedic Centre, Oxford OX3 7LD.
Typeset by Equipment for Disabled People, Mary
Marlborough Lodge, Oxford.
Printed in England by Cotswold Press Limited, Oxford.

CONTENTS

INTRODUCTION

Elderly and disabled people too weak or disordered in their movements to change their position in bed or transfer safely between two surfaces need assistance many times each day. In helping them their carers put their own health at risk in bearing heavy loads, often in positions which are mechanically inefficient, for example, reaching across a bed, lifting from the bath or into a car and turning in confined spaces. Accidental injuries to the cervical and lumbar spine are common - 40,000 nurses annually sustain back injuries and 750,000 nursing days are lost each year. (Finlay P.A. (1988)).

It is necessary for nurses and everyone who attends disabled people to practise correct lifting and handling techniques. In this way the person being helped is always comfortable, reassured and protected from injury and the carers provide the help that is required without harm to themselves. For speed and simplicity most of us choose to lift manually, because a hoist takes space, is not always at hand and positioning the slings takes a lot longer than putting ones arms around the person. This book reminds readers of the techniques; the methods have to become an unvarying practise. Success lies not so much in the programme of training but in the unvarying insistence on the application of what has been taught. The cost of injuries in personal discomfort, absence and throwing additional work on colleagues through incorrect lifting are obvious.

If a disabled person can stand with assistance, it is easier to transfer between bed, chair and lavatory perhaps with the help of a high chair, stout furniture or a turntable; this is clearly better than using a hoist. Those who are strong enough in their arms may learn to transfer without the help of others, using a sliding board if necessary. Those who are too heavy for their carers to lift and are completely dependent, need some form of hoist.

In selecting a hoist there are six determinants - patient, attendant, task, environment, equipment and cost. Making the right choice is crucial and before a decision is made careful consideration must be given to the person's health, the course of the disease, its likely outcome, and functional abilities now and those expected in the future. The amount of help that is available and the circumstances at home must be known. Many hoists, which are supplied with good intentions but without understanding the disabled person and his circumstances, remain unused and stored out of the way. When equipment is rejected the problem remains unsolved, money and effort have been wasted and someone else who might have benefited may go without. To be of real practical help a hoist must be fully accepted and the choice be founded on practical trial. Training should be given where the hoist is going to be used and continued until there is proven ability to position the slings and operate the mechanism. Besides being involved with the supply, installation and instruction in use of the hoist, the prescriber must go back every few months to ensure that the equipment is satisfactory and being well used.

Often a mobile hoist is provided by the health authorities through the community nursing services and the nursing aids store. In principle it can be supplied on loan without delay and returned to the store when the person no longer needs it. Lifts and fixed hoists may be supplied by the Social Services Department and part of the cost met by an Environmental Health Grant. A representative of the Social Services Department should be consulted before a decision is made. Whenever an Environmental Health Grant or the Social Services Department are involved in the supply and installation of equipment a community occupational therapist must be involved in making the decision.

Prices

Price guides are included to give a rough indication at the time of compilation. VAT, where applicable, has not been included. Some firms which supply to the public directly include carriage in their prices: unless this is appreciated comparison of different suppliers' prices may be inaccurate. Current details, availability, price and VAT should be checked with suppliers at the time of purchase.

Value Added Tax

Certain specialised goods and services that are for the domestic or personal use of a chronically sick or disabled person can be zero-rated. Those supplied to a charity can also be zero-rated if they are made available to chronically sick or disabled people. Goods include specialised beds, sanitary devices, lifts and hoists, and other equipment designed solely for use by a disabled person.

Services which can be zero-rated include constructing ramps or widening doors or passages to facilitate entry to or movement within a person's home and providing, extending or adapting a bathroom, washroom or WC in a person's home where this is necessary because of his condition.

Goods and services can only be zero-rated if the supplier is registered for VAT and if the person signs a declaration that he is chronically sick or disabled.

A form of declaration is usually provided by the supplier or it may be incorporated into an order form. Examples of declaration forms suitable for use by an individual or charity are given in the VAT leaflet 701/7/86: *Aids for handicapped persons* obtainable from local VAT offices.

The completed declaration should be kept by the supplier for inspection by Customs and Excise.

Help and advice can be sought from any local VAT office (see local telephone directory under Customs and Excise).

Safety of goods - *Consumer Protection Act 1987*

The Consumer Protection Act 1987 imposes strict or absolute liability upon a producer of goods for injury or damage which is suffered as a result of a defective product. People injured by defective products may have the right to sue for damages; product liability is the term given to laws affecting those rights. The injured person does not need to prove negligence. A customer can already sue a supplier without proof of negligence under the sale of goods law. The Act provides the same rights to anyone injured by a defective product, whether or not the product was sold to them. The Act does not affect any existing civil laws governing product liability. No liability is imposed under the Act in respect of products first supplied before 1 March 1988.

The general safety requirement means that since 1 October 1987 it is a criminal offence to supply unsafe consumer goods in the United Kingdom.
The Act provides that:
"a person should be guilty of an offence if he supplies consumer goods which are not reasonably safe having regard to all the circumstances"
These circumstances include
"the manner in which the goods are marketed and any instruction or warnings given with the goods
any published safety standards for those goods, the means, if any, and the cost of making the goods safer"
The general safety requirement applies to anyone who supplies the goods. It is restricted to consumer goods although not all are covered, e.g. growing crops, water, food, motor vehicles, controlled drugs.

The general safety requirement does not apply to the sale of secondhand goods.

The general safety requirement is closely linked to standards. Goods which meet an approved standard will satisfy the general safety requirement in respect of hazards covered by that standard. For any other hazards outside the scope of the approved standard the goods must be reasonably safe having regard to all the circumstances.

It is a criminal offence to give consumers misleading price indications about goods, services, accommodation or facilities. The *Code of Practice for traders on price indications* gives guidance about which practices are misleading.

Enforcement of the *Consumer Protection Act 1987* is the responsibility of local Trading Standards Officers. They may be contacted through the Trading Standards Department - see under Council in the local phone book.

Reference

Department of Trade and Industry (1988) *Guide to the Consumer Protection Act 1987. Product liability and safety provision.* DTI.
Department of Trade and Industry (1988) *Code of Practice for traders on price indications.* DTI.

Notes concerning electrical safety

Most types of electrical equipment offered for sale must comply with the *Electrical Equipment (Safety) Regulations 1975* and its amendments. These regulations are enforced by the Trading Standards Department of the Local Authority. Intending purchasers should check with the retailer that the equipment also complies with the appropriate British Standard.
Equipment which has been tested and approved by the British Electrotechnical Board carries the BEAB mark which indicates that the design complies with the appropriate British Standard.

Information

Information on aids and equipment is available from many sources. The Information Service of the Disabled Living Foundation issues to subscribers bi-monthly information lists and is prepared to answer enquiries on any non-medical matter affecting disabled people. Similar services are provided by Disability Scotland and by the Northern Ireland Council on Disability and the Wales Council for the Disabled.
The Disabled Living Centres (see below) also provide information.

Disablement Information and Advice Line (DIAL) is a countrywide network developed by volunteer disabled people for disabled people and others who require advice on any non-medical aspect of disability. Each group is autonomous and develops its own operational policy. Telephone numbers may be found in local phone books or obtained from DIAL UK.

Disabled Living Centres

Disabled Living Centres, where a selection of aids for disabled people can be seen and tried out, have been set up in Belfast, Birmingham, Caerphilly, Cardiff, Edinburgh, Exeter, Leeds, Leicester, Liverpool, London, Manchester, Newcastle Upon Tyne, Nottingham, Southampton, Stockport and Swindon. Centres offering a limited service are at Aberdeen, Aylesbury, Blackpool, Bodelwyddan,

Braintree, Colchester, Dudley, Huddersfield, Hull, Inverness, Macclesfield, Middlesbrough, Newcastle-under-Lyme, Paisley, Portsmouth, Swansea and Welwyn Garden City. Information is available to those professionally concerned with disabled people and their relatives and friends. An appointment is usually necessary. Visitors should always contact the Centre before visiting to check that the purpose of the visit can be fulfilled as the Centres vary in size, content and the type of services offered. There is a Mobile Centre organised by Disability Scotland. Addresses of the Disabled Living Centres are on page 130 and also available from the Disabled Living Centres Council.

REMAP

REMAP (Technical Equipment for Disabled People) is part of RADAR (Royal Association for Disability and Rehabilitation) and is a voluntary organisation having more than eighty branches across the country which specialise in designing, making and supplying an aid to satisfy the particular need of the disabled person.

Information about the nearest Panel may be obtained from the National Organiser, REMAP.

Disability Rights Handbook

The Handbook is intended to be an all-purpose rights guide for people with disabilities and their families. Sections include information on Income support, the Social fund, Housing, Community charge, Unemployment, Sickness and Invalidity benefits, Care needs, Mobility problems, Special compensation schemes, Children and young people, Practical help at home, Housing matters, Residential accommodation, Retirement, Money matters, Appeals and information and an extensive list of useful organisations is also given. The Handbook is revised annually and published in April. Three Disability Rights Bulletins to update it are issued during the year. The publications are obtainable from the Disability Alliance ERA. 15th edition. (1990) Price £4.

Directory for Disabled People

This is a comprehensive handbook of information and opportunities for disabled and handicapped people. Compiled by Ann Darnbrough and Derek Kinrade it covers the fields of statutory services, benefits and allowances, equipment and its availability, housing, education, employment, mobility, holidays, sports and leisure, sex and personal relationships, legislation affecting disabled

people, contact and tape organisations, information, legal and advisory services, helpful organisations. Two appendices contain further information on relevant government reports and the addresses of publishers and stockists mentioned in the text.

It is published in association with the Royal Association for Disability and Rehabilitation by Woodhead-Faulkner Ltd, Cambridge. 5th edition (1988) Price £17.50.

LIFTING AND HANDLING

Lifting and handling are part of the normal routine for nurses and carers.

Numerous surveys in hospitals over the last ten years have shown that this activity causes a high incidence of back pain which may lead to severe spinal injury. Figures quoted by Canterbury and Thanet Health Authority (1983) estimate that each year one nurse in six will suffer severe back injury. In addition a survey by the University of Surrey (1983) showed that 764,000 working days per annum were lost by nurses in the UK due to back pain.

In view of these facts it is very important that nurses and carers should understand the principles of lifting and be taught the correct techniques to avoid the risk of serious back injury. Refresher courses should be held regularly to encourage them to continue using the correct techniques.

Points to consider

✳ Lifting should not be carried out unnecessarily. The helper should consider how much a person can do for himself and show him how to be as independent as possible.

✳ The manual lift needs to be planned, the number of helpers decided, the use of aids such as belts and slings considered and the whole procedure explained to the person. There must be adequate space to allow the helpers to maintain the correct posture while carrying out the lift and any hazards such as mats should be removed. The lift should be carried out on an agreed signal between the helpers and the person to be lifted as it is essential to maintain good rhythm and timing.

✳ Two publications provide good clear information on lifting techniques and will be of value to those involved with moving people.

The booklet *Are you at risk?* concentrates on different manual methods of moving patients in bed and transferring, for example between bed and chair, using simple equipment such as lifting blocks or slings.

The handling of patients - A guide for nurses explores a greater range of lifting and transfer techniques, including the use of hoists.

Both publications are well illustrated and easy to follow with written guidance to complement the diagrams.

✳ If the person is too heavy or awkward to lift, or if the helper is unable to lift, a hoist will be necessary. It must be acceptable to the person and his family if it is to be used at home, and they should be involved in the discussions. The type of hoist, make and style of slings will be decided after practical trials.

References

1. Daws J. & Wright B. (1983) *Are you at risk? A guide to lifting techniques.* Canterbury & Thanet Health Authority. (Obtainable from Mrs J V Daws (see *Addresses*). Booklet: single copies 70p, discount for bulk orders. Poster: sold in multiples of 25, £5. Cheque, made payable to Canterbury & Thanet Health Authority, should be sent with order)

2. Lloyd P., Tarling C., Troup J.D.G. & Wright B. (1987) *The handling of patients: A guide for nurses.* 2nd ed. Back Pain Association in collaboration with Royal College of Nursing. pp64.

Grips and lifts

The following are some examples of the most common grips and lifts used by nurses.

Grips

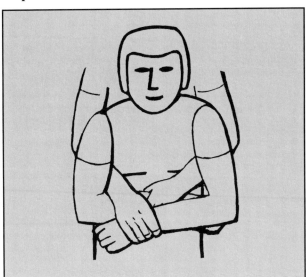

Through-arm wrist crossed-over grip

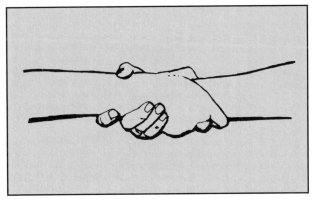

Wrist grip

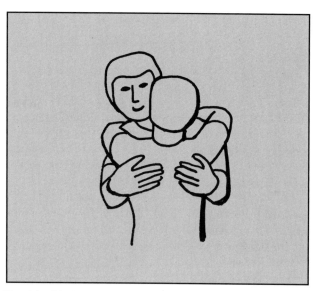

Shoulder-blade grip

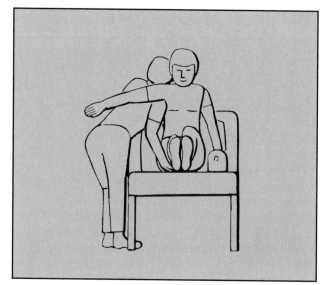

Partly assisted with block. Helper on weak side

Lifts

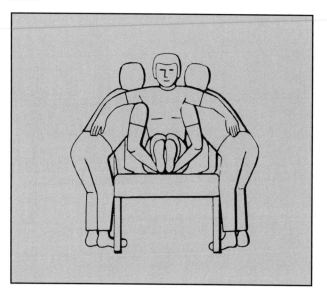

Shoulder lift

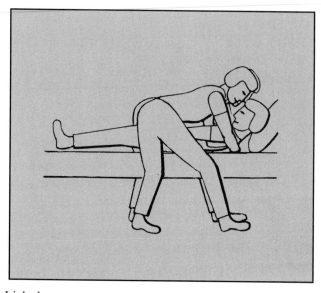

Linked arm support

Reproduced by kind permission of the authors from:
Pelosi T. and Gleeson M. (1989) *Illustrated Transfer Techniques for Disabled People* . Churchill Livingstone, London. UK. pp 180.

Additional references can be found on page 129.

Lifting aids

❏ **JARVIS MARY ROSE SLING**

This is a cheap, simple yet effective aid to lifting, suitable for use with the Australian and Through Arm lifts.

Made of nylon canvas, the sling is available in two sizes and is easy to wipe clean.

Size   small 380 x 155mm
        large 500 x 155mm

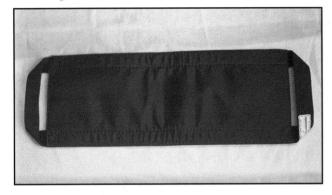

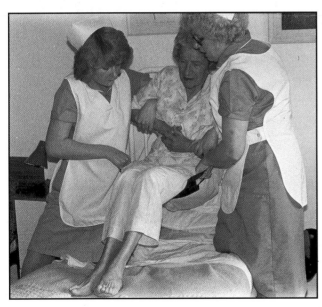

Obtainable from Jarvis Manufacturing Co
Price guide small £7, large £7
Export available

❏ **MEDESIGN PATIENT HANDLING SLING**

This sling can be used to lift a person up the bed or make a transfer from bed to chair.

It is made of thick, moulded plastic. The outer surface is slippery while the inner surface, which is in contact with the person, is textured. The handgrips have rounded edges and non-slip surfaces that are comfortable to hold. The sling is placed under the person's thighs when using the Shoulder lift, the Cross-arm lift and Through-arm lift. Instead of the orthodox method of lifting by two people when they lock their hands behind the person's back and under his thighs, the sling may be used, enabling the helpers to keep their backs straight when lifting and carrying out assisted standing transfers.

Positioning and removing the sling is easy. It does not slip during use but the patient should avoid wearing clothes of slippery material.

Clear, concise instructions are printed on the sling. The sling is simple but effective, quick to use and can be kept ready near the patient.

Size 510 x 200mm
Lifting capacity 200kg

Obtainable from MEDesign Ltd
Price guide £10
Export available

❏ **SPORTAG SLING SLS 508**

This band sling can be used in the home as well as in hospital, but guidance should be given by the therapist on the correct way to use it.

It is suitable for making transfers between chairs, bed to chair, chair to toilet etc.

The sling is made from woven nylon material with a polyurethane coating which stops it from fraying. It is fully waterproof, almost friction free, and can easily be wiped clean.

Size 600 x 190mm

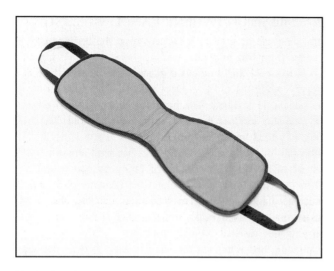

Obtainable from Agility Sports
Price guide £9
Export available

❑ ONWARD TRANSFER BELT

This grey nylon webbing belt can be used on its own or in conjunction with the Onward Transfer board as an aid to manual lifting.

It is soft and easy to fit and fastens with a black plastic clip buckle. It is adjustable to suit people of all sizes.
Size 1524mm x 50mm

Obtainable from Pear Associates Ltd
Price guide £5
Export available

❑ DUFFIELD PATIENT LIFT BELT AID04 AND LEG SLING AID05

The belt and sling are suitable for use with frail or elderly people and those with trunk weakness or poor balance.

The belt is made from a double layer of strong canvas fastened by Velcro and has two plastic-covered metal handles. The leg sling is made from a double layer of padded canvas, with double-stitched, strong nylon rope handles at either end.

The belt is positioned round the waist and the sling placed under the thighs when lifting a patient up the bed or during assisted transfers. The belt may be used by one attendant alone in standing transfers or to provide additional support for walking, but it is difficult to maintain the correct lifting position, support the patient's knees and lift the patient securely as the belt tended to slip and the handles dig in. The leg sling is too long for the handles to be used and is most effective when the wrist is passed through the handle or by holding the actual sling.

The belt and sling are cleaned by wiping with a damp cloth or scrubbing with soap using a soft brush.
Written instructions for use are supplied by the manufacturer.
Sizes
Belt   1480 x 115mm
Sling   620 x 120mm
Lifting capacity   115kg

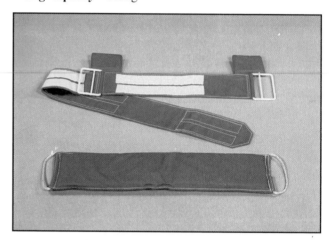

Obtainable from Chattanooga UK Ltd
Price guide Lift belt £22, Leg sling £13
Export available

❑ DUFFIELD PATIENT ROLL SHEET AID02

This large sheet is made from strong, durable, man-made fibre sail cloth with nylon loop handles and nylon webbing extensions. It is designed to turn unconscious patients and others who require carefully controlled, frequent turning, for lifting very heavy patients up the bed, making transfers from bed to trolley or for picking up patients from the floor after a fall.

The sheet is positioned under the supine patient by rolling him from side to side in a similar way to changing a draw sheet. Holding the sheet by the handles the patient is pulled to the opposite side of the bed and rolled on to his side. Nursing the patient on a sheepskin-lined sheet (extra) would reduce handling further.

The sheet can be wiped with a mild bactericidal agent or hand-washed in a detergent solution. It can be washed repeatedly in a domestic washing machine but is unsuitable for laundering in a hospital laundry.

Written instructions for use are supplied.
Size 1760 x 1020mm
Lifting capacity 152kg

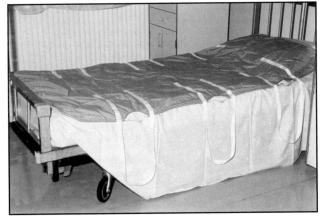

Obtainable from Chattanooga UK Ltd
Price guide £39
Export available

❏ ST ANDREWS MINI-LIFT SHEET AID03

The mini-lift sheet is made from strong, durable, man-made fibre sail cloth with double-stitched nylon loop handles and cross-bracing. Its main purpose is to replace the draw sheet when lifting a patient up the bed. It is unsuitable for those with poor head and trunk control or uncertain balance. The minisheet is positioned under the seated patient by rolling him from side to side in the same way that a draw sheet is changed. The sheet is held by the two lifters and the patient is slid up the bed without friction on his skin.

The sheet can be cleaned by wiping with a mild bactericidal agent or handwashed in a detergent solution. It will withstand repeated washing in a domestic washing machine but must not be laundered in a hospital laundry.

Nurses reported that using the sheet placed more strain on their arms than conventional lifting and that it was difficult to get sufficiently close to lift the patient. Patients tended to slip down the bed during the removal of the sheet and needed repositioning. A sheepskin-lined sheet on which the patient could be nursed might be more useful.
Size 870 x 870mm
Lifting capacity 115kg

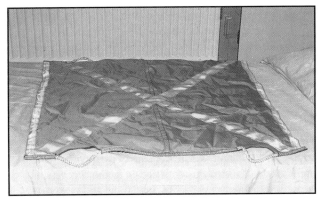

Obtainable from Chattanooga UK Ltd
Price guide £27
Export available

❏ SPORTAG LIFT SHEET SLS 506

This small lifting sheet can be used in the home as well as in hospital, but guidance should be given by the therapist on the correct way to use it.

It is suitable for moving a person up a bed, for use in a draw sheet lift or for the transfer of a more dependent patient.

The sheet is made from woven nylon material with a polyurethane coating which stops it from fraying. It is fully waterproof, almost friction free, and can be easily wiped clean.
Size 1000 x 750mm

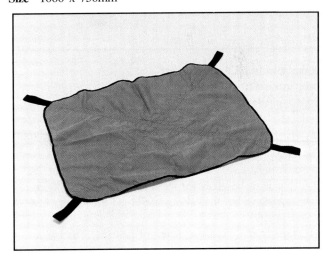

Obtainable from Agility Sports
Price guide £12
Export available

❏   SPORTAG LIFT SHEET SLS 507

This large lifting sheet can be used in the home as well as in hospital, but guidance should be given by the therapist on the correct way to use it.

It is suitable for lifting a more dependent person who needs turning regularly, for lifting a person off the floor or making a bed to trolley transfer where the equipment involved is the same height.

The sheet is made from woven nylon material with a polyurethane coating which stops it from fraying. Three safety straps are sewn to the sheet to secure the person during transfer and hand loops for lifting are located at each end and in the centre of the sheet. It is fully waterproof, almost friction free, and can be easily wiped clean.

Size   1800 x 600mm

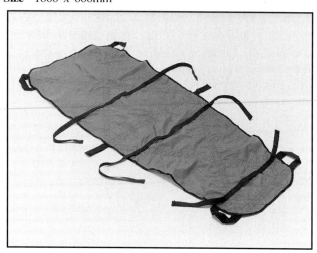

Obtainable from Agility Sports
Price guide £22
Export available

❏   EASYSLIDE

The Easyslide is designed to transfer people between two approximately level surfaces without the need to lift. Its main use is in hospitals for the transfer of patients from beds to trolleys but it is also a useful aid for turning bed-bound people.

It consists of a double cylinder of material. The inside cylinder is quilted with a low-friction fibre filling and the outer skin is made of low-friction fabric.

In use the person is rolled onto one side using a drawsheet. The Easyslide is placed beneath the drawsheet and the person is rolled back onto it and then slid across from one surface to the other without being lifted or dragged across the surface. The removable outer cover can be autoclaved and the quilted inside can be washed and tumble dried.

Size   2000 x 500mm

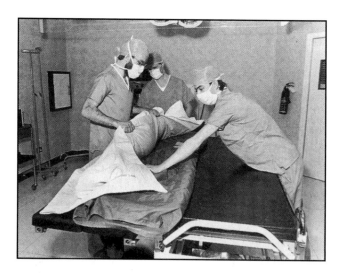

Obtainable from J Nesbit Evans & Co Ltd
Price guide £180-190
Export available

❏   ROTAPRONE

The Rotaprone is a simple aid to turning and positioning a patient in bed. It is moulded from heavy duty fibreglass with a low friction surface and looped webbing handles at either end. For conventional turning of a bed-bound patient the Rotaprone reduces the risk of skin damage from being dragged across a drawsheet.

The patient is rolled over on one side and the Rotaprone is placed behind and under his body. He is then rolled back and while he holds the webbing handle the attendant moves to the other side of the bed and pulls the Rotaprone towards her so turning the patient through 90°. This naturally turns the patient to his other side. The Rotaprone can now be gently eased out from underneath the patient.

Some people, particularly those who are rather bony, may find the device hard and uncomfortable. Easy removal of the device after turning is only possible if the patient's bedwear is dry and moves smoothly over the fibreglass surface. A towel or nursing fleece placed between the patient and the device will make it more comfortable and assist removal. It is easily cleaned but is rather unwieldy to store.

Size   560 x 380 x 560mm

The following sequence of diagrams illustrates the Rotaprone in use.

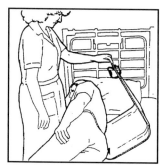 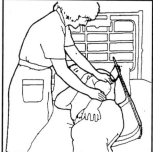

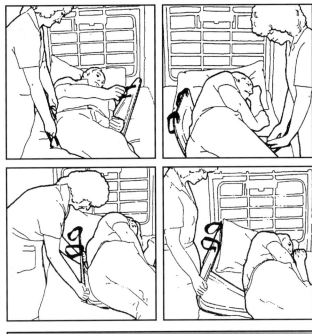

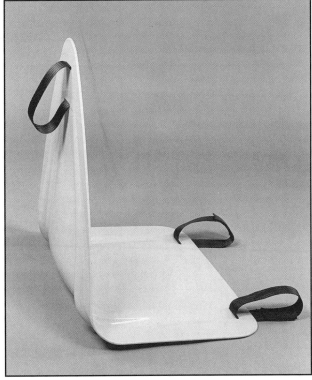

❑ BED ROPE LADDER

The ladder consists of four 25mm plastic rungs, 200mm wide and fitted on nylon cords 170mm apart .

The far end of the ladder is secured to the legs at the bottom of the bed and the other end is anchored to the strut of the headboard by a single piece of string. By moving his hands up the rungs of the ladder a person can gradually pull up into a sitting position and ease back up the bed.
Overall length 2150mm

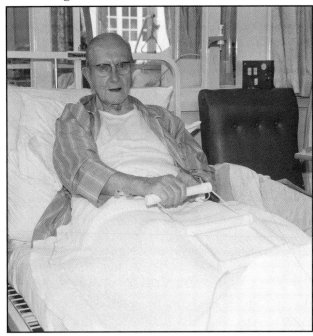

Obtainable from
Homecraft Supplies Ltd
  Price guide £3
Nottingham Rehab Ltd
  Price guide £3
Export available

Obtainable from Pear Associates
Price guide £105
Export available

Moving independently in bed

A rope ladder is a useful device to help a person pull up from a lying to a sitting position.

A lifting pole is another device used by a person to change position in bed. Several examples are given on pages 9-12.

Moving up and down the bed

Hand blocks held in each hand provide a firm base when pressed on the mattress and enable a person with strong arms to lift himself up and down the bed independently in hospital and at home. The blocks may be of particular assistance to lower limb amputees.

❑ DUFFIELD LIFTING BLOCKS

These lightweight but stable blocks have plywood ends with 25mm dowling handgrips. Because of their height the user requires considerable strength and shoulder mobility. They are unsuitable for a person with arthritis.
Handle height 140mm

Obtainable from Chattanooga UK Ltd
Price guide £24
Export available

❏   MEDESIGN PATIENTS' HAND BLOCKS

The resin blocks, lightweight but stable, offer a
comfortable grip and the height of the handles is
convenient for most users.
Handle height 115mm

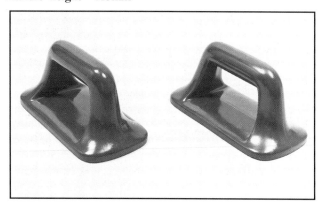

Obtainable from MEDesign Ltd
Price guide £20 per pair
Export available

Turning in bed

In some situations strategically placed grab rails fixed to
the wall can help a person to turn independently in bed.
(See *Equipment for Disabled People, Personal Care* 6th
edition 1990.)

Lifting the legs into bed

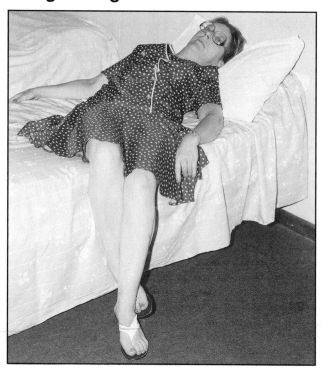

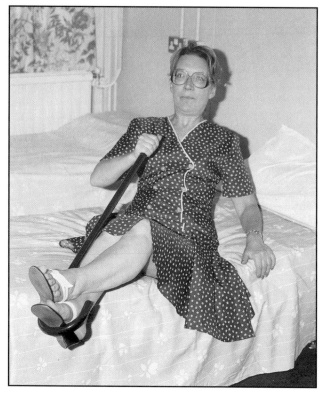

When only one leg is weak the unaffected leg can be
placed under the weak leg as a means of lifting it on to the
bed.

The crook of a walking stick can be used to lift a weak
leg on to the bed or a simple piece of equipment such as
the Nottingham Leg Lifter may be purchased (see page 9).

It may be easier to lift the legs in two stages: first to lift them on to a chair placed beside the bed and then to lift them from the chair to the bed.

A foot sling attached to a rope running over a pulley suspended from a fixed point can be used to lift paralysed legs into bed.

❑   **NOTTINGHAM LEG LIFTER**

The Leg Lifter is a simple piece of equipment designed to help people who have difficulty lifting their legs into bed, onto a footrest or into a car.

It is made of stiff, but bendable, steel wire with a cotton webbing cover and a loop at each end. One loop bent to fit the person's foot, is used for lifting the leg, the other loop, made of cotton webbing, forms a handle which slips over the user's wrist.

The webbing cover is loose. It is not easy to align and place the loop over the foot for lifting.

Length of lifter   900mm

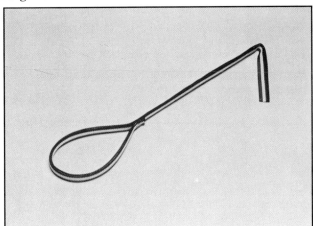

Obtainable from Nottingham Rehab Ltd
Price guide £9
Export available

Lifting poles

Points to consider

*   A fixed or free-standing lifting pole may help a person to move up and down the bed or to swing across from chair to bed.

*   Those with painful hands may prefer to use a wrist grip on the handle while those with high spinal lesions may hold by the crook of the elbow.

*   Lifting poles are available as optional extras for attachment to most hospital beds.

*   A free-standing lifting pole can be used with a divan or other bed at home. It *must* be stable and should not tip

when the user's weight is taken on the handle.

❑   **IMPROVED PATIENT HELPER C705**

This heavy, robust lifting pole is made from square section steel with a brown and cream epoxy-coated finish. The base is fitted with two rear castors and two anti-slip rubber feet at the front. An adjustable bed clamp is easily fitted on to a divan bed head up to 45mm thick to give extra stability. The triangular plastic handle is only large enough for use with one hand or arm, and the ridges at each end may cause some discomfort. Some users may find the handle slippery and the diameter too small. The height of the handle is easily altered by adjusting the height of the chain.

Stability   Although the base is rather narrow it is stable when attached securely to the bed.

Storage   The mast is easily unbolted from the base for storage.

Dimensions

Overall height	1810mm
Base width	470mm
Base length	650mm
Handle width	130mm
Handle diameter	22mm

Range of height of handle from floor   880-1500mm

Obtainable from Carters (J&A) Ltd
Price guide £150
Export available

❏   MASTERPEACE ANC004

This free-standing lightweight lifting pole is made of
tubular steel, painted cream, and comprises a mast which
slots into an extended base. The triangular plastic handle is
attached to the mast by an unnecessarily complicated
system of nylon straps, and care needs to be taken when
altering the strap length to ensure that it is secure.

Stability   The handle can be put into two positions on the
boom and is most stable nearer the mast.

Storage   The mast is detached from the base for storage.

Dimensions

Overall height   1850mm
Base width   690mm
Base length   680mm
Handle width   230mm
Handle diameter   20mm
Range of height of handle from floor   1270-1440mm

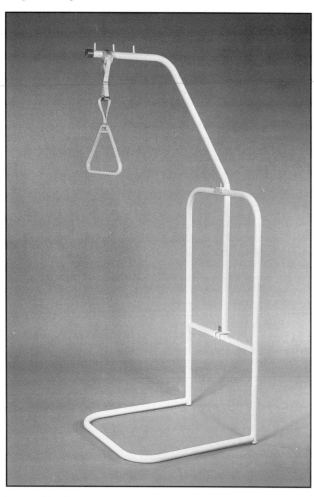

Obtainable from Masterpeace Products Ltd
Price guide £56
Export available

❏   PORTLIFT

The brown finished epoxy-coated steel lifting pole is light
and easy to move. The plastic handle is designed to be
comfortable and is ridged to give a good grip. It is
suspended from the pole by a webbing strap and is easily
adjusted with a buckle. The handle and strap can be hung
out of the way on top of the pole during nursing
procedures.

Stability   Suitable for lightweight use, but wobbles and is
unsteady with a heavy load.

Storage   The Portlift is easily slotted together and packs
flat for storage.

Dimensions

Overall height   1930mm
Base width   670mm
Base length   750mm
Handle width   230mm
Handle diameter   25mm
Range of height of handle from floor   1060-1340mm

Obtainable from Llewellyn-SML Health Care Services
Price guide £60
Export available

❑   SUPER PORTLIFT

This is similar to the Llewellyn Portlift but has a larger base and so is more stable. The base is finished with four rubber feet.

Stability   The handle can be suspended from several positions along the pole but is most stable in the middle.

Storage   The mast is detached and the whole packs flat for storage.

Dimensions

Overall height	2050mm
Base width	885mm
Base length	880mm
Handle width	230mm
Handle diameter	25mm
Range of height of handle from floor	950-1430mm

Obtainable from Llewellyn-SML Health Care Services
Price guide £61
Export available

❑   PULLMAN 411

This lifting pole is made of brown PVC-coated square section steel. A comfortable triangular handle is attached to the mast by nylon straps.

Stability   The swan-neck design of the mast flexes under a load and the base is only stable on a flat floor.

Storage   The mast is in two sections which slot together but when evaluated the top half was difficult to remove. The whole mast is bolted to the base and this is easily dismantled for storage.

Dimensions

Overall height	1830mm
Base width	630mm
Base length	800mm
Handle width	200mm
Handle diameter	22mm
Range of height of handle from floor	1280-1475mm

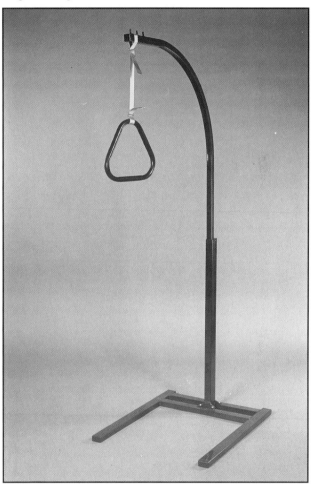

Obtainable from Roma Medical Aids Ltd
Price guide £57
Export available

The Manufacturer states that although the mast was difficult to dismantle when evaluated, they have noted this fact and it is being rectified.

❑   SPENCER CALDERDALE BEDLIFT

A lightweight free-standing lifting pole is made of tubular steel and painted cream. The ridged plastic handle is suspended from the mast by a webbing strap which is adjusted by means of a buckle. The mast slots into the frame and is easily removed or can be swung to one side during nursing procedures.

Stability The mast deflects under a load. The handle is more stable when positioned further back on the boom.
Storage The mast is easily removed from the base but it does not pack flat for storage.
Dimensions
Overall height   1910mm
Base width   690mm
Base length   690mm
Base height   50mm
Handle width   230mm
Handle diameter   25mm
Range of height of handle from floor   1050-1380mm

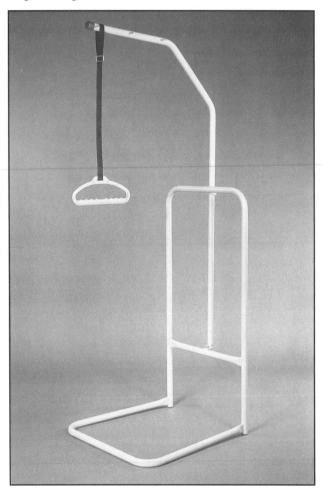

Obtainable from James Spencer & Co Ltd
Price guide £51
Export available

❑   WAINWRIGHT BEDLIFT

The heavy base gives good stability to this lifting pole which is made from square section steel with a grey epoxy powder-coated finish. The plastic handle is suspended by nylon webbing straps and the height is easily adjusted by a buckle. The handle is shaped to fit the fingers and is comfortable to use; it can be hung out of the way on top of the pole during nursing procedures.
Stability Stable on a level floor.

Storage The mast is bolted to the base and is simply dismantled using a spanner.
Dimensions
Overall height   1900mm
Base width   610mm
Base length   800mm
Base height   65mm
Handle width   230mm
Handle diameter   25mm
Range of height of handle from floor   1020-1350mm

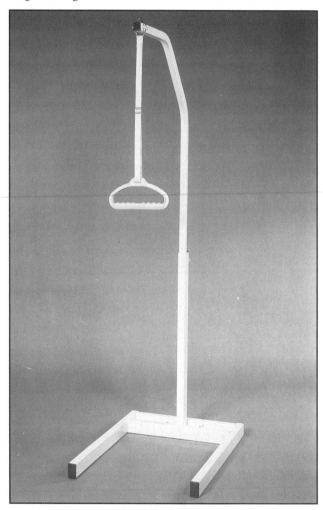

Obtainable from James Spencer & Co Ltd
Price guide £78
Export available

Free-standing over-bed hoist

❑   MEDECI HOPPER

The Medeci Hopper is a static hoist with limited use, but it has the advantage of taking up less space than a mobile hoist and costing less than an overhead track system. It is ideal for someone only requiring help in transferring between bed and chair.

   Made from 60mm box section steel, it stands permanently

behind the bed with the solid cross-shaped base out of the way under the bed. The base has adjustable feet to achieve stability on uneven floors.

This hoist is unsuitable for independent use since, although the lifting action is powered, the boom has to be swung round manually. The boom is long and the spreader bar is heavy and could be a hazard during a transfer. The spreader bar is suspended from the boom by nylon webbing which passes down the boom and mast to a spool on the motor. The hoist is used with a standard quick-fit-style sling and the attachment hooks are well made.

Hoisting action Smooth and controlled.

Power supply It is powered by a 12v electric motor which has a battery back-up permanently charged by the mains. This has sufficient power to make approximately five lifts in the event of a power failure.

Controls The hoist is operated by a hand-held pendant control box.

Dimensions

Hoist Height	2130mm
Boom projection	800mm
Range of lift	1300mm
Base length	1180mm
Width of cross bar	1600mm

Lifting capacity 114kg

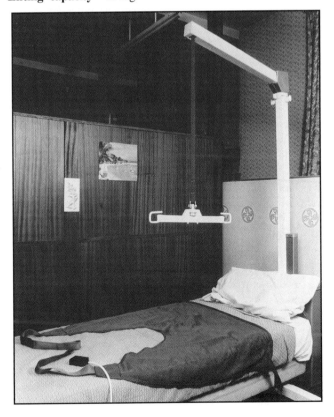

Obtainable from Medeci Rehab Ltd
Price £695
Export available

TRANSFER TECHNIQUES

'Transfer' is a term to describe the method used by a person to move from one surface to another, i.e. between bed, chair, wheelchair, bath, WC or car.

Points to consider

✳ A transfer can be made independently or with assistance from a helper and may or may not involve the use of equipment. The ability to transfer may determine the quality of life a person can enjoy.

✳ People can be taught to transfer in different ways depending on their functional abilities and their will to make what is often a considerable physical effort.

✳ A transfer is easier if the person can stand and take one or two steps. The installation of appropriate grab rails may help in some situations.

✳ The particular transfer techniques taught will depend on the relative positions of bed, chair, toilet, bath etc and the equipment used by the person, i.e. walking aid or wheelchair.

✳ The use of a hoist should be considered if the person needs total lifting, and is heavy and awkward to lift.

Critical factors

✳ The surfaces of each piece of furniture or equipment involved in a transfer must be the same height. The optimum height for an individual is determined by practical trials.

✳ The furniture or equipment must be in the best relative positions.

✳ The furniture and equipment must be stable and stationary.

✳ The person must be able to transfer across the gap between the two surfaces.

✳ The form and texture of the surfaces may assist or impede the transfer.

Bed transfers

Points to consider

✻ For some, the optimum height of the bed is when the feet just touch the floor as the person sits on the side of the bed. For others, the bed needs to be higher so that the buttocks rest on the edge of the bed when the person is standing. If the bed is too high its legs can be cut with a saw. If the bed is too low it can be raised by fitting blocks of the required height or by mounting on a Dexion frame.

✻ The position of the bed may be critical for ease of access. Placed against a wall, it can provide stable assistance to a person when getting in or out. Braking castors, if fitted, should be 'on' for extra stability during transfers.

✻ A firm mattress with a board underneath makes movement easier when transferring. The board can be made of 20mm block board, chipboard or seven-ply, or a series of planks edge to edge spanning the full width of the bed under the mattress from pillow to ankles.

✻ Nylon sheets may make movements easier because there is less friction.

✻ Sideways transfer is the usual method for a non-ambulant wheelchair user; a transfer board can be used to bridge the gap between wheelchair and bed. Some may transfer obliquely. A bilateral lower limb amputee with sufficient strength in his arms may be able to position his wheelchair at right angles to the bed and transfer forwards on to it. The arm rests are left in position but the footrests would normally be swung to either side out of the way.

✻ Use of a turning disc may be helpful if the person can stand for short periods.

✻ For some people a stand-up bed may provide the only means of independent transfer from a lying to a standing position.

Chair transfers

Points to consider

✻ The optimum height of a chair seat for an ambulant disabled or elderly person is usually 450-500mm with armrests at a height to support the arms comfortably, and extending forwards to assist when rising.

✻ A wooden raising unit (obtainable from Langham Products Ltd) can be fitted under the feet of an existing chair to lift it to the required height.

✻ A lifting seat unit or a manually or electrically-operated rising chair may be helpful to some who have difficulty in rising from a sitting position.

NOTE: High seat and rising chairs are shown in *Equipment for the Disabled: Housing and furniture* 5th edition, 1986.

Wheelchair transfers

Points to consider

✻ The brakes should be firmly 'on' during any wheelchair transfer.

✻ Wheelchair armrests must be detachable for transferring sideways.

✻ The type (hard-based or soft) and height of a wheelchair cushion are assessed for the user's comfort and ability to carry out transfers and other activities.

✻ A hard-based firm cushion covered with a slippery material is the easiest surface to slide on, but may be uncomfortable for those who are thin or unsuitable for those who lack sensation.

✻ A soft cushion impedes movement but will not affect the transfer provided the person has adequate strength in his arms to lift himself up and move across.

✻ Rear propelling wheels permit sideways transfers though very large wheels (600mm) may impede this movement.

✻ Front propelling wheels are not suitable if the person transfers sideways.

✻ Swinging detachable footrests lessen the risk of injury to the ankles and feet and are preferable to fixed footrests.

✻ Footrests must be adequately maintained so that they detach easily.

Bath transfers

Points to consider

✻ A bath board fitted across the back of the bath is useful for a person who has difficulty stepping over the side of the bath. The user sits on the end of the board with his feet on the floor, moves backwards along the board, lifts his legs over the side of the bath and turns to sit in the middle of the board. A wheelchair user can transfer sideways on to the board. Sometimes an extension bath board may be needed which is adjustable in height at one end. This enables the user to transfer on to the seat outside the bath and slide across. The wheelchair arm and footrest nearest the bath must be detached to make this transfer.

✳   A board can be used with a bath seat. A person with strong arms can lower himself from the board to the seat and then down to the bottom of the bath. The procedure is reversed to get out. For details of bath boards and bath seats see *Equipment for Disabled People: Personal care* 6th edition, 1990.

✳   A horizontal rail fitted on the wall beside the bath may be needed for support by an unsteady person.

✳   A non-slip mat should always be used in the bottom of the bath.

✳   A portable bath lift may be suitable for a person who has difficulty getting in and out of the bath but can manage other transfers.

✳   A person who cannot transfer independently will require hoisting. For details of bathroom hoists and portable bath lifts see section on Bathroom hoists p49.

WC transfers

Points to consider

✳   The height of a WC seat can be altered by fitting a raised seat of the required height. This can be easily removed so that the WC can be used by others (see *Raised WC seats* in *Equipment for Disabled People: Personal care* 6th edition, 1990.

✳   Sideways transfer is the usual method of moving between wheelchair and WC but it requires more space than is usually available.

✳   More space behind the WC pedestal will be needed if the help of an attendant is needed for personal cleansing.

✳   Where space is limited a forward transfer is sometimes possible and the person sits facing the wrong way on the WC.

✳   Occasionally backward transfer is used but this requires a special wheelchair canvas.

✳   A cantilever (wall-hung) WC allows easy access for transfer to and from a wheelchair.

✳   Horizontal or vertical handrails positioned to suit the

individual can be fitted for use with a raised seat or to aid transfers (see *Grab rails* in *Equipment for Disabled People, Personal Care* 6th edition, 1990).

✳   A combined raised WC seat with support rails may assist a person who needs help to get on and off the WC (see *Personal Care: Combined WC seats with support rails)*. NOTE: This type of aid is suitable for ambulant users and those who transfer obliquely from a wheelchair but is unsuitable for a wheelchair user who transfers sideways.

✳   The WC can be raised permanently by fitting it on a block to give the required height, but this requires structural and plumbing alterations and is a costly procedure.

Car transfers

Points to consider

✳   A rotating car seat or a swivelling sliding seat may be useful for an ambulant person who has difficulty getting in and out of the front seat of a car.

✳   An independent wheelchair user may find a transfer board (about 760mm long) helpful to bridge the gap between wheelchair and car seat.

✳   An electric wheelchair which fits into the car in place of the driving seat, or a pushchair which replaces the front passenger seat is available (see *Equipment for the Disabled: Wheelchairs* 6th edition, 1988).

✳   A severely disabled wheelchair passenger may need hoisting into the car. A mobile hoist may be suitable for some but for frequent use a car hoist fitted to the car roof will be more practical. (See chapter *Car Hoists* p80).

✳   A tail lift can be fitted to a van to lift a person in a wheelchair into the vehicle.

NOTE: Aids to car transfer are shown in *Equipment for the Disabled: Outdoor transport* 6th edition, 1987.

Transfer boards

A transfer board is useful in bridging the gap between two surfaces during sideways transfer, particularly if the user cannot support the weight of his body on his arms. The length of the board is determined by the gap it must bridge: a longer board is usually necessary for car transfers, a short board is most suitable for wheelchair to bed transfers. Sprinkling talcum powder on the board makes the surface more slippery. Care should be taken during transfer to avoid damaging the skin which might lead to a break in the surface and to a persistent sore.

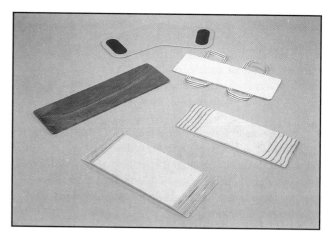

Table 1. Summary of various transfer boards available

Manufacturer	Construction	Size	Price	Comments
Onward transfer board				
Pear Associates	Fibreglass	730 x 250 x 8mm	£32	Angled-shaped with rubber pads on one side to prevent slipping. Bright yellow.
Butt board				
Butt Board	Formica laminated plywood	610 x 200 x 10mm	£30	Four nylon webbing handles incorporated in the board.
Chailey transfer board				
Rehabilitation Engineering Unit, Chailey Heritage	Polyurethane-coated birch face plywood	Various sizes available	£15 standard £20-140 special	Individual boards made for specific requirements (Not illustrated)
Transfer board				
Unit Installations	Polyurethane-coated birch face plywood	650 x 255 x 18mm	£10	Ends taper smoothly for easy transfer. May break if dropped because so thin.
Transfer board L98				
Homecraft Supplies Ltd	Polyurethane-coated birch face plywood	610 x 210 x 15mm	£9.10	Gradually tapered ends. Well finished board.
Transfer board MLP/128				
Langham Products	Stained basic plywood	755 x 222 x 12mm	£7.50	Ends not tapered. A very basic board.

Details of board ends

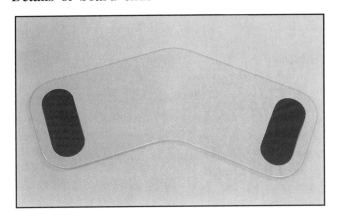

Onward Transfer Board

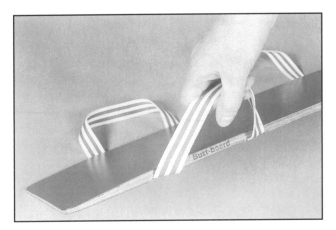

Butt Board

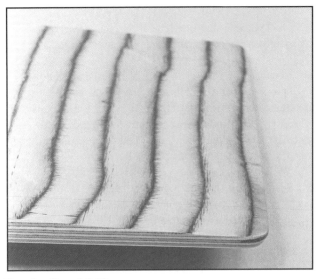

Transfer Board L98

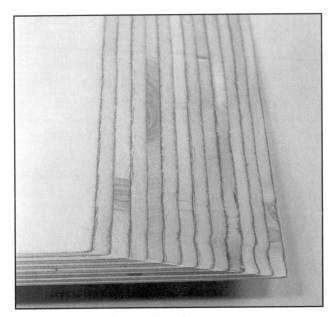

Unit Installations Transfer Board

Transfer Board MLP/128

Turn discs

Points to consider

A turn disc is used to rotate a person during an assisted standing transfer.

* A disc consists of two round plates, rotating one on the other with anti-slip outer surfaces. Some discs are identical on both sides and can be placed either way up, others have different surfaces and can only be placed one way up.

* Discs vary in diameter: check that the size chosen is sufficiently large to accommodate the user's feet.

* Heights of discs vary: a high disc may tip if the user's weight is not evenly distributed. The height also determines the ease of picking up the disc: a higher disc is easier to grasp, it is difficult to push the fingers under one which lies flat on the floor. Some discs have a lip or handle which aids picking up and carrying.

* Discs vary in weight: a heavier disc may be more secure but picking up, carrying and the frequency of use should be taken into account.

* Some discs may need to be taken apart occasionally for cleaning.

* To use, the disc is placed on the floor while the person is seated and he is then helped to stand on the disc. The helper holds the person in a 'bear hug' and shuffles round turning the person at the same time until he is correctly positioned for lowering to sitting (see diagram below). Then the disc is removed.

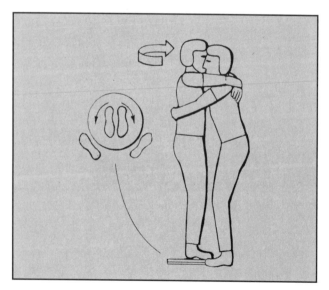

Reproduced by kind permission of the authors from:
Pelosi T. and Gleeson M. (1989) *Illustrated Transfer Techniques for Disabled People* . Churchill Livingstone, London. UK. pp 180.

❑   DERWENT GYRO TRANSFER DISC Z1442

The round plastic-coated metal base has eight small rubber pads, which hold it securely on different floor surfaces, and an upper surface of slip-resistant rubber. The disc is light and because the top plate is slightly larger than the lower, it is easily lifted and carried.

Diameter   340mm
Height from floor   30mm
Weight   2kg
Safe working load   127kg
Turning Movement is smooth and turning is easily controlled by the helper.
Instructions for use Not supplied.
Maintenance The disc can be dismantled for occasional cleaning by unscrewing a nut.

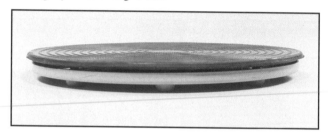

Obtainable from Nottingham Rehab Ltd
Price guide £40
Export available

❑   HEALTH AND COMFORT TURN DISC

The disc is constructed from two flat round nylon-coated steel plates which are pinned in the middle and slide over each other with no lubrication. Some people find it difficult to pick up because it is thin and close to the ground.

Diameter   355mm
Height from floor   10mm
Weight   4kg
Safe working load   150kg
Turning Movement is smooth and controlled.
Instructions for use Supplied by the manufacturer.
Maintenance Since the disc cannot be unscrewed any grit getting in between the plates can be removed by pulling soft string between them.

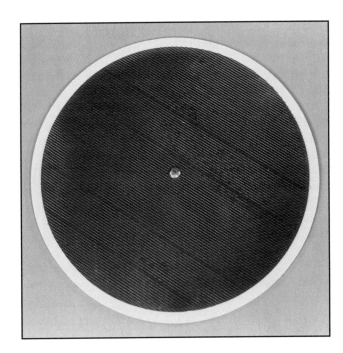

Obtainable from Health and Comfort Ltd
Price guide £30
Export available

☐ ORTHOTURN TURNTABLE

The disc is constructed from two round flat plastic discs
rotating on each other and separated by a non-stick surface.
The disc is light but hard to pick up because it is so thin
and close to the floor.

Diameter   380mm
Height from floor   12mm
Weight   1.36kg

Turning Movement is stiff but the helper did not find it
difficult to turn.

Instructions for use Not supplied.

Maintenance Any grit getting between the discs is not
easy to remove as the discs cannot be unscrewed.

Obtainable from Homecraft Supplies Ltd
Price guide £42
Export available

Other equipment to assist transfer

☐ EGERTON STAND UP BED MARK 2

This bed will help some people who have difficulty in
moving from a horizontal to a vertical position and for
various reasons wish to be independent.

The bed is three feet wide with a detachable footboard
which supports the user as the bed moves from horizontal
to vertical positions. The bed is powered by a small electric
motor and mounted on four 180mm diameter castors which
are braked. The mattress is secured to the base by tapes and
hooks. Detachable hand supports, which can be adjusted in
height, are fitted as standard. The manufacturer
recommends a duvet as the best bedding.

Controls Either a rocker switch operated by the user and
released at any time to stop the bed at a tilt or remote
controls operated by a helper.

Optional extras Soft latex foam rubber mattress,
washable mattress cover, back rest, tubular side rails,
lifting pole, retaining straps and a head down tilt
attachment.

Dimensions

Length   2130mm
Width   970mm
Height to top of mattress platform   690mm

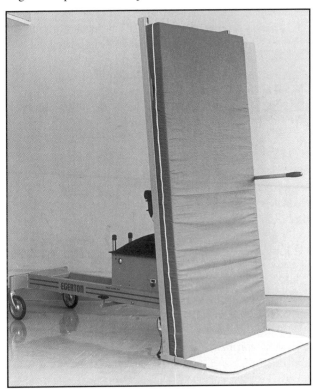

Obtainable from Egerton Hospital Equipment Ltd
Price guide £1430
Export available

ASSESSMENT FOR A HOIST

Several types of hoists are available to transfer those people who need full lifting to effect a transfer.

1 Mobile hoists - hydraulic/manually-operated
                 - electric
2 Overhead electric hoists
3 Bath hoists   - mobile
                  - fixed
                  - electric
4 Swimming pool hoists
5 Car hoists

Points to consider

* It is essential to consider first if the person can be taught to transfer independently, or if this can be achieved with minimal help or simple changes, such as rearrangement of the furniture in the room or the provision of a different type of wheelchair. If independent transfer is impossible, the use of a hoist should be considered.

* Assessment is usually carried out in the home by a community occupational therapist or, where there is very severe disability, the person may be referred to a specialist unit.

* A comprehensive assessment must be made of the illness; its expected course and response to treatment, the abilities and desires of the person and carers, the personal support which is available and the layout of the home.

* It must be established if there is a competent helper available to operate the hoist and cope with correct sling routine, or if it is necessary and possible for the person to operate it himself; if there is adequate space to manoeuvre a mobile hoist, particularly in the bathroom and round the WC; if there is adequate storage space for it; whether the building is suitable for the installation of an overhead track if an electric hoist is under consideration; if the local authority is able to supply the recommended equipment and how the installation can be financed.

* The disabled person and his family should be involved in the discussions and the hoist must be acceptable to them and prove itself to be of real practical value in the person's daily life. If it is not fully accepted it will be unused and the original problem will remain unsolved with unnecessary expense incurred.

* The type of hoist chosen will be influenced by the patient's needs and domestic arrangements.

* The availability of grants from local authorities and other sources to help with the basic cost and installation should be discussed with the disabled person. Mobile hoists with spreader bar and slings range from about £400 to £2000 depending on size and type.

Costs of electric hoists with spreader bar, slings, trolley, track and installation range from about £1600 upwards, excluding the cost of structural alterations.

* Before purchase practical trials are essential to select the most suitable type of hoist and sling techniques for the individual.

* The helper must be trained so that he or she is confident and capable of using the hoist and slings correctly and safely.

* Instructions for use and maintenance which the user may be required to carry out must be supplied. Servicing routines, usually arranged by the supplying authority, should be explained.

* A few weeks after a hoist has been supplied a further visit should be made by the prescriber to ensure that it satisfies the person's needs and is being used correctly.

* An overhead hoist which can be used independently may justify the high cost in cases where it is difficult to obtain help.

MOBILE HOISTS

British Standard specification

BS 5827: 1979 Specification for mobile, manually operated patient-lifting devices

Points to consider

∗ Different transfer techniques should be explored before a hoist is considered.

∗ The use of a hoist must be acceptable to the person and his family.

∗ The rooms, passages and doorways must provide sufficient space for manoeuvring and turning the hoist and there must be unimpeded level access in the areas where the hoist will be used.

∗ Adequate space will be needed at the front or side of the WC to accommodate the length of the hoist.

∗ The base of the hoist should be adjustable to fit round or under a chair.

∗ If the base of the hoist is too high to fit under the bath a section of the bath panel should be cut out to accept it.

∗ The base of the bed must be high enough to allow the legs of the hoist to move freely underneath.

∗ If the hoist is to be used in carpeted areas, it should be tried there to ensure that it manoeuvres smoothly.

∗ A helper will be needed who is strong enough to push and manoeuvre the hoist and is capable of managing the slings.

∗ If a hoist is used to lift a person out of bed, the one chosen should have an adequate range of lift to raise the person clear of the bed.

∗ Adequate space will be needed to store the hoist when it is not in use.

Types and features

∗ Large, rigid hoists are suitable for use in hospitals and residential homes where there is space to manoeuvre and store them. Smaller hoists, which require less room are available for use in private houses where space is restricted.

∗ Most hoists have an adjustable width base. This will determine whether the hoist will pass through doorways and passages and whether the legs will span or fit under the furniture.

∗ Wheels vary in size. Larger ones will make the hoist easier to push and manoeuvre but require greater clearance under furniture.

∗ Castors will run more freely over a hard, even floor than over a thick pile carpet. If carpet is wanted, castors move better over a dense weave.

∗ The hoisted person will tend to swing in transit if different types of floor surfaces must be negotiated.

∗ Braking castors are fitted to some hoists for stability during transfers. Some are more difficult to release than others and may damage the attendant's shoes.

∗ The range of lift of the hoist should be checked to make sure that the person can be lifted to and from different heights; not all hoists can lift a person from the floor. The purchasers should be shown the method of lifting from the floor.

∗ The lifting mechanism, depending on the model, is operated by a winding handle, hydraulic pump or electric motor.

∗ A hydraulic hoist is raised by pumping a handle and released by opening a valve. Valves with a controlled rate of descent leave the attendant with two hands free to position the person; some valves require fine adjustment during descent and leave only one hand free.

∗ The helper must be trained to manage the slings and operate the hoist correctly.

∗ Arrangements for servicing and repairs should be considered.

∗ Hoists with hydraulic rams should be kept dry to prevent the ram rusting. If stored or transported in the wet the hoist should be lowered completely.

All measurements in following diagrams are in mm.

Small mobile hoists

❑ DEXTRA

This small, compact hoist is suitable for use in the home or hospital for transfers between bed, chair and toilet. It can also be used for lifting a person from the floor.
    The design is unusual. The conventional spreader bar is replaced by a tilting frame which gives the helper more flexibility to position the person accurately.
    The hoist is simple to use. The slings are colour coded for

size with edging braid, and an explanatory key is attached
to the boom. Only Dextra or Maxilift slings can be used
with this hoist. When lifting from a bed or chair the tilting
frame should be wound down and angled so that the short
lifting straps can be attached correctly. Some users may
find the proximity of the tilting frame to the chest and
crotch a little alarming.

Construction The frame is made from epoxy-coated steel
and constructed from three parts, the base, the mast and the
boom. The standard base is unusual because it is "C"
shaped and the access is from the side. It is not adjustable
but an alternative conventional base, the same as used in
the Sara Lift, is available with adjustable legs. The base is
supported by twin-mounted castors 75mm in diameter at
the front and single ones of the same size, at the back. Each
castor has a buffer to save damaging skirting boards etc.

Brakes Effective rocker action brakes, which also stop the
swivel action, are fitted to the rear castors.

Tilting frame This is a four point steel frame which
swivels through 360° round a padded joint on the boom and
can be used to position the person from an upright to a
reclining position. The frame is directed by an integral
control handle.

Controls The hoist is raised and lowered by turning a
winding handle fitted on top of the mast. Some helpers
may find it tiring to wind with their arm raised.

Slings Page 61.

Movement Raising and lowering are slow but smooth.

Access The "C" shaped base will fit round most chairs
with hoisting from the side, and the frame is low enough to
fit under most wheelchair footrests and hospital beds. It
does not always give good access to toilets and if the
Dextra is required mainly for this use then the alternative
base is recommended.

Manoeuvring Fixed push-handles are mounted on the
mast. One of the castors on the back of the base has a flip-
over catch which locks it to stop the swivel action while
pushing in a straight line. The "C" shaped base allows the
hoist to be manipulated through doorways narrower than its
715mm width.

Stability Good.

Storage The mast unbolts from the base for storage and
transport.

Instructions for use Excellent written instructions with
good diagrams are supplied by the manufacturer.

Servicing and maintenance Can be arranged with the
manufacturer.

Optional extras A plastic sling holder for attachment to
the mast. Alternative base.

Dimensions

Total weight	39kg
Max. height of spreader bar	1420mm
Min. height of spreader bar	500mm
Overall range of lift	920mm
Width of closed legs	715mm
Height of base	115mm
Lifting capacity	160kg

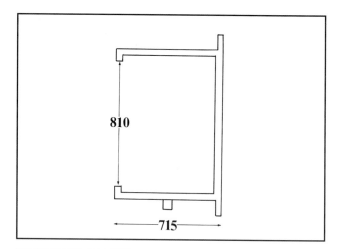

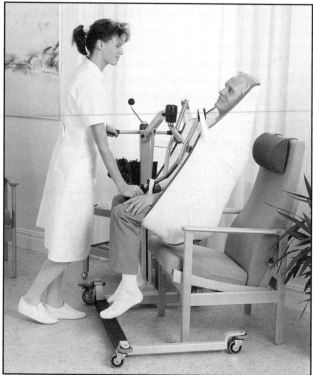

Obtainable from Arjo Mecanaids Ltd
Price guide £1349; with adjustable base £1460
Export available

❑ MECALIFT

This lightweight, compact hoist is most suited for use in
domestic situations where space is very limited. It can also
be used for making transfers to and from a car and lifting a
person from bed.

Construction The frame is made up of three main parts,
the base made of tubular steel, a mast of box section steel
and a boom of tubular steel. The base is supported by two
tandem wheels of 95mm diameter at the front and a single
swivel castor of 100mm diameter at the rear.

Brakes None

Spreader bar Can be turned through 360°. Made from
steel tube, the "coat-hanger"-shaped spreader bar
incorporates a hook at each end and one in the centre for

attachment of the slings. It is quite close to the user during lifting so it is important for the helper to position him either facing sideways or with legs each side of the mast.

Controls The hoist is raised and lowered by turning a winding handle fitted on top of the mast. Some helpers may find it tiring to wind with their arm raised despite the low effort required.

Slings Pages 59-61.

Movement The boom is lifted vertically, not through an arc like most other hoists. Raising and lowering are slow but require little effort. The helper only has one hand free to position a person when lowering. The spreader bar does not rock from side-to-side.

Access The base is fixed so the legs do not spread. The manufacturer suggests a sideways or frontal approach depending on the construction of the chair. The base will fit under most beds. To give some flexibility two different widths are available.

Manoeuvring The hoist is easily manoeuvred once the helper has got used to the rear wheel steering. Fixed push-handles are mounted on the mast, and the hoist is easy to move along the straight. The castors are a good size for use on carpets.

Stability Usually stable but can sometimes be unbalanced. Not as stable as four-wheeled models.

Storage Easily dismantled for storage or transportation.

Assembly Simple. No tools are needed to fit the mast to the base.

Instructions for use Comprehensive written instructions are provided by the manufacturer.

Servicing and maintenance Can be arranged with the manufacturer.

Optional extras Different width bases and a 100mm mast extension for use on higher beds.

Dimensions

Total weight	21kg
Max. height of spreader bar	1430mm
Min. height of spreader bar	630mm
Overall range of lift	800mm
Width of closed legs	690mm
Height of base	110mm
Lifting capacity	127kg

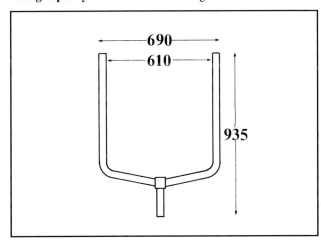

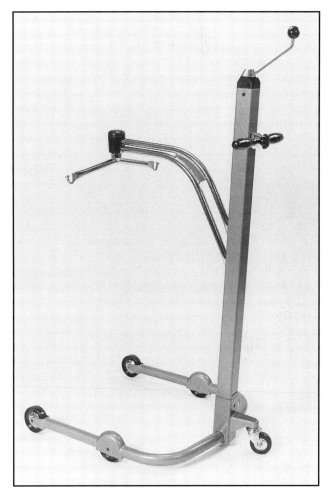

Obtainable from Arjo Mecanaids Ltd
Price guide £580
Export available

❑ CARTERS HOISTS

Carters make a range of five hoists, based on two different size chassis powered by either a hydraulic lift or an electric motor.

For the purposes of this book we have chosen to include the COMPACT C360 below and the ELECTRALIFT C352 (see p33) as representative of the range.

❑ CARTERS COMPACT C 360

This robust and well made hoist is suitable for use in hospitals and residential homes. The manufacturer states that it complies with BS 5827:1979.

Construction The frame is made of box section steel with a white plastic coating. The base is supported by a pair of twin 75mm diameter castors at the front and two single 125mm diameter castors at the back. It can be adjusted to three different positions using a lever at the back of the mast. The boom is angled to allow easy turning of the user at full lift.

Brakes The rear castors are fitted with brakes which are effective and only require a light touch to operate.

Spreader bar Made of steel and padded with plastic it swings front-to-back and swivels round 360°. Two hooks are situated at both ends of the bar which give secure attachment for the slings.

Controls The efficient hydraulic pump is operated by a handle which can be rotated through 180° for use from either side. To lower the boom the pump handle is pushed in against a button at the base of the pump. This is a constant pressure system so one hand will be needed to operate it all the time leaving the helper only one hand free to position the person. This system has the advantage of always being ready to raise as there is no valve to close. Electric models are powered by one or two 12v batteries.

Slings Pages 62-63.

Movement Raising and lowering are smooth. The lowering system is sensitive to load so that it lowers slowly to start with but once the weight is reduced by the person touching a surface, it drops quickly.

Access The base width can be easily adjusted with a lever at the back of the mast. It will span most chairs and fit under a divan bed provided there is clearance of 110mm for the base.

Manoeuvring Fixed, upright push handles are attached to the mast. The large rear castors make the hoist easy to push over carpeted floors.

Stability Stable during transfer and manoeuvring.

Storage The mast lifts from the base for storage and transportation.

Assembly Instructions are supplied.

Instructions for use Supplied by the manufacturer.

Servicing and maintenance A warranty is given for the first twelve months. The manufacturer offers an annual servicing scheme. Hydraulic seals in the pump should be replaced every five years.

Dimensions

Total weight	34kg
Max. height of spreader bar	1660mm
Min. height of spreader bar	670mm
Overall range of lift	990mm
Width of closed legs	600mm
Height of base	110mm
Lifting capacity	127kg

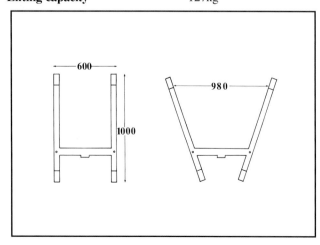

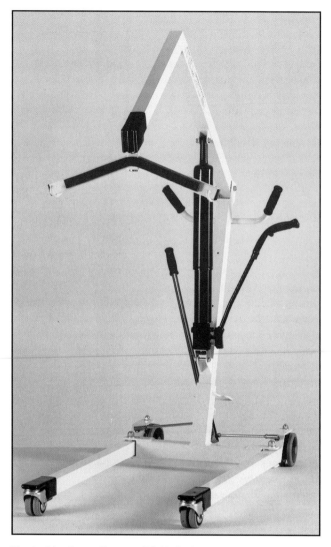

Obtainable from Carters (J&A) Ltd
Price guide £495
Export available

❑ MOBY IMP (RH 501)

This small compact hoist is best suited for use in domestic situations, where space is limited, to transfer people between bed, chair and toilet.

Since the hoist is small, the person is lifted very close to the mast and must be positioned either facing sideways or with legs each side of the mast.

Construction The hoist is made of two main parts, a variable base, mounted on four castors, and an angled mast which supports the spreader bar. The frame is made from light weight box section steel with a cream epoxy finish.

Brakes Flimsy wire brakes, which are difficult to operate, are fitted to the rear castors.

Spreader bar It can be turned through 360° and during moving rocks a little from side to side. The bar is padded to protect the user. Integral hooks at each end provide secure attachment for the slings.

Slings Pages 67-68.

Controls The hydraulic pump is operated by a long handle which can be rotated through 180° for use from either side. The hoist is lowered by turning a release valve which is easy to control. The pump and all potentially sharp parts are covered with moulded plastic.

Movement Raising and lowering are smooth, although the person may need steadying as the spreader bar sometimes swings a little from side to side.

Access The arms of the base are opened and closed by a telescopic lever at the back of the base. It will span any wheelchair and fit under a divan bed or bath provided there is clearance of 110mm. When set in the down position the lever locks the base in the unopened position.

Manoeuvring Two handles for manoeuvring the hoist are fixed half way up the mast and a straight wheel is mounted centrally on the base to help keep the hoist moving in a straight line. It is easy to steer round furniture.

Stability Stable under load.

Storage The mast lifts easily out of the base for storage.

Assembly Simple.

Instructions for use Written instructions supplied by the manufacturer.

Servicing and maintenance 12 months guarantee.

Dimensions

Total weight	27kg
Max. height of spreader bar	1588mm
Min. height of spreader bar	445mm
Overall range of lift	1143mm
Width of closed legs	610mm
Lifting capacity	127kg

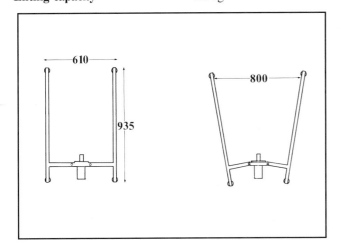

Obtainable from Llewellyn-SML Health Care Services
Price guide £360
Export available

❑ MOBY MINOR

This hoist is very similar to the Moby Imp but has a taller mast and a different base. It is more robust than the Imp and so is suitable for use in nursing homes as well as domestic situations, to make transfers between bed, chair, wheelchair and toilet. It has a greater range of lift than the Moby Imp. When fully raised the user is lifted very close to the mast, and must be positioned either facing sideways or with legs each side of the mast.

Construction The mast and base are made from cream coated box section steel. The base has parallel opening legs which are operated smoothly by using a telescopic lever on the back of the base.

Brakes Flimsy wire brakes, which are difficult to operate, are fitted to the rear castors.

Spreader bar It can be turned through 360° and during moving rocks a little from side to side. The bar is padded to protect the user. Integral hooks at each end of the bar provide secure attachment for the slings.

Controls The hydraulic pump is operated by a long handle which can be rotated through 180° for use from either side. The hoist is lowered by turning a release valve which is easy to control. The pump and all potentially sharp parts are covered with moulded plastic.

Slings Pages 67-68.

Movement Raising and lowering are smooth, although the person may need steadying as the spreader bar can swing a little from side to side.

Access The legs of the base are opened and closed by a telescopic lever at the back of the base. It will span any wheelchair and fit under a divan bed or bath provided there is clearance of 110mm. When set in the down position the lever locks the base in the unopened position.

Manoeuvring Two handles for manoeuvring the hoist are fixed half way up the mast and a straight wheel with two spindle positions is mounted centrally on the base to help keep the hoist moving in a straight line. This is not entirely successful. The high position is too high to make contact with the floor, and the low position is below the level of the other castors making the hoist rock around the centre wheel.

Stability Stable under load.

Storage The mast lifts easily out of the base for storage.

Assembly Simple.

Instructions for use Written instructions are supplied by the manufacturer.

Servicing and maintenance 12 months guarantee.

Dimensions

Total weight	31kg
Max. height of spreader bar	1715mm
Min. height of spreader bar	572mm
Overall range of lift	1143mm
Width of closed legs	610mm
Lifting capacity	127kg

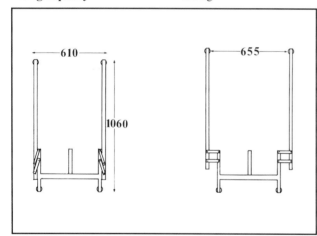

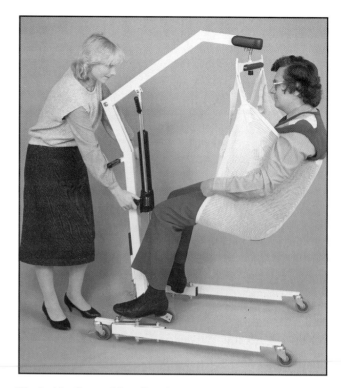

Obtainable from   Llewellyn-SML Health Care Ltd
Price guide £380
Export available

❑   BODYMOVE MAXI

This well made heavy hoist is designed for the transfer of people between bed, chair, toilet and bath in a domestic or hospital situation. It is also suitable for lifting someone off the floor.

The manufacturer states that it conforms to BS 5827:1979.

Construction The frame is made from box section steel finished with a beige nylon coating. It is assembled from three main parts, the base, the angled boom and the mast. The base is adjusted using a lever at the back of the mast.

Brakes Effective "see-saw" action brakes which act on the rear castors and brake their swivel action.

Spreader bar Made from a steel core covered by moulded polyurethane, the spreader bar is 160mm long and has three hooks at either end for attachment of the slings. It swivels through 360° and swings from back to front.

Controls The efficient hydraulic pump is operated by a handle, which can be rotated through 180° for use from either side. The handle can be operated one-handed and is not tiring to use. The hoist is lowered by pushing the pump handle in towards the mast.

Slings Pages 67-68.

Movement Raising and lowering are smooth. The hydraulic pump is sensitive to load so it descends slowly as the person is lowered but when he reaches the surface the load is reduced and the boom descends more quickly.

Access The base width can be easily adjusted with a lever at the back of the mast. It will span most manually propelled wheelchairs and fit under a divan bed, provided that there is clearance of 120mm to accommodate the base.

Manoeuvring Push handles are fixed to the mast. A fifth wheel fitted to the centre of the right arm of the base is available as an optional extra. This makes it easier to steer the hoist in a straight line.

Stability Stable during transfer and manoeuvring.

Storage The mast lifts off the base for storage and transport.

Assembly Simply screws together, (Allen keys provided).

Instructions for use A comprehensive booklet is supplied by the manufacturer.

Servicing and maintenance Regular maintenance of the hydraulic pump, pivots, castors and slings are recommended. Servicing can be arranged by the firm but in the UK only. The hoist is sold with a one year guarantee.

Dimensions

Total weight	40kg
Max. height of spreader bar	1870mm
Min. height of spreader bar	770mm
Overall range of lift	1100mm
Width of closed legs	690mm
Height of base	120mm
Lifting capacity	145kg

Since this photograph was taken the bracket which retains the handle to manoeuvre the lift has been lowered 200mm. This has not altered the operation of the hoist.

Obtainable from J Nesbit Evans & Co Ltd

Price guide	Four castors £398
	Five castors £425

Export available

❑ BODYMOVE MINI

This is a smaller, more compact version of the Bodymove Maxi hoist suited is for use in domestic situations, particularly where space is limited.

The research findings for the two hoists were so similar that only the dimensions for the Bodymove Mini are given here, with reference to the full report on the Bodymove Maxi.

Dimensions

Total weight	39kg
Max. height of spreader bar	1690mm
Min. height of spreader bar	750mm
Overall range of lift	940mm
Width of closed legs	665mm
Height of base	120mm
Lifting capacity	145kg

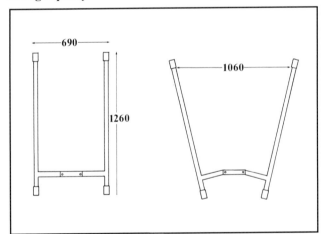

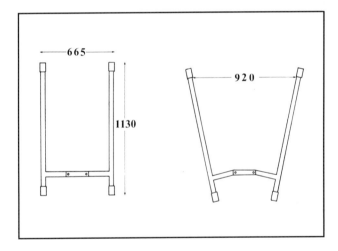

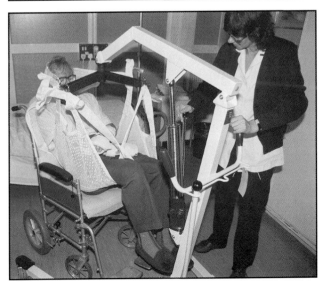

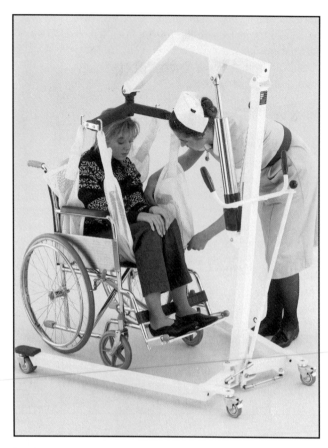

Obtainable from J Nesbit Evans & Co Ltd
Price guide   Four castors £365
                     Five castors £392
Export available

❑ OXFORD 125 MINI

The Oxford 125 Mini is a small and lightweight hoist
suitable for use in a confined space. It can be used for all
transfers including lifting a person from the floor. The
manufacturer state that it conforms to BS 5827:1979.

Construction The frame is made from box section steel
with an off white nylon coating. The base is supported by
twin castors of 75mm diameter at the end of each arm in
front and two single ones of the same size at the back. It is
adjusted using a lever at the back of the mast. The boom
and mast are both angled and the end of the boom is
padded to protect the user.

Brakes Fitted to the rear castors they are easy to operate
but do not brake the swivel action .

Spreader bar This is a straight steel bar padded with
plastic foam. The three hooks attached at each end give
secure points of attachment for the slings. The bar swivels
around 360° in a horizontal plane and swings back to front.

Slings Pages 68-70.

Controls The lifting action is powered by a simple
hydraulic pump with a knob release valve to lower the
boom.

Movement Raising and lowering are smooth.

Access The base width can be altered using a lever at the
back of the mast to span wheelchairs and most armchairs.

Manoeuvring Straight push handles are situated on the
back of the mast. A non-retractable straight line wheel is
mounted on the left arm of the base to aid straight line
running and acts as a pivot wheel when there is weight on
the hoist.

Stability Stable during transfer and manoeuvring.

Storage The mast and boom separate from the base for
storage and transportation.

Assembly Instructions are supplied.

Instructions for use Supplied.

Servicing and maintenance The manufacturer offers an
annual servicing scheme.

Dimensions

Total weight	25kg
Max. height of spreader bar	1610mm
Min. height of spreader bar	420mm
Overall range of lift	1190mm
Width of closed legs	650mm
Height of base	110mm
Lifting capacity	127kg

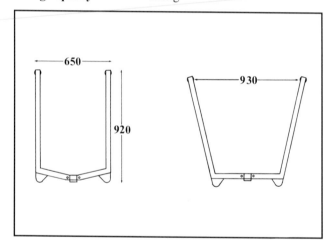

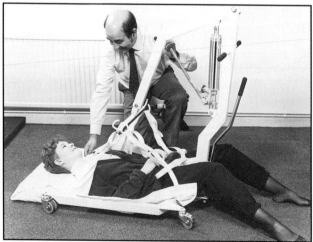

Manufactured by F J Payne (Manufacturing) Ltd
Obtainable from
F J Payne (Manufacturing) Ltd and NOPAC Healthcare
Services Ltd
Price guide £395
Export available

❏ ISIS HOIST

This small hoist is specially designed for use in a confined or limited space.

Construction The chassis is assembled from three main parts, a base, an angled boom and a mast. These are made of good quality white plastic-coated box section steel. The base is easily adjusted using a lever at the back of the mast.

Brakes Effective "see-saw" action brakes which act on the rear castors. They do not brake the swivel action of the castors and can be difficult to release as they tend to swivel under the base of the hoist.

Spreader bar The bar is made from chrome plated steel wire with a triple hook at each end for attachment of the slings. The bar can be turned through 360°.

Controls The efficient hydraulic pump is operated by a handle which can be rotated through 180° for use from either side. The handle can be operated one-handed and is not tiring to use. The hoist is lowered by a release valve which has a graduated control so that it can be released slowly leaving the helper's hands free to position the person.

Slings Pages 68-70.

Movement Raising and lowering is smooth though the person may be lowered too quickly if the valve is opened too far.

Access The base width can be easily adjusted with a lever at the back of the mast. It will span most manually propelled wheelchairs and fit under a divan bed provided there is clearance of 100mm to accommodate the base.

Manoeuvring Push handles are fixed to the mast and the hoist is easy to push in straight lines and manoeuvre in a confined space.

Stability Stable during transfer and manoeuvring. A fifth castor is fitted at the back of the base to prevent the hoist tipping when being pulled backwards.

Storage The mast lifts off the base for storage and transport.

Assembly Simply bolts together.

Instructions for use Supplied by the manufacturer.

Servicing and maintenance Instructions are included in the manufacturer's leaflet. Servicing can be undertaken by the firm. The hoist is sold with a one year guarantee.

Dimensions

Total weight	29kg
Max. height of spreader bar	1490mm
Min. height of spreader bar	615mm
Overall range of lift	875mm
Width of closed legs	635mm
Height of base	110mm
Lifting capacity	127kg

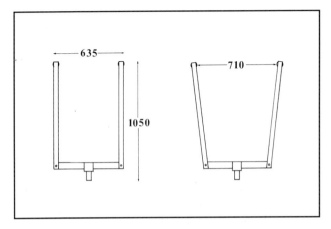

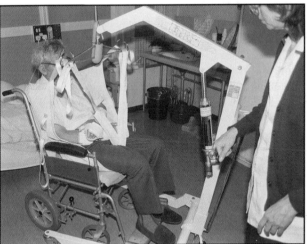

Obtainable from F J Payne (Manufacturing) Ltd
Price guide £382
Export available

Large mobile hoists

❏ AMBULIFT MODEL D

This large heavy duty, but compact hoist is suitable for use in hospitals and residential homes where there is adequate space for manoeuvre. Model D covers all the features of the Ambulift range. Other models with fewer accessories and static bases for floor-fixing in bathrooms are also available. These are listed at the end of this report.

The chair unit can be fitted to the hoist for transfer of a person in and out of the bath. The user is rolled on to the seat while lying on the bed, or alternatively, slings can be fitted to the hoist. A stretcher frame is available to lift those who must remain in a supine position.

Construction The seat unit is easily detached from the hoist unit by releasing a catch. The backrest does not support the lumbar spine and forces the person into a flexed position. The hard, moulded plastic seat has a concave surface, with a pear-shaped aperture, narrow at the front which is an adequate size for washing the perineum.

This can be done easily by raising the person just above the level of the bathwater. The armrests provide all-round security, latch securely in position and can be easily detached or swung back for independent washing.

Brakes Fitted to rear castors, effective, easy to put on and release.

Spreader bar This has hooks at each end for sling attachments.

Controls The hoist is raised and lowered by means of an easily turned handle which can be operated one-handed.

Slings Pages 59-61.

Movement Raising and lowering is smooth.

Access The base width must be adjusted for the work area before hoisting is started: the hoist is tipped on to its side, and the bolts unscrewed and relocated. The hoist fits under a King's Fund bed.

Manoeuvring Easy to push straight but not to manoeuvre in a confined space. The push handles are attached to the turning handle and this does not assist manoeuvring.

Stability The hoist is stable but the seat wobbles during transferring and this may be disconcerting.

Storage Bulky and awkward to store, space is also required for any accessories used.

Accessories Leg extension to support the legs, length 690mm; commode pan and holder which hooks on to the back of the seat; wheeled sub-chassis which slides into tubes beneath the seat and converts the unit into a commode or shower chair (width 450mm, clearance for WC 425mm) - fitting and removing of this sub-chassis must be done from the back and can be awkward.

Optional extras A safety chain which holds the ends of the armrests together.

Assembly Assembled by Arjo Mecanaids

Instructions for use Clear instructions are provided by the manufacturer.

Servicing and maintenance Annually, maintenance instructions provided. A servicing scheme is offered by the manufacturer who recommends monthly inspection checks by hospital engineers.

Dimensions

Overall height (boom fully raised)	1535mm
Length	1065mm
Width adjustable from (see Access above)	680mm
Internal width from	560 to 760mm
Height of base	105mm
Diameter of wheels	75mm
Range of lift	135 - 985mm from ground
Weight	69kg
Lifting capacity	160kg

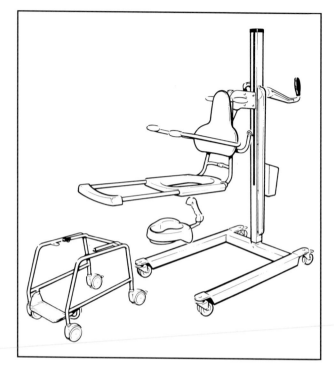

Ambulift Model D

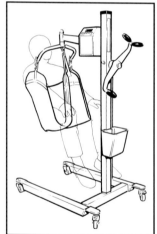

Model C3

Model BME

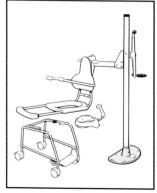

Model BSE

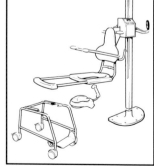

Model BSQ

Obtainable from Arjo Mecanaids Ltd
Price guide   Model D £2240
                   Other models from £1230
Export available

Other models

C3 Mast and boom with sling lifting facility only.
     (Diagrams show version with electronic scale).
BME Mobile bath seat only. End loader.
BSE Static bath seat only. End loader.
BSQ Static bath seat only. Side loader.
Please note All the above are offered complete with the
sub-chassis transporter/commode/shower unit, commode
pan and attachment and a scale is a useful option.

❏ NEW STEEL NURSE PATIENT HOIST HN750

This robustly built hoist is suited for use in hospitals and
nursing homes, but its size makes it unsuitable for use in
most private houses. It has a greater lifting capacity than
any other portable hoist, and is excellent for transferring
very large and heavy people. It is not attractive to look at
and some people may find this disconcerting especially
when using it for the first time.
Construction The heavy duty well made frame is
constructed from white epoxy coated steel. The base is
supported by four 50mm diameter castors, all with a swivel
action, and it is adjusted by winding a handle fitted onto
the mast. As the legs are widened the height of the chassis
is lowered.
Brakes Optional extras. As the hoist is so solid and stable
they are seldom necessary.
Support frame for slings This is a complex structure
which is quite different from the conventional spreader bar.
A single bar is attached to the boom and this supports the
back and head/neck slings. Attached to the centre bottom
of this bar is a three pronged support frame to which is
fixed the leg support and the knee block.
Slings The head and back slings are padded vinyl band
slings. The head support has a strap each side which
contains six eyelet holes to give flexibility for attachment
to the spreader bar. The back sling is fixed to the spreader
bar by two large metal "D" rings. The thigh support, also
made from padded vinyl, is attached permanently to the
support frame at a central point leaving the two ends free.
To fit, these are passed under the user's thighs and attached
to the support arms by two metal "D" rings. The knee
block is mounted on a metal bar which slides in and out of
the support frame. It is fully adjustable and is held in place
by a screw.
Positioning the slings
Fitting to a person in a chair: The thigh support is fitted
first and then the support frame is tilted, by releasing a
handle, to bring the spreader bar close to the person's chest

for attachment of the back and head slings. The person is
then lifted clear of the chair and moved into an upright
position by pressing down on the support frame until it
clicks into position.
   Fitting to a person on a bed: The back sling is placed in
position before the support frame is tilted and lowered into
position over the person who is lying supine. After lifting
clear of the bed the person is swivelled round and moved
into an upright position. Care must be taken as there are no
brakes on the standard model.
Support When lifting, the New Steel Nurse supports a
person's body round the back and under the arms with the
back sling and under the thighs with the leg support. In
addition a neck/head support and a knee block give extra
security. Some people will find that the lifting position puts
strain on the lower back but, although this is not supported,
it would be difficult to fall through.
Toileting and personal cleansing Very good. Clothes can
be easily adjusted with the slings in position. The hoist is
suitable for toileting and personal cleansing in bed.
   All the slings are waterproof, so they can also be used for
bathing.
Controls The hydraulic pump has an easy action with a
knob release valve. Care should be taken to open the
release valve gradually as it is sensitive to small
movements.
Movement Raising and lowering are smooth.
Access The hoist will span most manually-propelled
wheelchairs and fit under a King's Fund bed. It can be used
to lift a person from the floor.
Manoeuvring The pushing handles are fitted too low to
the mast making them awkward to use. The hoist
manoeuvres well on smooth floors but is difficult to push in
a straight line with a heavy passenger.
Stability Stable during transfer and manoeuvring.
Storage The chassis splits into three parts for storage or
transportation: the base unit; the mast, boom and hydraulic
pump and the patient support frame.
Assembly Not difficult but the parts are heavy to handle.
The diagrams supplied by the manufacturer are clear.
Instructions for use Pictorial instructions are supplied by
the manufacturer which are not very clear. Trial before
purchase is strongly recommended.
Servicing A six-monthly maintenance scheme is available
on request.
Optional extras Braked castors, 100mm castors and extra
large slings for heavy weights.
Dimensions

Total weight	49kg
Overall range of lift	1010mm
Width of closed legs	540mm
Height of base	100mm
Lifting capacity	250kg

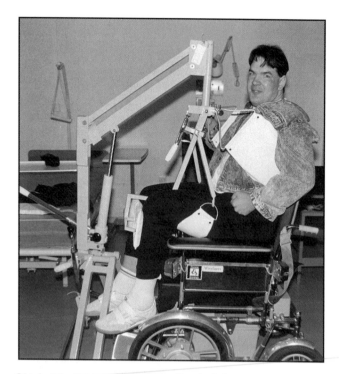

Obtainable from The Holborn Surgical Instrument Co Ltd
Price guide
Standard hydraulic model £1310
Electrified model £2286
Export available

❏   OXFORD HOIST 175 MAJOR

This hoist is suitable for use in hospitals, residential homes
and larger private houses. This new, updated model has a
larger lifting capacity than earlier models and its stepped-
back mast and angled boom allows easy manipulation of
the person even at full lift.

Construction   The hoist is assembled from three main
parts, the base, the angled boom and the stepped-back
mast. These are made of good quality·white plastic coated
box section steel. The base is adjusted easily using a lever
at the back of the mast.

Brakes   Effective "see-saw" action brakes act on the rear
castors. They do not brake the swivel action of the castors.

Spreader bar   This is made from square section steel with
three hooks at each end which provide secure attachment
for the slings. The front and back hooks on each side are
275mm apart. This allows a person to be lifted in a more
reclined position if required, without the use of extra side-
suspenders. The bar is padded in the centre to protect the
user and can be turned through 360°.

Controls   The efficient hydraulic pump is operated by a
handle which can be rotated through 180° for use from
either side. The handle can be operated one-handed and is
not tiring to use. The hoist is lowered by an easily operated
release valve.

Slings   Pages 68-70.

Movement   Raising and lowering are smooth though the

person may be lowered too quickly if the valve is opened
too far.

Access   The base width can be easily adjusted with a lever
at the back of the mast. It will span most manually
propelled wheelchairs and fit under a King's Fund bed. The
hoist can be used to lift a person from the floor.

Manoeuvring   Upright push handles are fixed to the mast
and the hoist is easy to manoeuvre over smooth surfaces.

Stability   Stable during transfer and manoeuvring.

Storage   The mast lifts off the base for storage and
transport.

Assembly   Simply bolts together.

Instructions for use   Supplied by the manufacturer.

Servicing and maintenance   Instructions are included in
the manufacturer's leaflet. Servicing can be undertaken by
the firm. The hoist is sold with a one year guarantee.

Dimensions

Total weight	32kg
Max. height of spreader bar	1765mm
Min. height of spreader bar	635mm
Overall range of lift	1130mm
Width of closed legs	635mm
Height of base	110mm
Lifting capacity	175kg

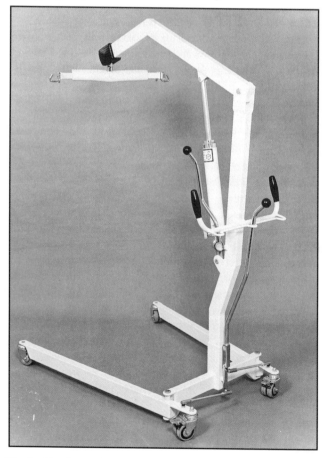

Obtainable from F J Payne (Manufacturing) Ltd
Price guide £475
Export available

Electrically operated mobile hoists

❑ ARJO MAXI LIFT

This hoist is specially designed to give a large range of lift. It is suitable for making transfers between bed and chair or toilet and particularly useful for lifting a person off the floor, or onto a high bed.

The slings used are the same as those for the Dextra hoist but with quilted leg supports. They crease less as the person is lifted but are more difficult to fit to someone in a wheelchair.

Construction The hoist consists of three main parts, a base of similar size to the Sara lift, an electrically powered telescopic mast and the modified tilting frame of the Dextra hoist.

Brakes Fitted to the rear castors.

Tilting frame This has been modified so that the tilting bar is supported by an arched frame. In consequence there is more room between the person being lifted and the frame than in the standard Dextra hoist, which reduces the risk of knocking the user's head against the bar.

Controls The hoist is raised and lowered by an electric motor fixed to the top of the mast and powered by two rechargeable batteries. A wall-mounted charger and a second battery module are supplied so that one unit is permanently charged. The remote control handset is attached to the motor by a lead and hooks on either side of the mast when not in use.

Slings Page 61.

Movement The boom is lifted vertically not through an arc like most other hoists. Raising and lowering are smooth and comfortable and there is an automatic cut-out if the frame meets an obstruction as it lowers.

Access The base legs can be difficult to adjust as they are opened and closed by pushing with a foot. The base will fit under most beds.

Manoeuvring Fixed push-handles are mounted on the mast and the hoist is easy to move along smooth surfaces.

Stability Good.

Storage Mast unbolts from the chassis for storage and transport.

Instructions for use Comprehensive written instructions are provided by the manufacturer.

Servicing and maintenance Can be arranged with the manufacturer.

Dimensions

Total weight	70kg
Max. height of spreader bar	1575mm
Min. height of spreader bar	175mm
Overall range of lift	1400mm
Width of closed legs	680mm
Height of base	115mm
Lifting capacity	160kg

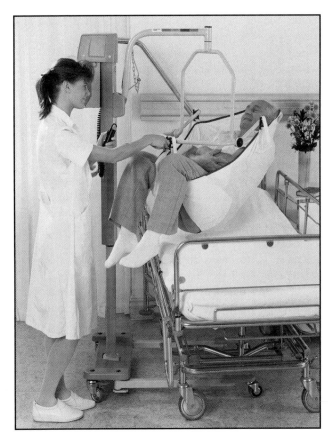

Obtainable from Arjo Mecanaids Ltd
Price guide Including one sling, spare battery unit and charger £2300
Export available

❑ ELECTRALIFT C352 12v

This robust and well made hoist is suitable for use in hospitals and residential homes. The manufacturer states that it complies with BS 5827:1979.

Construction The frame is made of box section steel with a white plastic coating. The base is supported by a pair of twin 75mm diameter castors at the front and two single 125mm diameter castors at the back. It can be adjusted to three different positions using a lever at the back of the mast. The boom is angled to allow more headroom when turning a person at full lift.

Brakes The rear castors are fitted with brakes which are effective and only require a light touch to operate.

Spreader bar Made of steel and padded with plastic it swings front-to-back and swivels around 360°. Two hooks are situated at both ends of the bar which give secure attachment for the slings. (Pages 62-63.)

Controls The lifting is powered by two completely sealed 12v batteries which are supplied with a purpose made electronic battery charger. The batteries are fitted at either side of the mast. Raising and lowering are manually controlled with a coiled cable extending to the batteries. The back of the control box is magnetic so that it may be attached to any point on the frame when not in use.

Movement Raising and lowering are smooth.

Remote control of the lift allows the attendant to stand in the most suitable position for raising or lowering the patient.

Access The base width can be easily adjusted with a lever at the back of the mast. It will span most chairs and fit under a divan bed provided there is clearance of 110mm for the base.

Manoeuvring Fixed, upright push handles are attached to the mast. The large rear castors make the hoist easy to push over carpeted floors.

Stability Stable during transfer and manoeuvring.

Storage The mast and motor unbolt from the base and the wires unplug for storage and transportation. As the batteries are sealed they can be transported by car if necessary.

Assembly Instructions are supplied.

Instructions for use Supplied by the manufacturer.

Servicing and maintenance A warranty is given for the first twelve months. The manufacturer offers an annual servicing scheme.

Dimensions

Total weight	52kg
Max. height of spreader bar	1640mm
Min. height of spreader bar	650mm
Overall range of lift	990mm
Width of closed legs	620mm
Height of base	110mm
Lifting capacity	140kg

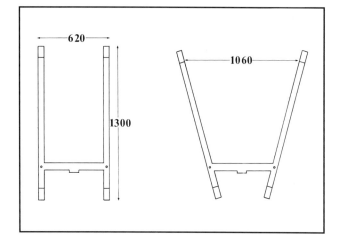

Obtainable from Carters (J&A) Ltd
Price guide £895
Export available

❏ MOLIFT

Molift is a versatile, battery-operated hoist with a low base which enables it to be used under most beds. It is easy to use and handle and can be used to lift a person to and from bed, WC, chair (front or side transfer) and from the floor.

Construction The legs and mast are made from red polyester-coated box section steel and the upper surface of the base has an anti-slip coating. The mast is mounted on a fixed base with parallel legs. It extends telescopically and two main support arms can be fitted to either of the cross bars which are attached to the main mast. The two, well-padded support arms have integral push handles. These slide over the ends of the cross beams and lock firmly when a load is placed on the hoist. There are no positive fixing points and no marking on the cross beams to show that the support arms have been pushed far enough onto the beams. Care must be taken to check this before lifting is undertaken. The U-strap slings are suspended from the support arms by nylon webbing loops.

Brakes Fitted to the rear castors the brakes are easy to apply and release. They prevent the castors from swivelling and stabilize the base during transfer.

Controls A remote hand control allows the attendant to stand in the most convenient place to position the person.

Access The base is not adjustable in width but the hoist will span most wheelchairs or chairs since one leg of the base fits inside the chair and the other outside. The support arms can be positioned on the cross beam to compensate for the off-set legs to ensure the person is lifted up in a good position.

Manoeuvring The hoist is easily directed and the double front castors, although small, are able to negotiate uneven ground and changes in level.

Stability Manoeuvring is smooth as there is no spreader bar or swivel joint to cause swing.

Storage/transport The two cross bars and support arms are detachable and the mast can be folded flat. Having a number of separate components may be inconvenient if the hoist is dismantled frequently as there is the possibility of a piece being mislaid.

Optional extras These include toilet straps, lifting straps, back strap, horizontal strap, knee support, standing platform, flatlifter and rotary support for flatlifter.

Instructions for use A comprehensive set of instructions with diagrams is supplied.

Dimensions

Overall length	1060mm
Overall width	695mm
Height of mast	1250 - 1940mm
Range of lift	680mm
Height of base	80mm
Front castor diameter	50mm
Rear castor diameter	125mm
Lifting capacity	150kg

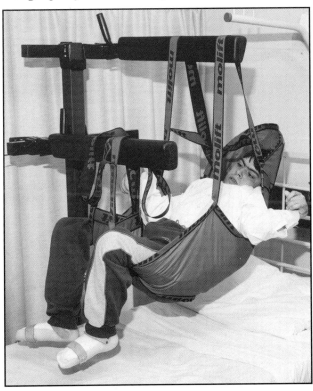

Slings

Material Cotton and polyester net for bath use.

Size Small, medium and large, with or without head support.

Attachment The sling has single loops at the lower end and can be used in cross-over, divided leg or full support ways. Two loops at the head end enable the person to be lifted in a reclined or sitting position. The position of recline can also be adjusted by moving the height of the support arm. The U-strap special provides good leg support without creasing, but the head support is only suitable when lifting from a bed and provides little support in the sitting position.

U-strap slings can be used for toileting, but a special toilet strap, with or without a support belt, is available. It offers less support than the U-strap sling but allows clothing to be adjusted more easily.

Horizontal lifting straps have a metal insert within the webbing loop to aid the fit of the strap when lifting a person, so that a bedpan can be used or bedding changed. A flatlifter, a solid stretcher which is split into two halves, is available for transferring a person from bed to trolley. The person is rolled from one side to the other so that the two halves can be placed underneath and clipped together. It is used with the rotary support.

A lifting strap used with a back-restraining strap is designed for chair to car transfer.

The straps are machine-washable.

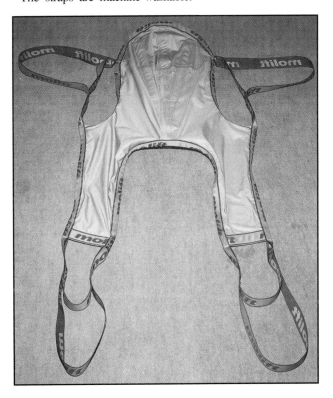

U-strap with head support

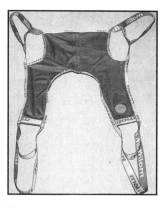

Toilet strap

U-strap

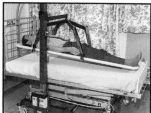

Flatlifter

Horizontal lifting straps

Obtainable from Samson Products (Dorset) Ltd
Price guide Molift U-strap special, battery and
charger £1750
U-strap special in cotton or polyester £75
U-strap special with head support £89
Flatlifter £390
Rotary support for flatlifter £135
Export available

❏ OXFORD 140 ELECTRIC HOIST

This hoist is suitable for use in hospitals, residential homes
and larger private houses.

Construction The hoist is assembled from three main
parts, the base, the angled boom and the mast. These are
made of good quality white plastic coated steel. The base is
adjusted easily using a lever at the back of the mast. The
batteries are fitted at the bottom of the mast and the top of
the housing can be used as a footrest by the user.

Brakes Effective "see-saw" action brakes act on the rear
castors. They do not brake the swivel action of the castors.

Spreader bar The bar is made from chrome-plated steel
wire with three hooks at each end to provide secure
attachment for the slings. The bar is padded in the centre to
protect the user and can be turned through 360°.

Controls The electric motor is fitted to the mast and
covered with a loose PVC cover to protect the user from all
sharp edges. It is powered by two batteries sited at the base
of the mast. A battery charger is supplied. The on/off
switch is located on the mast and the lift is operated using a
pendant control. This has a magnetic back which attaches it
to the frame when not in use.

Slings Pages 68-70.

Movement Raising and lowering are smooth.

Access The base width can be easily adjusted with a lever
at the back of the mast. It will span most manually
propelled wheelchairs and fit under a King's Fund bed. The
hoist can be used to lift a person from the floor.

Manoeuvring Upright push handles are fixed to the mast
and the hoist is easy to manoeuvre over smooth surfaces.

Stability Stable during transfer and manoeuvring.

Storage Mast lifts off base for storage and transport.

Assembly Simply bolts together.

Instructions for use Supplied by the manufacturer.

Servicing and maintenance Instructions are included in
the manufacturer's leaflet. Servicing can be undertaken by
the firm. The hoist is sold with a one year guarantee.

Dimensions

Total weight	50kg
Max. height of spreader bar	775mm
Min. height of spreader bar	660mm
Overall range of lift	1115mm
Width of closed legs	660mm
Height of base	110mm
Lifting capacity	145kg

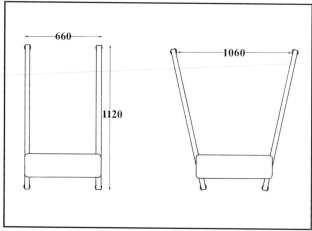

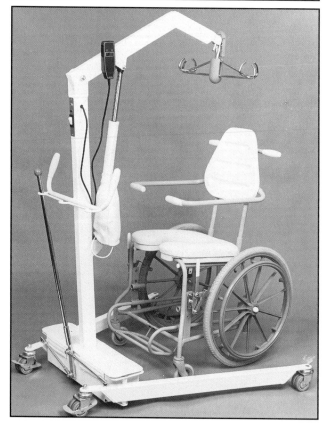

Obtainable from F J Payne (Manufacturing) Ltd
Price guide £745
Export available

Mobile seat lifts

This small section includes pieces of equipment which
have been designed principally for people who need some
assistance in making a transfer from bed to chair or toilet
but do not require full lifting, as they are able to stand and
take some weight through their bodies.

❑   **MOBILAID**

Mobilaid is designed for home use to transfer a person
from bed to chair or for toileting. It is not a lifting aid and
the person making the transfer must be able to stand and
transmit some load through his arms for short periods.

Construction   The seat unit clips to the epoxy-coated steel
frame at the desired height. The frame is made up of two
parts, a flat seat and a backrest upholstered in padded
vinyl. These are easy to remove and replace in the frame,
which is mounted on four castors, with a non-slip footrest
fitted at the base. Brakes which stop the swivel action are
fitted to the front castors. A removable table top slots into
the frame in front of the chair and the height of this can be
changed to suit the user. The legs of the frame can be
adjusted to fit round a wheelchair.

Use   With the padded vinyl seat and backrest removed, the
frame is wheeled up to a person sitting on the side of a bed,
who then leans across the table and grips its outer edge. In
this position the person is raised sufficiently to put the seat
under his buttocks, or for a helper to carry out dressing or
personal care. When the backrest is slotted into the frame
the seat is fixed in position and the person is ready for
transfer. The seat cushion can be removed and a commode
pan (optional extra) inserted for toileting. Handles for
pushing the chair are incorporated in the backrest.

Manoeuvring and stability   The Mobilaid is easy to push
and is stable in use.

Optional extras   Backrest extension, table top with cut-out
for a large person and a commode pan with stainless steel
fittings.

Storage   The seat and backrest are removed and the frame
is easily dismantled by unscrewing four screws.

Instructions for use   Provided by the manufacturer.

Servicing and maintenance   None required

Dimensions

Backrest height		425mm (extension optional extra)
Seat height	460 - 680mm (adjustable)	
width		460mm
depth		355mm
Table height	750 - 1100mm	
Footrest width		460mm
depth		410mm
Total weight		27kg
Lifting capacity		102kg

Obtainable from AMP Services
Price guide £695
Backrest extension £20
Table top with cut-out £50
Commode pan £35
Export available

❑   **ARJO-MECANAIDS SARA**

This hoist is principally a standing and raising aid. It is
designed to simulate a "bear-hug" lift and is used primarily
for transfers from wheelchair to chair or toilet. Because of
its size it is most suited for use in a nursing home or
hospital situation, particularly for those people who need
frequent toileting. It is not always suitable for a person
with a hemiplegic condition as without the support of a
second attendant there may be a risk of injuring the
shoulders. Many hemiplegic patients can be lifted if they
have control of one side and the sling is placed well down
the back. The person being lifted should have some ability
to bear weight in at least one leg and be moved quickly to
avoid discomfort in standing.

The advantages of this hoist are that it is quick and simple
to use. It is ready assembled, there are no slings to attach,
and it is very easy to remove clothes for toileting.

Construction   The chassis of the hoist is made of a coated
steel frame with padded vinyl handgrips and knee
restraints. The legs are adjustable within a range of 680-
960mm.

Sling   Padded and covered with synthetic sheepskin, it is
easily removed for washing. The cords which attach it to
the chassis lock automatically when tightened.

Controls   The hoist is operated by a hand-winding system
which requires the minimum of effort as there is good

leverage on the winding handle.

Brakes Fitted to the rear castors and operated by foot flaps, the brakes lock both the wheels and their swivel action.

Hoisting action Smooth and easily controlled by the attendant. It should be done quickly as it is not comfortable to be held by the sling for long periods.

Manoeuvring Travels easily over smooth ground.

Range of lift Suitable for tall and short people.

Storage Dismantles for storage or transportation.

Optional extras A white plastic seat and frame mounted on the closed chassis legs which fits directly over the toilet, and bedpan for use with the seat.

Lifting capacity 160kg

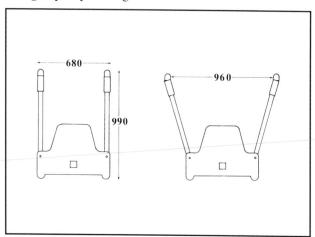

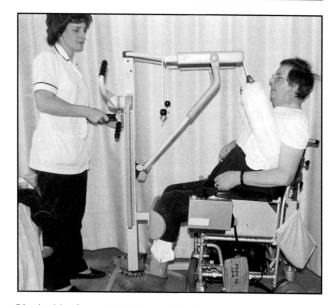

Obtainable from Arjo-Mecanaids Ltd
Price guide Hoist £1805
Seat accessory £89
Bedpan holder £31
Bedpan £10
Export available

❑ LIC LIFTING STOOL

The Lic lifting stool is designed to transfer a person in a sitting position, from chair to chair or toilet, or to move someone seated on the side of a bed.

Construction The device comprises a chest cushion, knee support and footrest based on an adjustable height frame, and mounted on a mobile base. The main support for the body is a large seat sling which is positioned on the lower back. The lifting stool slides under the chair so that the person's feet are above the footrest and his knees are firmly blocked against the knee supports. Once in position the footrest is raised by rotating the crank so that the knees are flexed to 90°. The patient then leans forward against the chest cushion and a strap is placed round his back to hold him in place. While he is in this position the main support strap can be fitted over his buttocks. Further rotation of the crank handle lifts the person off the seat. Held firmly in this position he can then be moved to another seat or over the toilet. For toileting the clothing can be adjusted before the back strap is fitted and modesty can be retained by pulling the shirt or dress over the lifting strap whilst moving. The seat is comfortable for short transfers or toileting, but would not be suitable for those with painful hips or knees.

Manoeuvring It manoeuvres easily on smooth level surfaces as the castors move well and straight ahead. Because the base is narrow it is advisable for safety to move a person in the lowest position.

Dimensions

Seat height Adjusts from 340 to 770mm

Overall length	900mm
Height	1000mm
Width	550mm
Base Inner width	250mm
Outer width	340mm
Castors diameter	80mm
Rear castors braked	

Lifting capacity 120kg

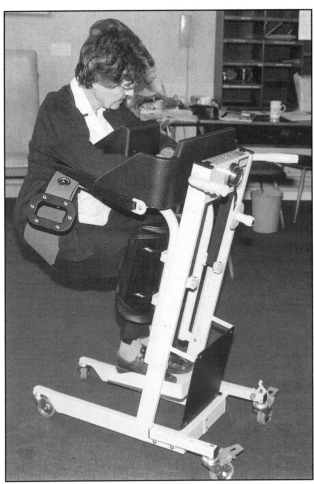

Obtainable from PowerTech (UK) Ltd
Price guide Standard stool £1375
Adjustable stool with splayed leg base £2180
Export available

❏ MOVEE

The Movee is a mobile chair for use in the home to help those requiring assistance in transferring from bed to chair or for toileting. It is specially designed to fit in unobtrusively amongst the household furniture. The Movee is only suitable for those who can transmit some load through their legs as it is not strictly a lifting aid, and it is not suitable for independent use.

Construction   The brown epoxy-coated steel frame has a detachable upholstered sling seat and an integral table fitted across the front. The table can be lifted out and underneath is a handle for altering the height. The frame moves easily on two sets of wheels. The rear wheels do not swivel so it is easier to pull than push the chair. An elderly person may find it difficult to manoeuvre over a deep pile carpet.

Use   A person using this chair must have the ability to move to the side of the bed and sit. The seat slings are first removed and the frame is wheeled up to the seated person, who then leans forward over the table while the seat sling is positioned and attached to the support arms. The backrest is then dropped into place and finally the person's

feet are rested on the cross bar of the frame ready for moving. During the evaluation of this equipment an alternative method of using this chair (not recommended by the manufacturer) was tried for people who are not comfortable leaning over the table. The seat sling was put under the person as he moved to sit at the side of the bed and swung his legs down. The Movee was then wheeled up round him to attach the seat sling to the arms and fit the backrest. The seat was wound up to clear the bed and the table fitted before moving the person. This method of use was satisfactory.

Storage   Collapses easily and folds flat for storage. A carrying bag is available as an optional extra.

Servicing and maintenance   None required

Dimensions

Base	width	51mm
	depth	78mm
Weight		21kg
Seat height	40 - 62mm	

Lifting capacity   115kg

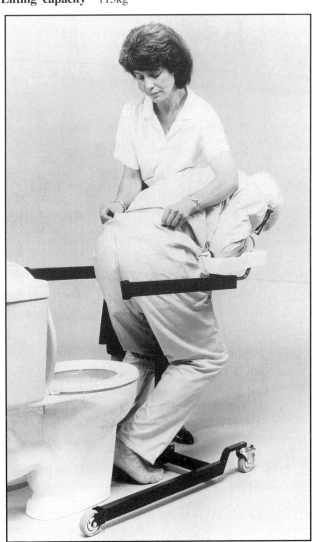

Obtainable from Parker Bath Developments Ltd
Price guide £475
Export available

ELECTRIC OVERHEAD HOISTS

Points to consider

∗ An electric hoist consists of a hoist motor attached to a traversing trolley, a spreader bar with sling or other attachments which is fixed at the lower end of a spool of tape fitted in the motor box, and pull-cords or a pendant control box.

∗ It runs on an overhead track which is either ceiling or wall-mounted, or on a track fitted to a portable 'A' frame gantry.

Use

∗ An overhead electric hoist is suitable for use by a helper who is not strong enough to push a portable hoist, but can manage the slings.

∗ It can be used where space is too restricted for a portable hoist.

∗ An electric hoist gives a smoother lift than a portable hoist and is more comfortable for a person with severe pain.

∗ In a hospital or residential home an electric hoist which is permanently available on an overhead track is more likely to be used by nursing staff than a portable hoist which is stowed away.

Installation

∗ An electric hoist must be operated from mains electricity: pre-payment meters are unsuitable.

∗ The hoist must have upper and lower safety limits for movement of the spreader bar and a brake which operates automatically in the event of a power failure.

∗ A step-down transformer must be fitted outside the room if an electric hoist is installed in a bathroom, WC or swimming pool.

∗ Other equipment which will be used with the hoist, e.g. grab rails in the bathroom, should be suitably positioned.

∗ The electric socket outlet used should be at least 1000mm away from the track so that the amount of suspended flex is kept to a minimum. If the socket is too close the flex may become entangled with the motor as it passes.

∗ Movement of the trolley along the track can be noisy and it may be inappropriate to install an electric hoist in a flat or terrace house. Some trolleys have aluminium tracks and rubber-bonded or nylon wheels to minimize noise.

∗ Most suppliers offer servicing arrangements.

Controls

∗ Controls for raising and lowering the hoist are either pull-cords or push-buttons fitted on a handset attached to a pendant lead.

∗ Beads can be knotted down the thin nylon cords, or knots can be made, to provide a better grip.

∗ Pull-cords tend to tangle and may be a hazard if pulled inadvertently.

∗ Handsets with push-buttons are easier to manage. They vary in design and it is suggested that before purchase the operator makes sure that the shape and size are comfortable to hold and that the buttons can be reached easily.

∗ Both pull-cords and push-buttons require only a light touch to operate and may be managed by a severely disabled person. His ability to use the hoist independently will depend on his ability to attach and remove the slings.

∗ The direction of movement controlled by the push-buttons is indicated by arrows, colour or layout. This should be clear and unambiguous whichever way the handset is held.

∗ An emergency lowering device must be fitted for use in the event of a mains power failure. It is recommended that the user checks that the device is easy to operate and that it is supplied when the hoist is installed.

∗ Some means of moving the hoist sideways along the track must be provided. This may be a cord and pulley system operated by hand, or an electric traverse unit. Some manufacturers supply a cord and pulley system as an extra; electric traverse units are also available for use with each model of hoist.

Overhead track

Points to consider

∗ Track is available in straight or curved runs and the choice will depend on the shape and layout of the room. Curved track may be more suitable in some rooms, for example the bathroom, where space may be limited.

✳ Before installation the ceiling joists must be checked to ensure that they are capable of supporting the track and its moving load.

Length of track

✳ The path of the track should be carefully considered to ensure that all items of furniture and equipment needed by the user will be adequately covered.

✳ Approximately 1000mm of track should be allowed for each item of furniture or equipment.

✳ When measuring the length of run, approximately 160mm should be allowed at either end for the terminal brackets.

Height of track

✳ The height of the track above the floor should allow sufficient clearance to lift the user between the highest and lowest pieces of equipment.

Position of track

✳ The distance of the track from the wall behind it is determined by the person's position in bed or chair and his hoisting techniques. About 1000mm clearance is usually adequate but for an attendant to position and lower the person from behind more space will be needed.

✳ Over the bed, bath or WC the track should be mounted so that the hoist is positioned over the person's hips to ensure that the lift will be vertical and the person will not swing.

Supply and installation of track

✳ Most manufacturers of electric hoists, or their agents, will advise on installations and will supply and install track and fittings.

✳ Before ordering four pieces of information are required: (i) the purpose for which the track will be used, (ii) the maximum weight to be carried (iii) a plan of the track giving dimensions (iv) the height from floor to track.

✳ The cost of track and fitting is variable and may be obtained from the manufacturer.

✳ Installation is extra and a quote should be obtained.

Sideways movement along track

✳ An electric traverse unit or hand-operated pulley is needed to move the person along the track. These are supplied as extras by the manufacturer although in some hoists they are built-in.

Portable gantry

✳ A free-standing, portable 'A' frame gantry can be used where the ceiling is unsuitable for the installation of an overhead track. It is also convenient when an overhead electric hoist is required for temporary use; it saves the expense of installing track and the supplying authority can remove it quickly and easily when it is no longer required and reissue it elsewhere.

✳ Portable gantries are obtainable from electric hoist manufacturers (see below).

For use on curved or straight track

❑ CARTER HOIST 2

Two versions of this hoist are available, the C800 CV with a manual traverse and the C800 CH which has an integral powered traverse. Both these versions are driven by a 24v motor and are suitable for use with straight and curved track which can be wall, ceiling or gantry mounted.

The main feature of this re-designed hoist is the position of the webbing strap which supports the spreader bar. It has been moved from the centre of the hoist unit to the side to allow easier manoeuvring close to walls, for example in the bathroom, and where space is limited.

Construction The hoist unit runs on rubber wheels along an aluminium track which incorporates a built-in conducting strip. This eliminates the need for trailing wires. In the motorised traverse version, the motor and the traverse modules are enclosed in a single unit. A transformer with an integral battery pack can be provided to give limited use of the hoist in an emergency.

Spreader bar This is the same as for Carters mobile hoists, a curved padded bar with two hooks at either end for attaching the slings. The hoisting action is smooth.

Controls Hand-held pendant control with a splash-proof cover.

Slings Uses the full range of Carters slings as on pages 62-63.

Instructions for use Provided by the manufacturer.

Servicing and maintenance A warranty is given for the first twelve months. The manufacturer offers an annual servicing scheme.

Range of lift 2000mm

Lifting capacity 127kg

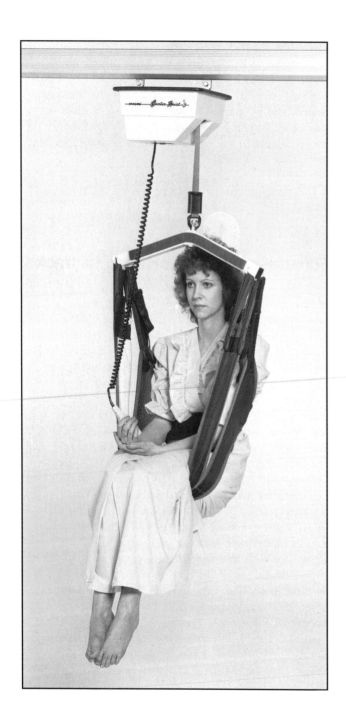

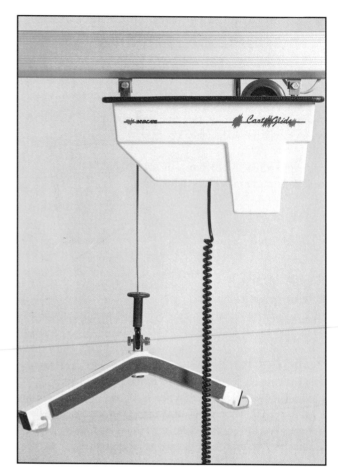

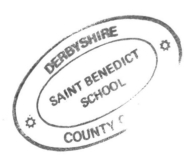

Obtainable from Carters (J&A) Ltd.
Price guide   800CV £365
                      800CH £535
Export available

❑   CARTER MASTER HOIST 2

This hoist is almost the same as the Carter Hoist 2 except it is heavy duty and has a larger lifting capacity of 170kg. Two versions are available, the C800 MV with a manual traverse and the C800 MH with a powered traverse.

It is more suitable for installation in a hospital or a residential home, for example in a bathroom or toilet, where it will have frequent use.

Obtainable from Carters (J&A) Ltd
Price guide   C800MV £525
                      C800MH £695
Export available

❑   CHILTERN WISPA AND WISPALONG

These two electric overhead hoists are identical except that the Wispa has a manual traverse and that of the Wispalong is power assisted. Both versions are suitable for installation in living and bedrooms, bathrooms and swimming pools, on either straight or curved track.

Construction The hoist and traverse motors are encased together in a single unit. This unit runs on a white coated aluminium track which can be mounted unobtrusively on the wall or ceiling, or on a gantry.

Three different drives are available:

1 Standard drive linked via a step down transformer to the 240v mains supply

2 Standard drive with battery backup

3 Cordless drive with battery recharger at the end of the track. This version is the most suitable for installation in bathrooms and swimming pools.

Each drive system has a small rechargeable battery with enough power to lower the hoist in case of emergency.

Spreader bar Suspended centrally on a nylon webbing strap it has two hooks at each end for attachment of the sling. The hoisting action is smooth unless the person is lifted off centre; then the webbing suspension strap catches on the edge of the casing causing an irritating noise. This has now been modified by the manufacturer.

Controls Large air switches in a pendant box which is safe even when entirely immersed in water.

Slings The range of Chiltern slings for use with this hoist is shown on pages 64-65.

Instructions for use Provided by the manufacturer.

Servicing and maintenance An extended warranty can be arranged with the manufacturer.

Range of lift 2000mm

Lifting capacity 130kg

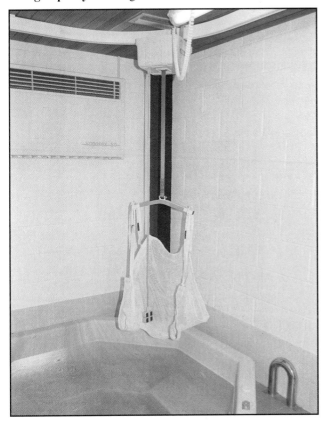

Obtainable from Chiltern Medical Developments Ltd.
Price guide

Wispa	W	Standard drive (24v via transformer)
	WE	Standard drive (battery backup)
	WB	Cordless drive
Wispalong	WL	Standard drive (24v via transformer)
	WLE	Standard drive (battery backup)
	WLB	Cordless drive

Export available

❑ CHILTERN WISPA TURBO (WT)

This overhead hoist is almost identical to the Wispa. The difference is that it is a heavy duty hoist and has a lifting capacity of 230kg.

Obtainable from Chiltern Medical Developments Ltd.
Price guide £750 Special transformer £100
Export available

❑ COMMODORE MAJOR

This hoist is suitable for curved or straight track. The standard 240v model is converted by a transformer to a 24v version for use in wet areas such as bathrooms and swimming pools.

Construction The hoist and traverse motors are enclosed together in the hoist unit which is encased in a fire retardant moulded plastic cover. It runs on nylon wheels along a steel track which is mounted on the ceiling, wall or a gantry. The unit incorporates a rechargeable battery which will provide enough power to lower the hoist in emergency, in addition to a hand winding mechanism. As standard the hoist is fitted with an overspeed governor safety device to stop the user falling if there is mechanical damage.

Spreader bar A swivel type spreader bar with three hooks at each end for attachment of the slings. The hoisting action is smooth.

Controls Hand-held pendant control. An optional time delay can be incorporated without cost to the hand control unit, to eliminate an immediate reverse of the hoist when the control buttons are pressed accidently.

Slings The range of SML Llewellyn slings for use with this hoist is shown on pages 65-67.

Instructions for use A comprehensive instruction manual is provided by the manufacturer.

Servicing and maintenance This can be arranged with the manufacturer at the time of installation. The hoist is guaranteed for twelve months.

Lifting capacity 130kg
Range of lift 3650mm

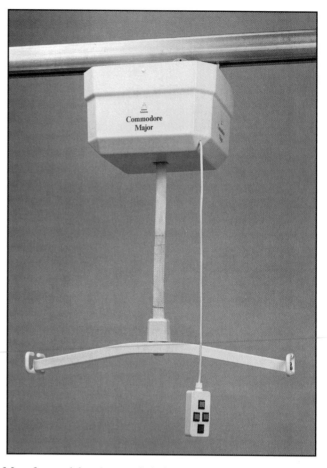

Manufactured by Access Solutions, a division of Llewellyn-SML Health Care Services, part of the Nesbit Evans Group
Supplied and installed by Access Solutions
Price guide £750
Export available
This hoist was not evaluated in use so the report is based only on the manufacturer's technical literature.

❑ COMMODORE HOIST

This hoist is suitable for curved or straight track. Two versions are available, the standard 240v and a 24v version for use in wet areas such as bathrooms and swimming pools.

Construction The motor unit is enclosed in a steel cover and is supplied with or without a separate traversing unit and an overspeed governor safety device. This stops the user falling if mechanical damage occurs within the hoist. It runs on nylon wheels along a steel track which is mounted either to the ceiling or on a gantry. A hand-winding mechanism is incorporated in the motor unit for emergency use.

Spreader bar A straight steel bar has a range of holes at each end for the attachment of the slings. These fit onto the bar with "S" hooks fastened by spring clips to make them safe. The hoisting action is smooth and rather noisy.

Controls Four thin nylon cords operate the hoist. They are fiddly to use and tangle easily. There is a danger they may get pulled and operate the hoist while the sling is being positioned.

Slings   The range of Llewellyn-SML slings for use with this hoist is shown on pages 65-67.

Instructions for use   A comprehensive instruction manual is provided by the manufacturer.

Servicing and maintenance   The hoist is guaranteed for twelve months. Service and repair information is provided by the manufacturer.

Range of lift   3650mm
Lifting capacity   127kg

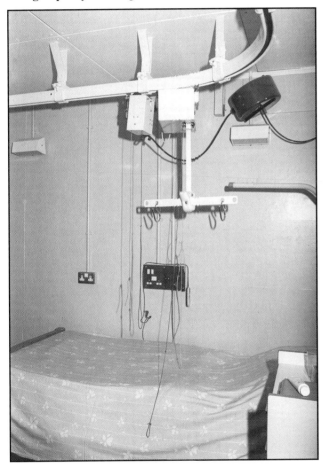

Manufactured by Access Solutions, a division of Llewellyn-SML Health Care Services and part of the Nesbit Evans Group.
Supplied and installed by Access Solutions
Price guide £750
Export available

❑   SPECTRA HOIST

This hoist can be installed on curved or straight track. The standard model is powered by a 24v motor and is suitable for use in wet areas such as bathrooms and swimming pools. It is available with or without a motorised traverse.

Construction   The hoist and traverse motors are encased in a fire retardant moulded plastic cover. This unit runs on rubber wheels along a steel track which is mounted either on the ceiling or on a gantry. It incorporates a small rechargeable battery which will provide enough power to lower the hoist in emergency. A battery power pack is available as an optional extra. This can be used to operate the hoist and eliminate the need for trailing wires. A battery charger is fitted to the end of the track and when not in use the batteries are automatically put on charge.

Spreader bar   The straight steel bar with a swivel joint has a range of holes for the attachment of the slings. These fit onto the bar with "S" hooks fastened by spring clips to make them safe. The hoisting action is smooth.

Controls   Hand-held pendant control.

Slings   The range of Spectra slings for use with this hoist is shown on pages 70-71.

Instructions for use   Instructions are provided by the manufacturer.

Servicing and maintenance   This can be arranged with the manufacturer at the time of installation. The hoist carries a one year guarantee.

Range of lift   2000mm
Lifting capacity   127kg

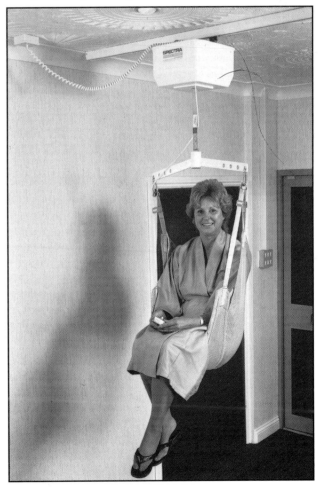

Obtainable from Southern Lift Co Ltd
Price guide £700
Export available
This hoist was not evaluated in use so the report is based only on the manufacturer's technical literature.

❑ WESSEX PATIENT HOIST

This overhead hoist is suitable for straight track. Two versions are available, the standard 240v and a 24v version for use in wet areas such as bathrooms and swimming pools.

Construction The motor unit is enclosed in a steel cover and can be supplied with or without a separate traversing unit. It runs on nylon wheels along a steel track which is mounted on the ceiling, wall or a gantry. A hand-winding mechanism is incorporated in the motor unit for emergency use.

Spreader bar An angled steel bar has two holes at each end for the attachment of the slings. These fasten onto the bar by spring clips which stop the slings slipping off. The hoisting action is smooth if rather noisy. A "coat hanger" spreader bar is also available.

Controls Four thin nylon cords operate the hoist. They are fiddly to use and tangle easily. There is a danger they may get pulled and operate the hoist while the sling is being positioned.

Slings The range of Wessex slings for use with this hoist is shown on pages 71-74.

Instructions for use The user is given instructions on the correct way to use the hoist after installation.

Servicing and maintenance Arrangements can be made with the manufacturer.

Range of lift   2435mm
Lifting capacity   115kg

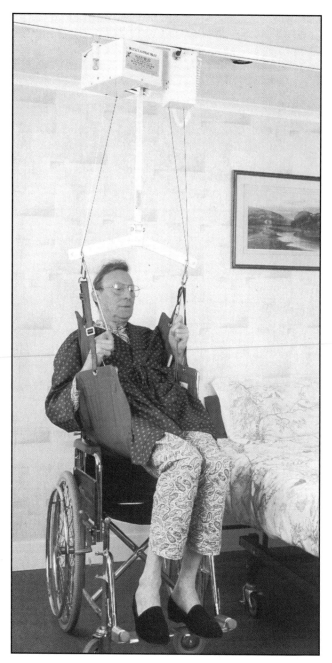

Obtainable from Wessex Medical Equipment Co. Ltd.
Price guide £394   Traverse £190
Export available

❑ WESSEX TRAVELMASTER HOIST

This hoist is well-suited for installation in hospitals, residential homes and domestic situations. It is suitable for use on straight and curved tracks and with the Wessex Orkney Tracking System (described below). The standard 24v version can be fitted in all areas including wet places such as bathrooms and swimming pools.

Construction The hoisting and traverse motors are enclosed together in a moulded cover. The unit runs on wheels along a steel track which is mounted on the ceiling, wall or a gantry. The motor is fitted with an overspeed governor as an additional safety feature. A hand-winding mechanism is incorporated in the motor unit for emergency use. An emergency power supply is also available as an optional extra.

Spreader bar The straight steel bar has four holes at each end for the attachment of the slings. These fasten onto the bar by spring clips which make the slings safe. The hoisting action is smooth. A "coat hanger" spreader bar is also available.

Controls Constant pressure push buttons are fitted in a hand-held pendant control.

Slings The range of Wessex slings for use with this hoist is shown on pages 71-74.

Instructions for use The user is given instructions on the correct way to use the hoist at the time of installation.

Servicing and maintenance Arrangements can be made with the manufacturer.

Range of lift 2435mm

Lifting capacity 115kg

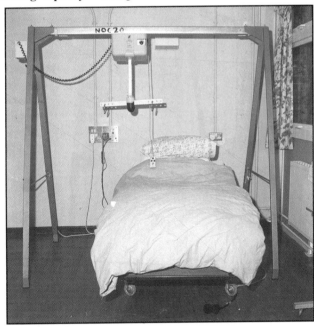

Obtainable from Wessex Medical Equipment Co. Ltd.
Price guide £750
Export available

❑ WESSEX ORKNEY TRACKING SYSTEM

The Orkney Tracking System has been developed for use in conjunction with the Travelmaster hoist. It is a specialist system for use where a curved track does not cover all options. It is the only system to offer two dimensional tracking with powered traversing, which is suitable for an independent user.

Construction The system consists of a pair of parallel tracks which are mounted on opposite walls or opposite ends of the ceiling, with a crossbeam running between them. The Travelmaster hoist unit is mounted on the crossbeam. The drive motor which moves the crossbeam

along the parallel tracks is mounted on the end wall.

This arrangement allows the user to move anywhere within the room, and covers an area up to 6 x 3m.

Controls Hand-held pendant controls with four direction buttons and two other buttons to control the hoisting action.

Slings The range of Wessex slings for use with this hoist is shown on pages 71-74.

Instructions for use The user is instructed in the correct use of the system at the time of installation.

Servicing and maintenance Arrangements can be made with the manufacturer.

Range of lift 2435mm

Lifting capacity 115kg

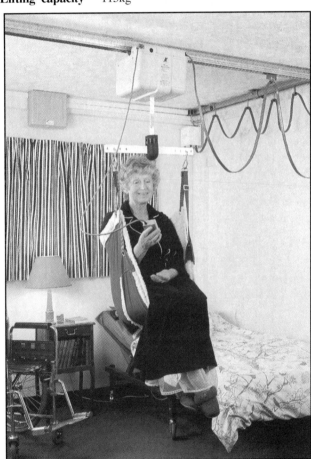

Obtainable from Wessex Medical Equipment Co. Ltd.
Price guide £3500
Export available

For use on special tracks

❑ SCANDILIFT

This hoist is specially designed for lifting and transferring people in confined spaces, where it is difficult to accommodate mobile hoists and it is not possible to install a single track system.

The tracking system is wall mounted using specially

designed brackets which distribute the weight evenly so that the wall does not require reinforcement.

Construction The hoist unit is mounted on a carriage track which can be up to 4.2m wide. This track runs along parallel traversing tracks fixed to the wall and can be up to 6m long. This arrangement allows the user to move anywhere within the room. The hoist is driven by a 24v motor and the traverse is manually controlled by the attendant. The motor stops automatically on reaching the upper and lower limits of the lifting range. A built-in accumulator operates automatically to provide power in an emergency.

A model suitable for use in bathrooms is also available.

Controls Hand-held pendant controls attached to the motor by a coiled wire.

Slings The range of Arjo Mecanaids slings for use with this hoist is shown on pages 59-61. A special bathing sling of waxed open weave polyester is also available.

Instructions for use Provided by the manufacturer.

Servicing and maintenance Can be arranged with the manufacturer.

Range of lift   Set to individual requirements.

Lifting capacity 170kg

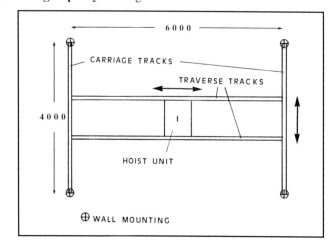

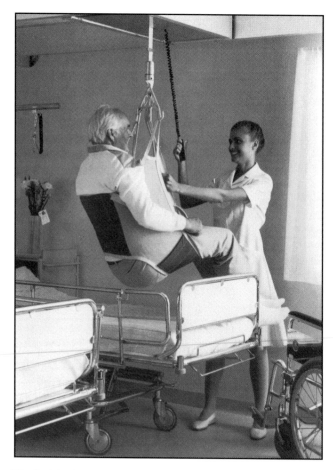

Obtainable from Arjo Mecanaids Ltd.
Price guide For room 4 x 3m £4300
(all rooms require separate quotations)
Export available

This system was not evaluated in use and the report is based on the manufacturer's technical literature.

❑   NEW CHILTERN TRACKING SYSTEM

A new Chiltern tracking system is under development but was not available for evaluation for the purposes of this book. This is a point system which will allow the hoist unit to stop and change direction onto another track giving the user greater flexibility while making the best use of the space available.

More details are available from Chiltern Medical Developments Ltd

BATHROOM HOISTS

Points to consider

* A person who cannot transfer independently in and out of an ordinary bath will need help. A more mobile person will manage with a bathboard or seat and the assistance of a bath attendant, a less mobile person will require lifting either manually or with equipment.

* Manual lifting is quicker but there is a risk of injury to the attendant's back. Hoisting reduces this risk and is more comfortable for the person.

* Choice of equipment is between a hoist, mobile, floor-fixed or overhead, or a portable bath lift.

* The mobile and floor fixed hoists are either manually or electrically-operated.

* A **mobile hoist** (see *Mobile hoists* pages 21-39) can be used in the bathroom provided that there is sufficient space to manoeuvre and adequate clearance under the bath to accommodate the legs.

* A **floor-mounted hoist with a seat** (see below) may be suitable for those who lack confidence in getting in and out of the bath unaided, and may enable them to bathe independently.

* Where there is insufficient space a floor-mounted base plate or socket can be fixed at the side of the bath and the mast and boom of a mobile hoist inserted into it. Before installation a builder should check if the floor is sound.

* The base plate can be fitted at the end or side of the bath.

* The width of the seat should be checked to ensure that it can be lowered to the bottom of the bath.

* The range of lift of the hoist should be checked to see that it is adequate to clear the bath rim.

* The lower limit of the seat should be set to prevent damage to the bath.

* Fixings for wood or concrete floors can be supplied.

* Some lifts which fit to the side of the bath are described as 'portable'. Strengthening wedges must be inserted if the lift is attached to a plastic bath and although not a permanent installation the lift cannot be removed

quickly and easily.

* Grab rails may have to be fitted on the wall within reach of the independent bather to help pull the seat round (See *Equipment for Disabled People Personal Care* 6th edition 1990).

* An **electrically-operated overhead hoist** (see *Electric Overhead hoists* pages 40-48) can be fitted for bathroom use. It must operate on low voltage (24v) supplied from the mains through a transformer which is enclosed and installed outside the bathroom.

* A **portable bath lift** (all reviewed in *Personal Care* see above) is an alternative to a hoist. It can be used independently or with attendant help. Some types may be practical for use by a district nurse or bath attendant and they can be transported to different homes.

* The lifting mechanism may be provided by water pressure, a compressor, battery-pack or counter-balanced springs.

* Some water-powered bath lifts require permanent plumbing, others can be attached to the bath or basin taps provided that the pressure is adequate.

* Most bath lifts rest on the bottom of the bath and some are attached by large suction feet which can be difficult to remove.

* The user sits on a seat or a cushion depending on the type of lift. The choice will depend on the person's disability and the amount of support needed: the cushion provides no back support and good sitting balance is necessary.

* Controls may be a lever or a handset with push-buttons. Some need one hand and others both hands to operate. The user should make sure that he can reach the controls and operate them easily.

* The different types of bath lifts all raise and lower smoothly.

* None have an aperture for washing the perineum.

* The choice of equipment, whether hoist or bath lift, will be determined by the bathroom layout, the person's independence or need for help, the attendant's abilities and the use of the bathroom by other members of the family. The appropriate choice will be made after discussion with the person, his family and helpers.

Mobile bathroom hoists

❏ ARJO MECANAIDS AMBULIFT

This large, heavy duty compact hoist is suitable for use in hospitals and residential homes where there is adequate space for manoeuvre. Model D covers all the features of the Ambulift range. Other models are available with fewer accessories and these are reviewed in *Mobile hoists* on page 29. Static bases for floor-fixing in bathrooms are also available.

❏ ARJO MOBILE BATHING HOIST

Simple and easy to use this mobile hoist is particularly suitable for use in hospitals and residential homes to transfer a person from a bed or wheelchair to the bath or WC or to lift a person from the floor. It can also be used as a shower and commode chair.

The manufacturer states that the hoist complies with BS 5827:1979.

Construction The steel chassis is coated with epoxy polyester and the seat and backrests are moulded polypropylene. The backrest provides comfortable support and can be removed easily and clipped to either arm so that the person can sit facing right or left. The arms, fitted with handgrips, serve as push handles. The oblong seat has a smooth, hard surface. It is made in two parts which can be detached for cleaning. A removable insert fits into the seat and, if necessary, can be removed when washing the perineum (it was found that washing is possible with the insert in place).

A safety belt is supplied as standard. It is simple to fit and has alternative fixed positions.

The brakes fitted to the back castors are easy to use.

Controls The seat is raised by operating a hand pump at the top of the mast. This can be reached easily and managed one-handed. It is lowered by pressing a button on top of the mast. A battery-operated hoist is also available with the capacity to make 80 lifts before recharging.

Transfer To lift a person from the bed, the arms are swung out of the way for access. The seat is raised until it slides over the mattress and the user is rolled on. The arm is lowered in front of the user, who is then helped into a sitting position. The backrest is put into place, the safety belt is attached and the seat is raised for lifting. The user sits facing sideways, supported by the backrest and holding the arms. The bath is approached from the side so that the user is in the correct position for transfer, remaining on the seat while being lowered into the bath. A section may need cutting out of the lower part of the bath panel to accommodate the hoist legs.

Hoisting action Raising and lowering are smooth and there is no movement of the seat during transit.

Manoeuvring The hoist is easy to position and to manoeuvre and use in confined space. The helper's view is not obstructed.

Stability The hoist is stable during transfer and transit.

Optional extras A leg support fixes into the seat of the chair with adjustable straps to hold the legs in place. A commode pan and holder hook under the seat and are easy to remove and replace.

Assembly The hoist is delivered ready assembled. It is recommended that it should *not* be dismantled for transport.

Instructions for use A demonstration is given with directions during practice by the user and helper. Comprehensive instructions are printed on the hoist and written instructions are supplied.

Servicing and maintenance A maintenance checklist is provided; servicing and maintenance are available on request.

Dimensions

Hoist

Height	1400mm
Length	690mm
With leg extension	1020mm
Width	680mm
Base height	115mm
Diameter of castors	100mm

Seat

Height of seat	0 to 900mm, width 400mm, depth 465mm.
Seat aperture	310 x 70mm
insert removed	420 x 200mm
Backrest from seat	340mm
Weight of hoist	39kg
Range of lift	500mm
Lifting capacity	150kg

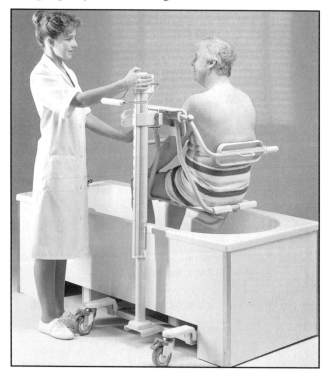

Obtainable from Arjo Mecanaids Ltd
Price guide   Hydraulic £1500
                    Electric   £2360
Export available

❏ KEBO 9650

The Kebo system is used principally as a bathing hoist but can be used for other transfers and for lifting a person from the floor.

It is most suited for use in residential homes, hospitals and large bathrooms because it requires space for manoeuvring.

It is well-suited for people with all kinds of disability as both a chair and stretcher are available for transfer.

Construction The base and mast are made of steel with a blue epoxy finish. The base is mounted on two braked castors at the back and smaller twin castors at the front. The legs of the base are splayed and will easily pass through the standard 762mm door. Handles for manoeuvring the hoist are fixed to the mast. The basic frames of the chair and stretcher units are made of tubular steel and finished with removable polyurethane units. The chair has two armrests which swing out of the way for transfer. The user sits sideways on the chair and an interchangeable back pad is attached to either armrest for support. The seat of the chair is flat and has an aperture for personal cleansing which some people may find uncomfortable. Each end of the stretcher, which is fitted with two safety belts and a single armrest, can be adjusted as required.

The hoist is electrically powered and the motor, 24v sealed battery and belt drive are all housed in the base. A fully charged battery is expected to power 80 lifts. The hoist is supplied with a battery charger.

Controls The hoist is controlled by two large rubber air buttons situated on the base and operated by the foot.

Transfer The bather can be transferred from bed or chair to the bath using the stretcher or the chair as appropriate. The hoist is easy to manoeuvre and will fit under the bath provided there is clearance of 120mm. The hoisting action feels very smooth and secure. When picking a person up from the floor the seat can be lowered to floor level, but the stretcher can only be lowered to 160mm above floor level because of the base.

Optional extras Mattress for the stretcher and solid seat and stainless steel bedpan for the stretcher and chair.

Storage The components are not disassembled for transport or storage.

Instructions for use No written instructions are provided by the manufacturer.

Cleaning The components are easily removed for cleaning.

Servicing and maintenance Can be arranged with the manufacturer.

Dimensions

Overall length of base	875mm
Overall width of base	755mm
Range of lift	950mm
Lifting capacity	150kg

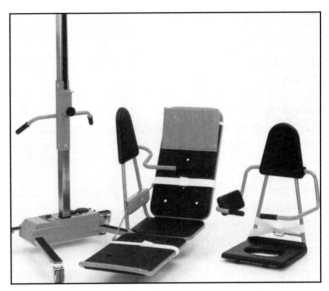

Obtainable from Parker Bath Developments Ltd
Price guide Kebo 9560 (stretcher and chair) £2250
9652 (stretcher only) £665
9653 (chair only) £219
Export available

Fixed bathroom hoists

❏ AUTOLIFT

This floor-mounted bathing hoist is well-suited for installation in hospital and private houses particularly where space is limited. It can be used independently or with attendant help and is suitable for those who need assistance to transfer in and out of the bath and require support during bathing. Several versions of the Autolift are available from the basic standard to the complete F1 which includes all the optional extras. This report is based on the F1 model.

Construction The base plate is bolted to the floor at the side of the bath (specify whether wood or concrete floor) and the mast can be mounted for right- or left-handed operation. All metal parts are made from coated steel and are corrosion proof. The mast height can be adjusted to suit the height of the bath. The seat is made of moulded white plastic with an aperture for personal cleansing and fitted to a metal frame. It slots into the seat pick-up arm on the angled boom for lifting and transfer into the bath. The armrests, which fold out of the way for transfer, bend round in front of the bather. The chair can be mounted on a frame which is supported by braked castors. A leg rest which only supports the calves is also available. This slots into the frame of the chair to extend the support available for the bather should it be needed. On the standard model a basic chair is available without an aperture. Strategically placed grab handles will be needed for independent use of the standard model.

Controls The chair is lifted by a horizontal winding handle which is fitted on top of the mast and can be adapted for right- or left-handed use by the bather or a helper. Raising and lowering are smooth; winding the handle with the arm raised is tiring but the arm can be rested on the curved boom while doing this.

Transfer The bather is transferred to the chair and wheeled to the bath edge. The chair is reversed to the seat pick-up arm ready for lifting into the bath and lifted just enough to allow the metal base frame to be detached by releasing a catch under the seat and withdrawing it from the prongs. The transfer into the bath is then completed. The chair and wheeled frame can also be used as a commode.

Optional extras A pan and holder are also available.

Storage The mast and seat can be lifted from the socket but are heavy and bulky to store elsewhere. The seat can be kept inside the bath when not in use to give adequate circulation space in the bathroom. It can be swung outside the bath while other members of the family are bathing.

Installation Carried out by the manufacturer.

Instructions for use Verbal instructions are given at the time of installation and written instructions are provided.

Cleaning Can be cleaned with a bath cleaner.

Servicing and maintenance Unnecessary in a private house; where it is in more frequent use regular inspection by the manufacturer is recommended. If installed on a wooden floor this should be inspected regularly.

Dimensions

Seat unit Overall width 750mm (with leg extension fitted minimum distance between edge of bath to nearest obstruction 900mm); overall depth 650mm

Backrest Height 360mm

Arms Length 170mm; distance between arms 420mm.

Seat Height adjustable from 230 to 660mm; width 460mm; depth 380mm.

Weight 27kg

Range of lift 430mm

Lifting capacity 127kg

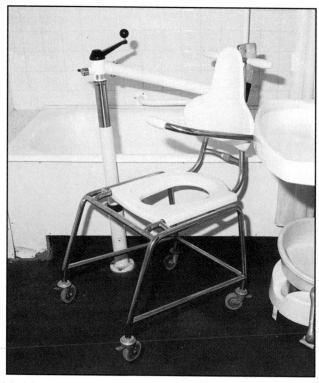

Model F1 with base for concrete floor, commode seat and trolley

(1) Static base for wood floor with solid seat

(2) Static base for wood floor with commode seat and leg support

Obtainable from Arjo Mecanaids Ltd
Price guide depending on model £710 - 1399
Export available

❏ STATIC BASE FOR MECALIFT

A static base plate can be bolted to the floor at the side of the bath to accept the mast unit of a Mecalift hoist (see *Mobile hoists* page 22).

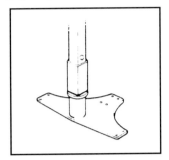

Obtainable from Arjo Mecanaids Ltd
Price guide Static base and fittings £153
Export available

❏ REGAL BATH AID

This bath aid is similar to the Royal (see Electric bath hoists page 56) but has a manually operated hydraulic lifting system. The pump handle can be operated by the patient or alternatively can be swung through 180° to allow attendant operation. The basic white plastic seat can be rotated through 360° and has one fixed armrest.

Lifting capacity 127kg.

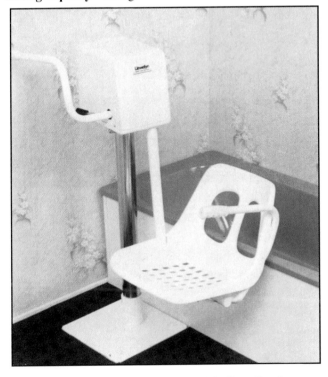

Obtainable from Llewellyn-SML Health Care Services
Price guide   Standard £775
                    Locking   £872
Export available

❏ OXFORD MERMAID AND MERMAID RANGER

This range of floor-mounted bathing hoists is designed for hospitals, residential homes and private homes, especially where space is limited. The Mermaid is the basic bath hoist while the Ranger is the more complex model including several optional extras. Three versions of each are available:

1   Standard for independent use
2   Attendant operated
3   Traversing for independent use.

All versions can be used independently or with help and suit those who need help to transfer in and out of the bath and support during bathing.

This report is based on the Standard Mermaid model but includes details of all the options.

Construction The base plate is bolted to the floor at the side of the bath (specify whether wood or concrete floor) and the mast can be mounted for right- or left-handed operation. All metal parts are non-corrosive. The mast height is adjusted to suit the height of the bath, and an adjustable clamp is set to prevent the seat damaging the bottom of the bath. The standard seat is moulded white plastic with fold-up armrests and drainage holes but no aperture. It slots into a seat pick-up arm on the angled boom for lifting and transfer into the bath. A seat with an aperture for personal cleansing is available as an optional extra. The Mermaid Ranger is fitted with a flat plastic seat with armrests which fold round the front of the user when bathing, and fold back out of the way when not in use. This seat incorporates an aperture as standard, which some thin people may find uncomfortable. Optional extras are a castor-mounted chassis for the seat and a calf-rest which slots into the frame of the chair to extend the support.

Controls The chair is lifted by a horizontal winding handle which is fitted on top of the mast. The position of the winding handle varies in different models. In the standard model it is positioned for independent use but the user must be able to swing manually over the bath after lifting. Appropriately placed grab handles may be required.

The position of the winding handle in the traversing model is the same but the mechanism is different and swings the user over the bath automatically.

The attendant-operated Mermaid and the Mermaid Ranger have the winding handle on top of the mast, so they cannot be used independently.

Raising and lowering with all versions are smooth.

Transfer In using all versions of the Mermaid the bather is transferred to the chair in the bathroom. For transfer from the Ranger, the chair is detached from the pick-up arm in the bathroom, mounted on the chassis, and the bather is transferred to the chair in the bedroom and wheeled to the bathroom. The chair is reversed onto the pickup arm and lifted just enough to allow the metal base frame to be detached by releasing a catch under the seat. An autolock system prevents the chassis being detached before the seat is securely attached to the pick-up arm. The transfer into the bath is then completed. After bathing the chair is lowered onto the chassis until it clicks into place. The chair and wheeled frame can also be used for toileting. A self-propelled chair is available as an optional extra.

Optional extras A slot-in calf support, a self-propelled chassis, a padded seat and the option to have four brakes on the chassis instead of two.

Storage The mast and seat can be lifted from the base but are heavy and bulky to store elsewhere. The seat can be kept in the bath when not in use. It can be swung aside for other members of the family to use the bath.

Installation Carried out by the manufacturer.

Instructions for use Full written instructions are supplied by the manufacturer.

Cleaning Can be cleaned with a bath cleaner.

Servicing and maintenance Unnecessary in a private house; where it is in more frequent use regular inspection is recommended by the manufacturer. If installed on a wooden floor this should be inspected regularly.

Dimensions

Seat unit
Overall width
Standard 460mm   Commode 360mm
Overall depth
Standard 560mm   Commode 460mm
Backrest height
Standard 360mm   Commode 390mm
Arms
Length   450mm
Distance between arms
Standard 390mm   Commode 390mm
Weight

Mermaid		Ranger	
Attendant model	28kg	Attendant model	38kg
Standard model	29.5kg	Standard model	39.5kg
Traversing model	32.5kg	Traversing model	42.5kg

Range of lift   615mm
Lifting capacity   127kg

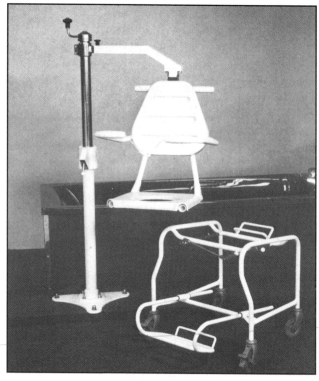

Mermaid Ranger Standard Model

Mermaid Traversing Model

Mermaid Attendant-operated Model

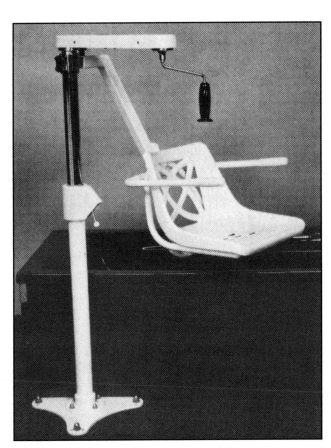

Mermaid Standard Model

Obtainable from F J Payne (Manufacturing) Ltd
Price guide
Standard Mermaid £635
Commode chair £65 (additional)
Attendant model £595
Traversing model £745
Mermaid Ranger Complete £965
Self propelled chassis £330
Padded seat kit £79
Calf support £65
Four brakes on chassis £10 (additional)
Export available

❏   OXFORD AND ISIS BATHROOM
TURNTABLE
The Oxford (pages 28 and 32) and Isis (page 29) hoists can
be converted into bath hoists by substituting the base for a
floor-mounted turntable.
   This can be fitted either at the side or end of the bath and
is bolted to the floor. Separate versions are available for
wood and concrete floors. The floor should be checked by
a builder before installation.
   The hoist mast fits into the turntable sleeve and can be
rotated through 360°, to allow full access for the user.

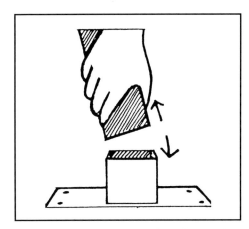

Manufactured by F J Payne (Manufacturing) Ltd
Details of stockists available from F J Payne
Price guide Concrete floor £195
              Wooden floor £184
Export available

Electric bathroom hoists
(See also Electric overhead hoists pages 40-48)

❏   BELL CLASSIC BATH HOIST
This floor-mounted bathing hoist is suitable for installation
in hospitals and private homes, particularly where space is
limited. It can be used independently or with attendant help
for those who need help to transfer in and out of the bath or
support during bathing.
Construction The chrome-plated mast is fixed to the floor
at the back or side of the bath. The lift is powered by an
electric hydraulic pump which is fitted under the bath, and
the 12v battery pack is sited outside the bathroom. A
trickle charger to keep the batteries topped up is included
in the price of the hoist.
   The plain white moulded fibre glass seat has no drainage
holes or cut-away for personal cleansing. It lacks armrests
but is fitted with a safety belt. The chair is swivel-mounted
on the boom which rotates on the mast to give the best
access during transfer. To help the independent user grab
rails should be fitted for manoeuvring and safety.
Controls Hand-held pendant controls.
Storage The chair can be swung over the bath when not in
use.
Installation Undertaken by the manufacturer.
Range of lift   914mm
Lifting capacity   127kg

Obtainable from F M Bell Ltd.
Price guide £1586
Export available

❏ ROYAL BATH AID

This bath lift is suitable for use in nursing homes, hospitals
or private houses.

Construction The hydraulic lifting unit is powered by a
12v DC supply in the bathroom. The main support pillar
can be mounted at the side or end of the bath. The white
moulded plastic seat has two fold-away armrests with
vertical rubber grip handles. The seat has drainage holes
but allows no access to wash the perineum. As the seat can
be fully rotated access is available from any position in the
bathroom. A locking device is available as an optional
extra to limit rotation when the patient is transferring to the
seat. For independent use well placed grab rails will allow
the user to manoeuvre into the correct position.

Controls Hand-held pendant control.

Lifting capacity 159kg

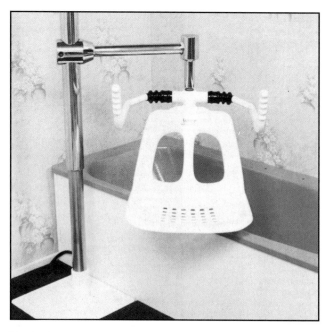

Obtainable from Llewellyn-SML Health Care Services
Price guide   Standard £1699
                    Locking   £1799
Export available

❏ SPECTRA BATH LIFT

This lift is suitable for use in residential homes, hospitals
and private houses. It is principally used as a bathing hoist
but can also be used for other transfers such as those
between bed and chair or toilet. It is supplied with a rigid
plastic seat or a spreader bar and Southern Lift slings. In
many respects it is very similar to the Wessex Romsey
Bath Hoist.

Construction The hoist is electrically operated and the
24v transformer is installed wherever convenient outside
the bathroom. The mast is mounted at the side of the bath
and fixed to both the floor and ceiling. The moulded plastic
seat is flat with an aperture that thin people may find
uncomfortable. The seat has armrests which fold up for
transfer. It is attached to the boom and rotates through 360°
to give good access and can be stored in the bath when not
in use. An adjustable limit switch is fitted to the mast and
is set to stop the seat hitting the bottom of the bath. If the
descending seat is obstructed it will stop automatically.
When the spreader bar is used the slings are attached by
metal hooks which slot into holes in the bar.

Controls Hand-held pendant controls

Transfer The bather transfers in the bathroom from the
shower seat or wheelchair.

Installation Carried out by the manufacturer. The
equipment is guaranteed for one year.

Servicing and maintenance Recommended every year for
private installations and every six months in residential
homes and hospitals.

Slings For details see Spectra Slings pages 70-71.

Dimensions
Range of lift   700mm
Lifting capacity   127kg

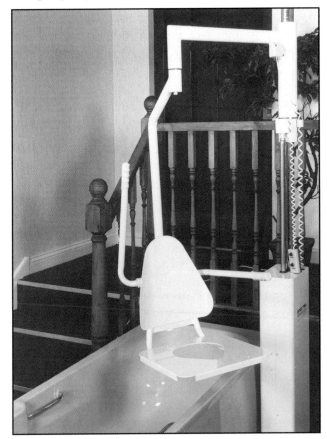

Obtainable from The Southern Lift Co Ltd.
Price guide With fixed seat £1900
With spreader bar and slings £1800
Export available

❑   WESSEX ROMSEY ELECTRA BATH HOIST
This lift is principally used as a bathing hoist but is suitable
for other transfers such as those between bed and chair or
toilet. It can be used in residential homes, hospitals and
private houses. It is supplied with a rigid plastic seat or a
spreader bar and hammock sling and it suits a wide range
of disabled people.
Construction The hoist is electrically operated and the
24v transformer is installed wherever convenient outside
the bathroom. The mast is mounted on the floor at the side
of the bath and is fixed to the ceiling. The moulded plastic
seat has drainage holes and armrests which fold up for
transfer, but no aperture for washing the perineum. It is
attached to the boom and rotates through 360° to give good
access. It can be stored in the bath when not in use. An
adjustable limit switch is fitted to the mast and set to stop
the seat hitting the bottom of the bath. If the descending
seat should be obstructed it will stop automatically. A
detachable shower seat is available, which clips into a
mobile carriage, and can be used to transfer from the

bedroom.
    When the spreader bar is used the sling is attached by
metal hooks which slot into holes in the bar.
Controls   Hand-held pendant controls
Transfer   The bather transfers in the bathroom from the
shower seat or wheelchair but disabled people use the
hammock sling, put in position in the bedroom before
transfer.
Optional extras   An automatically rechargeable battery
pack for emergency use. A detachable shower seat with
mobile carriage.
Installation   Carried out by the manufacturer. The
equipment is guaranteed for one year.
Instructions for use   Comprehensive demonstration and
full instructions are given when the hoist is installed.
Servicing and maintenance   Recommended every year for
private installations and every six months in residential
homes and hospitals.
Slings   For details see Wessex Hammock Sling page 72.
Dimensions
Range of lift   635mm
Lifting capacity   With seat 115kg
                                  With spreader bar and sling 222kg

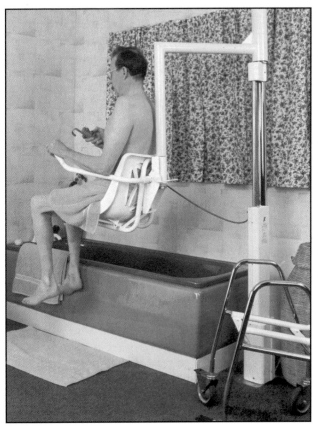

Obtainable from Wessex Medical Equipment Co Ltd.
Price guide With fixed seat only £1300
With fixed seat and shower seat and mobile carriage £1300
With spreader bar £1050
Net Hammock sling £62
Export available

SLINGS

Points to consider

✻   The choice of sling is one of the most important factors affecting the use of a hoist.

✻   Practical trials are necessary to select the most suitable slings and techniques for the individual. During the assessment the therapist and the user must consider the purpose for which the sling will be used, the user's comfort and the required suspension posture e.g. reclined, seated, legs apart or together, and the ease of positioning and removing the slings.

✻   The areas of support required will narrow the choice, e.g. a person with poor head control will require a sling with head support.

✻   Care should be taken when selecting a sling that it does not interfere with any drainage bags or catheters the person may be wearing.

✻   User and helper should be taught how to use the slings correctly and the therapist should visit a few weeks later to check that the recommendations were appropriate and the hoist is used frequently and satisfactorily.

✻   Suitable storage space will be needed for the slings.

Style of sling
✻   **It is important that the only slings used with a hoist are those recommended by the manufacturer.**

✻   Several different styles of sling are available:

Hammock sling with or without head support and commode aperture

A one-piece hammock sling gives full body support and is probably the most suitable choice for a severely disabled person; it is available with head support for those who lack head control, or an aperture or divided legs for toilet purposes. A sling with an aperture is difficult to position accurately and a quick-fit sling may be more practical.

Quick-fit sling

A quick-fit sling provides separate support for each thigh and enables the sling to be removed or repositioned easily under a user when he is in a wheelchair. This saves him

from sitting on it throughout the day. The legs may be held together or apart depending on the way the sling is positioned.

Band slings

Two band slings (backrest and seat support) provide a safe and comfortable method of lifting for the person who is able to position the slings himself. Some people with stiffness or contractures may also find them suitable. Band slings are unsuitable for a person with extensor spasm, a floppy person who may fold and fall through or for a confused person.

Specialised slings, e.g. long seat, amputee slings, walking harness.

✻   Slings are available in various materials for different purposes e.g. nylon mesh allows water to drain easily and is suitable for bathing.

✻   Most manufacturers can supply slings fully or partly lined with synthetic sheepskin for those at risk of pressure sores.

✻   Some manufacturers offer a range of sizes to suit different ages and weights of users.

✻   Each sling should carry a label showing its type, size, the manufacturer's name and address and the safe working load. Some manufacturers use colour coding to help with identification.

✻   Any alteration to slings must be made by the manufacturer.

✻   Handles on outside of sling are helpful in manoeuvring a suspended person to a final destination.

Attachments
✻   Attachments to the spreader bar by chains are more complicated and difficult to get evenly balanced than nylon webbing hooks.

✻   The security of the attachments of the hooks on the spreader bar is important.

✻   Most band slings are attached to the spreader bar by loops of nylon webbing. Varying the length of the loop changes the comfort and position of the user from upright, to semi-sitting or lying.

✻   S-hooks should be fitted with safety clips to prevent the slings from slipping off. They are difficult for those with disabled hands to manage but such people are unlikely to be independent users.

✳ Hammock slings are usually attached to the spreader bar by metal side suspenders and chains or webbing straps.

✳ Some straps are adjustable in length by a buckle: they are less suitable for slings used for many people as precise adjustment is time-consuming.

❏ ARJO MECANAIDS SLINGS

Arjo Mecanaids make four main styles of sling with several variations to use with all their hoists except the Dextra and Maxilift hoists which have special slings. Three styles of sling are described here and the fourth style, a stretcher sling, is not included.

General points

Material All the slings are available in polyester material, except the two-piece back and thigh slings which are only available in PVC-coated nylon.

Special modifications Slings can be modified to suit the user.

Cleaning The PVC slings are stain resistant and can be wiped clean with warm water and detergent or disinfectant. The polyester slings are machine washable. Any metalwork must be removed before washing.

Instructions The leaflet available from the manufacturer does not give full instructions on the use of all styles of slings available. It is advisable to arrange a demonstration before use. The GP sling is now used for almost all general lifting except when using the Dextra and Maxilift.

Obtainable from Arjo Mecanaids Ltd
Export available

❏ ARJO ONE PIECE SLING

This sling is very versatile. An all-in-one hammock style sling with a perineal aperture, it is suitable for those who require full body support but can control their own head.

Sizes Small, medium and large.

Positioning and removal The sling is positioned and removed in bed by rolling the user. Positioning in a chair is unsuitable as the user must be manually lifted to insert the sling. The user's arms can be inside or outside the sling and the knees are held firmly together as this is not a divided leg sling.

Attachment The sling has four webbing straps, one at each corner, each with two loops for making adjustments.

Support It supports the trunk and thighs satisfactorily, but may cause discomfort to some people as the thighs are held firmly together.

Toileting and personal cleansing Clothes must be adjusted before fitting the sling but correctly fitted it gives good access. Not suitable for bathing as drainage of water is a problem.

This sling is also available with divided legs which allows easier personal cleansing.

Another variation is a synthetic fleece lining for pressure relief and comfort through long periods of sitting. The sling

can be put in a wheelchair and with all the straps tucked in the user can sit on it all day.

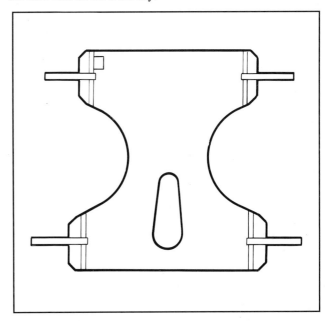

One Piece sling

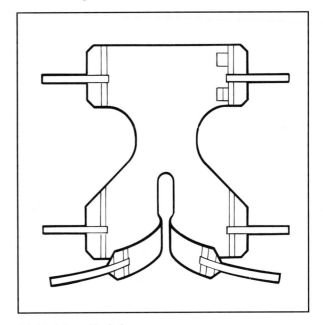

Divided Leg Variation

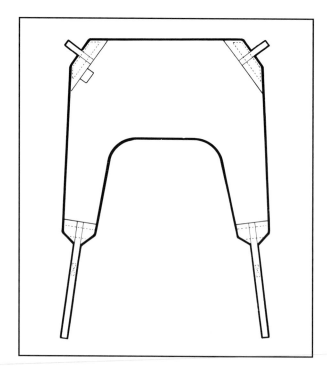

Price guide £62

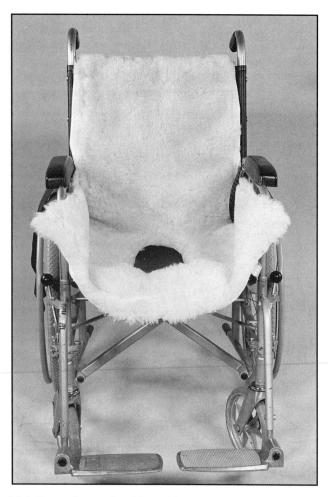

High Dependency, One Piece Sling with sheepskin lining

Price guide   Standard one piece £64
               With divided leg £67
               With fleece lining approx. £100

❏   ARJO GP SLING

This sling is a general purpose quick fit design and gives
good support to those with a weak trunk.
Sizes Small, medium and large.
Positioning and removal It can be positioned in bed or
sitting in a chair. It tends to crease under the thighs during
the initial lift and needs adjusting before lifting is
completed. The sling can be fitted in the cross-over or
divided leg positions.
Attachment Two nylon webbing straps are fixed to each
side of the sling, each with two loops to give flexibility for
adjustment. There are no metal parts on this sling. To use
with the Mecalift the two lower straps can be connected to
the central hook of the spreader bar giving the divided leg
position with less abduction.
Support Good to the trunk and legs but none to the head.
Toileting and personal cleansing Clothes need to be
adjusted before fitting. Access is not impeded if the sling is
arranged with the legs apart.

❏   ARJO GP SLING WITH HEAD SUPPORT

This sling is similar to the GP sling described above but
has an integral shaped and ribbed head support to hold up
those with no head control.
Sizes As for GP sling.
Positioning and removal As for GP sling.
Attachment As for GP sling. It does not require any extra
straps for attachment.
Support Good support to the head. Lifts well from a bed.
Toileting and personal cleansing As for GP sling.

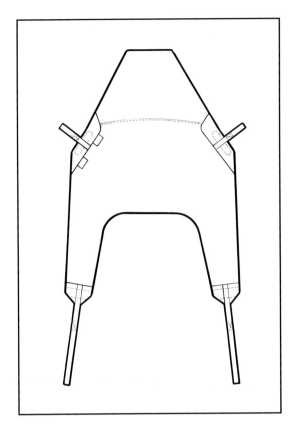

Price guide £84

❏ ARJO TWO-PIECE SLINGS

The back and thigh slings are suitable for those with good head and trunk control and strong upper arms as the back sling is held in place under the arms. The slings are not suitable for floppy people who may fold and fall through them, for those with extensor spasm who may slide off them or for those with painful shoulders.

Sizes Small, medium and large.

Positioning and removal Can be positioned and removed in bed or in a chair.

Attachment The chain hooks are easily attached and detached from the spreader bar of the Mecalift and the models of Ambulift which use slings.

Support The slings are comfortable provided that they are used correctly.

Toileting and personal cleansing Access is good. Clothing is easier to adjust than in a hammock sling.

Lifting capacity 127kg

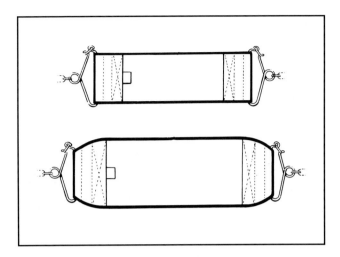

Price guide Back sling £28
　　　　　 Thigh sling £28

❏ DEXTRA SLING

The Dextra sling is specifically for use with Arjo Mecanaids Dextra and Maxilift hoists.

This quick-fit style sling has an integral head support which is stiffened with removable polythene ribs.

Sizes Four sizes are available. Each size is easily identified by a colour coded binding.

Positioning and removal The quick-fit design is easy to fit in a wheelchair. For those who are in bed the sling is fitted in the usual way by rolling the person from one side to the other.

Attachment Four single keyhole fittings clip firmly to the tilting frame of the hoist. This prevents the sling unhooking while the slack is taken up at the beginning of the lift.

Support Good support to the trunk and thighs once the creasing is straightened after an initial lift. Support for the head is excellent in both the sitting and reclined positions. The shaped headrest gives good lateral support.

Toileting and personal cleansing Clothes must be adjusted before the sling is fitted for toileting. There is no drainage so this sling is unsuitable for bathing.

Instructions for use Provided by the manufacturer.

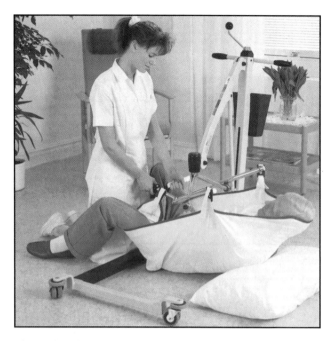

Price guide £91

❏ CARTERS SLINGS

Carters make three different styles of slings for use with their mobile and electric overhead hoists. All slings have colour-coded bindings which help rapid identification. The nylon webbing is more pliable than that used previously, so the slings are easier to attach to the spreader bar.

General points

Material Blue polyester mesh.

Special modifications Synthetic sheepskin linings are available for all slings if required.

Cleaning All slings are washable.

Instructions for use Provided by the manufacturer.

Obtainable from Carters (J&A) Ltd.
Export available

❏ CARTERS HAMMOCK SLING

This sling is available in standard (C257) and commode (C258) versions. This style of sling is suitable for people who need full head and body support.

Size One size only.

Attachment Four nylon webbing straps are attached to each corner of the sling. Each strap has two loops for flexible attachment to the spreader bar.

Positioning and removal The sling is placed on the bed so that the user's buttocks are aligned with the perineal aperture. When fitting the standard version the top of the sling should be aligned at the top of the user's head. The straps can then be attached to the spreader bar.

Support Good support to all parts of the body. The knees are forced together and the back of the thighs are squeezed. Some people may find this uncomfortable. The head is lifted off the bed first and some people may require a little extra support from the helper at this stage.

Toileting and personal cleansing Only possible using the version with the perineal hole. Clothing must be adjusted before fitting the sling.

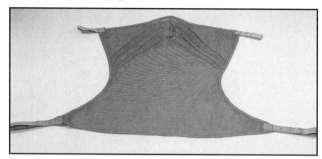

Hammock sling - standard version (C257)

Price guide   C257 £65
                 C258 £70

❏ CARTERS UNIVERSAL SLING

This is a split leg sling with a perineal aperture.

Size Standard (C 254), junior (C255) and large (C256).

Attachment Six nylon webbing straps are sewn to the sling for attachment to the spreader bar, two to each leg support and one at each shoulder. Each strap has two loops for flexible adjustment.

Positioning and removal The sling can be used in the divided leg, cross over or full support positions. It is easy to fit to a person in a chair or bed. The twin leg straps are divided between the front and back hooks of the spreader bar and the shoulder straps are attached to the back hook. This spreads the thigh straps and helps to prevent the material of the sling creasing under the legs.

Support Good to the trunk and legs.

Toileting and personal cleansing Can be used in the divided leg or cross-over positions, but clothes must be adjusted before fitting the sling.

Price guide   C254 £50
                 C255 £45
                 C256 £75

❑ CARTERS UNIVERSAL WITH HEAD SUPPORT

This sling is similar to the Universal but with head support.

Size Standard (C 254H), junior (C255H) and large (C256H).

Attachment Eight nylon webbing straps are sewn to the sling for attachment to the spreader bar, two to each leg support, one at each shoulder, and one each side of the head support. The head support straps are single but can be adjusted. They clip together around the swivel joint of the spreader bar. The remaining straps each have two loops for flexible adjustment.

Positioning and removal The sling can be used in the divided leg or cross over positions. It is easy to fit to a person in a chair or bed. The twin leg straps are attached to the front and back hooks of the spreader bar and the shoulder strap is fixed to the back hook. This method of attachment spreads the thigh straps and helps prevent creasing under the legs.

Support Good to the trunk, legs and head. The strap of the head support requires adjusting during lifting. It should be tightened as the person is lifted higher off the bed and finally moved into an upright position. The sling gives some lateral head support due to its central attachment on the spreader bar.

Toileting and personal cleansing The sling can be used in either the divided leg or cross-over positions, but clothes must be adjusted before fitting the sling.

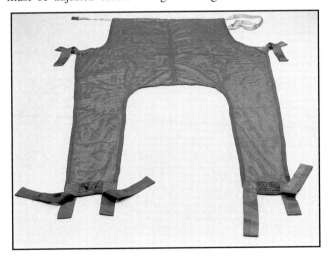

Price guide   C254H £80
              C255H £75
              C256H £85

❑ CARTERS UNIVERSAL COMMODING SLING (C250 UCS)

This is a new sling which is similar to the Universal Mesh Sling. It has a larger cut away area round the buttocks and back, and a wide nylon webbing strap fastens tightly round the user's chest with velcro. During lifting the person is supported round the chest and under the thighs. This sling is not suitable for those people with little trunk control who may slip through, nor for those with wasted chests and distended stomachs as these conditions make it difficult to fasten the belt tightly round the chest.

Size One size only.

Attachment As for Universal.

Positioning and removal As for Universal but with additional chest straps.

Support Good for the right person. Best used for short transfers.

Toileting and personal cleansing Access is excellent. Clothing can be easily adjusted while the sling is in position.

C250UCS

Price guide £85

This sling was not evaluated and this report is based on the manufacturer's technical literature.

❑ CHILTERN SLINGS

Chiltern Medical make three different styles of sling for use with the Wispa and Wispalong electric overhead hoists.

General points

Material All slings are available in woven polyester or nylon net. The band slings are padded polyester and the hammock sling has quilted thigh supports to help prevent creasing under the legs.

Special modifications Synthetic sheepskin linings are available for use with the slings if required. Specialized slings can be made to order.

Cleaning All slings are washable.

Instructions for use The manufacturer provides an instruction manual on the use of the slings.

Obtainable from Chiltern Medical (Developments) Ltd
Export available

❑ CHILTERN HAMMOCK SLING

This sling is suitable for people who require full body support.

Sizes Small, medium and large.

Attachment Six nylon webbing straps, each with two loops to give alternative positions for attachment to the spreader bar, are sewn onto the sling. Alternate loops are white and black for ease of identification.

Positioning and removal The sling can be used in the divided leg or cross over positions.

To fit in the divided leg position the sling is placed around the person in a chair or more usually when lying on a bed. The head straps are attached to the spreader bar before the outer leg straps are passed through the inner straps and fixed to the spreader bar. This helps to prevent the sling creasing under the thighs.

To fit in the cross over position the procedure is the same until finally the outer strap from the right side is passed through the inner strap from the left side and vice versa before attachment to the spreader bar. This keeps the legs together in the sling.

Support The sling gives good support to the trunk and legs. Quilting on the leg supports prevents creasing under the thighs. There is no lateral support to the head.

Toileting and personal cleansing Clothes must be adjusted before the sling is fitted in the divided leg position for toileting.

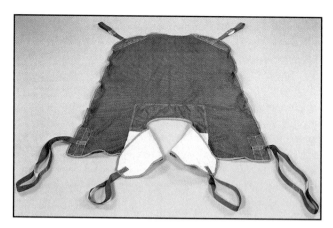

Price guide   Standard £70
                Quilted £75
                Specialized slings by quotation

❑ CHILTERN UNIVERSAL SLING

A quick fit style sling.

Size One size only.

Attachment Four nylon webbing straps, each with two loops to give alternative positions for attachment to the spreader bar, are sewn onto the sling. Alternate loops are colour-coded for ease of identification.

Positioning and removal The sling can be used in the divided leg or cross over positions and can be fitted to a person in a bed or chair.

Support Good support to the trunk and legs but no support for the head.

Toileting and personal cleansing Clothes must be adjusted before the sling is fitted in the divided leg position for toileting.

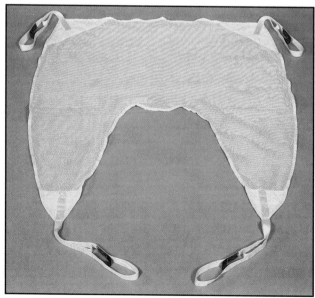

Price guide £55

❑ CHILTERN BAND SLINGS

These two slings are quilted diagonally to strengthen them and prevent creasing during use.

Size One size only.

Attachment Four nylon webbing straps, each with three loops to give alternative positions for attachment to the spreader bar, are sewn onto the sling. Alternate loops are colour-coded for ease of identification.

Positioning and removal The band slings are easy to fit to a person in bed or a chair.

Support The slings give support to the trunk and legs and the padding gives extra comfort.

Toileting and personal cleansing Clothing can easily be adjusted with the slings fitted, and access for personal cleansing is good.

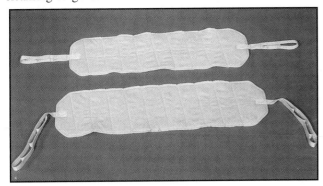

Price guide £60

❑ LLEWELLYN-SML SLINGS

Llewellyn-SML make a comprehensive range of slings which are for use with their Commodore and Moby range of hoists. All Llewellyn-SML slings are made with a twist in the webbing loops so that they are always open and easier to fit on the hooks of the spreader bar.

General points

Material All slings are made in polyester nylon net except for the padded version of the two-piece sling and all the versions of the dressing slings which are made only in polyester.

Special modifications All slings can be partly or fully lined with synthetic sheepskin and the split-leg slings can be fitted with padded leg sections to help prevent creasing.

Cleaning All slings are washable.

Instructions The manufacturer provides a leaflet giving good instructions on use of the slings. The slings are labelled for size and supplied with washing instructions.

Obtainable from Llewellyn-SML Health Care Services
Export available

❑ LLEWELLYN-SML LONG SEAT SLING WITH COMMODE APERTURE SP06

This sling is designed specifically for the care of somebody in bed or for transferring a person to a commode or toilet. It is normally used with two side suspenders, but a version (S33) is available without side suspenders. The sling is suitable for use by somebody who needs body support but can control their head. Demonstration before use is strongly recommended.

Size One size only.

Positioning and removal Can be positioned and removed in bed by rolling the person from one side to the other.

Attachment The sling is used with two side suspenders. On each side of the sling are two nylon webbing straps for attachment to the suspenders. The sling also incorporates a velcro fastened chest restraining strap which fastens with velcro.

Support Good trunk and thigh support but no support for the head.

Toileting and cleansing Access is good. Clothing must be adjusted before fitting the sling. A net version is available for bathing.

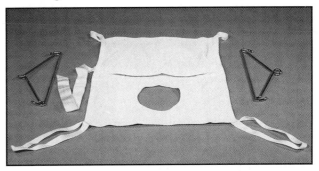

Price guide   Mesh sling   06M £62
               Polyester sling 06P £58

❑ LLEWELLYN-SML EASY-USE SLING WITH COMMODE APERTURE S19, S20, S21 and S34

The divided leg sling with perineal aperture is suitable for those who need full body support but can control their head.

Sizes Small, medium, large and extra large.

Positioning and removal Can be positioned and removed in bed by rolling the user from one side to the other or fitted in a chair.

Attachment The sling is attached to the spreader bar with four nylon webbing straps, each of which has two loops for adjustment.

Support Good trunk and thigh support. The sling is uncomfortable if used in the cross-over position. When lifting a person from the bed the sling needs adjusting after an initial lift to make the person comfortable and straighten out any creasing of the sling fabric under the thighs.

Toileting and personal cleansing Access is good if the sling is arranged with the legs apart. Clothing must be adjusted before the sling is positioned.

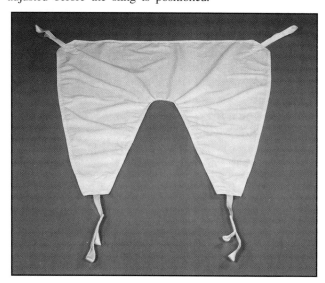

Price guide   Mesh   S19M £50   Polyester S19P £46
                     S20M £60   S20P £55
                     S21M £50   S21P £46
                     S34M £66   S34P £60

❑   LLEWELLYN-SML EASY-USE FULL BODY SLING WITH COMMODE APERTURE S22, S23, S35
The divided leg sling with perineal aperture and head support is suitable for those who need full body and head support. Demonstration before use is strongly recommended.
Sizes   Small, medium, large and extra large.
Positioning and removal   Can be positioned and removed in bed by rolling the user from one side to the other or fitted in a chair.
Attachment   The webbing straps are attached to the spreader bar. The top and bottom straps each have two loops for adjustment but the head straps have only a single loop.
Support   Good trunk and thigh support. When lifting from the bed the sling pulls the head up first but this is not uncomfortable.
Toileting and personal cleansing   Access is good if the sling is arranged with the legs apart. Clothing must be adjusted before the sling is positioned.

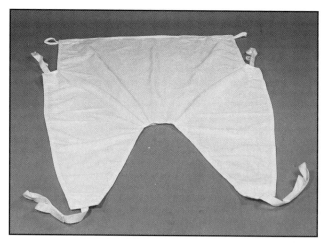

Price guide   Mesh   S22M £60   Polyester S22P £55
                     S23M £60   S23P £55
                     S24M £72   S24P £72
                     S35M £79   S35P £70

❑   LLEWELLYN-SML EASY-USE SLING WITHOUT COMMODE APERTURE S25, S26, S27
The divided leg sling is suitable for those who require full body support but can control the head. Demonstration before use is strongly recommended.
Sizes   Small, medium and large.
Positioning and removal   The sling can be positioned and removed in bed by rolling the user from one side to the other, but cannot be fitted to someone in a chair.
Attachment   Four webbing straps are fixed to the sling for attachment to the spreader bar. Each strap has two loops for adjustment.
Support   Good trunk and thigh support. When lifting a person from the bed the leg supports should be adjusted before the transfer is completed to prevent creasing of the sling fabric under the thighs.

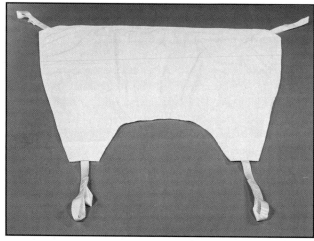

Price guide   Mesh   S25M £56   Polyester S25P £47
                     S26M £60   S26P £50
                     S27M £62   S27P £53

❑ LLEWELLYN-SML TWO-PIECE SLING WITH ARM CUTOUTS SP32

The Two-piece padded band slings are suitable for those with good head and trunk control and strong upper arms as the back sling is held in place under the arms. They are not suitable for those with painful shoulders or extensor spasm.

Sizes One size only.

Positioning and removal The sling can be positioned and removed in bed or chair. The back sling is clearly identified by the cut-out arms. The slings are attached to the spreader bar by nylon webbing straps. Each strap has two loops to give a range of adjustment for an upright or reclined position.

Support Good back and thigh support. The padded cut-out design is more comfortable than the standard band sling.

Toileting and personal cleansing Access is good and clothing can be adjusted while the user is in the slings.

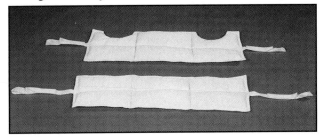

Price guide £70

❑ NESBIT EVANS SLINGS

Nesbit Evans make two slings, the Main Stay and the Fast Fit to be used with their Bodymove hoists.

General points

Material Nylon mesh or full fabric versions.

Cleaning The slings can be washed by hand.

Instructions for use A comprehensive and well explained leaflet is available from the manufacturer.

Obtainable from J Nesbit Evans & Co Ltd
Export available

❑ MAIN STAY SLING

This one piece sling is for use with both the Maxi and Mini models of the Body Move hoist. It can be used in the divided leg or cross-over positions and is most suitable for lifting a person off a bed. Using this sling it is difficult to lower a person into a chair because of the reclined position and it is better to use the Fast Fit sling for such a transfer.

Sizes One size only.

Positioning and removal The sling can be positioned or removed in bed or on a chair. When positioning the sling it is essential to ensure that the perineal aperture is in the correct place.

Attachment The sling is attached to the hoist by four nylon webbing straps on each side. Each strap has two loops to give some means of adjustment.

Support The sling provides good support to the head, trunk and thighs, and is comfortable to use.

Toileting and personal cleansing The perineal space is good. Clothes need to be adjusted before fitting but it may be difficult to position a person on the toilet because of the reclining position when lifted. Drainage after bathing is good.

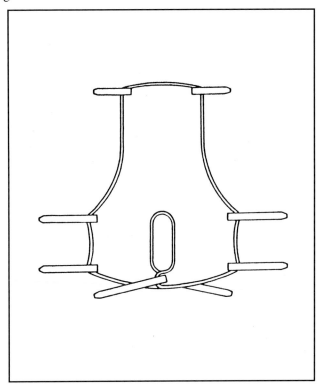

Price guide　Mesh £68
　　　　　　　Cloth £63

❑ FAST FIT SLING

This sling is suitable for use with people who have limited use of the trunk or those with extensor spasm.

Sizes Small, medium and large.

Positioning and removal Can be positioned or removed in bed or on a chair. The user should lean forward in a sitting position and make sure that the sling is fitted to the base of the user's spine. The leg supports are crossed over under the person's thighs.

Attachment Four nylon webbing straps, each with two loops to give flexibility for adjustment.

Support Good to the trunk and legs.

Toileting and personal cleansing The sling must be removed first.

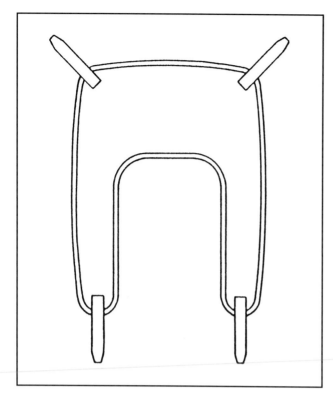

Price guide   Mesh £46 - 57
             Cloth £41 - 52

❏   PAYNE SLINGS

The manufacturers F J Payne make a comprehensive range of slings which are for use with their own hoists and the Chiltern Wispa electric hoist.

General points

Material   Polyester or nylon net.

Special modifications   Slings can be made to suit the individual. Added padding, extended straps or sheepskin inserts are some of the many modifications that can be provided by the manufacturer.

Cleaning   All slings are washable

Instructions   A wall chart identifying the different styles of slings is available from the manufacturer. The slings are labelled and supplied with fitting instructions.

Obtainable from F J Payne Manufacturing Ltd
Export available

❏   PAYNE NEW HAMMOCK SLING WITH HEAD SUPPORT

This divided leg sling with an aperture for personal cleansing and head support is designed for those who need full body and head support. A nylon net version is available for bathing.

Sizes   small, medium and large.

Positioning and removal   The sling can be positioned and removed in bed by rolling the user from one side to the other.

Attachment   The sling is fixed to the spreader bar by three

nylon webbing straps on each side of the sling. Each strap has two loops for adjustment. When attaching the legs the outer thigh strap is passed through a loop on the inner strap and connected to the spreader bar. The inner thigh straps must not be linked to the spreader bar, and only two straps are hooked to the spreader bar on either side. If the inner straps are crossed over the legs are held together when the person is lifted.

Support   Very good head and body support. The sling is comfortable to use and head support is good even when lifting from a bed.

Toileting and personal cleansing   Access is not obstructed when each leg is supported individually. The sling is unsuitable for personal cleansing if the leg supports are crossed over. Clothing must be adjusted before the sling is positioned.

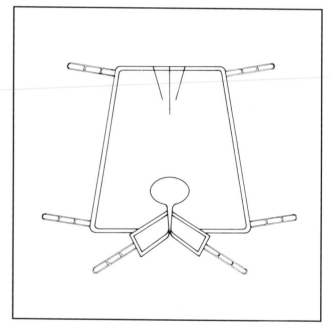

Price guide £70

❏   PAYNE LONG SEAT SLING - PLAIN AND COMMODE

The all-in-one long seat sling available with or without an aperture for personal cleansing is suitable for those who require full body support but have control of the head.

Sizes   Small, medium and large.

Positioning and removal   The sling can be positioned and removed in bed by rolling the user from one side to the other.

Attachment   Four nylon webbing straps at each corner of the sling are attached to two chrome side suspenders which hook into the spreader bar. These spread the load and make the sling more comfortable in use.

Support   Generally good support to the body and legs.

Toileting and personal cleansing   The plain model is unsuitable for toileting. Access is good in the model with the aperture but clothing must be adjusted before positioning the sling.

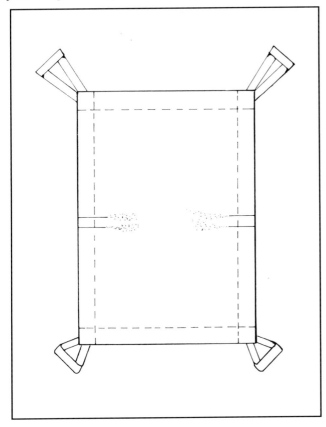

Price guide   Plain £43
                    Commode £48

❏   PAYNE QUICK-FIT SLING

This is a one-piece basic quick-fit sling. It is a divided leg design with an aperture for personal cleansing and is suitable for those who need full body support but have control of their head.

Sizes Small, medium and large.

Positioning and removal The sling is easy to position and remove in bed or when the user is sitting in a chair. It can be fitted in the divided leg, cross-over or knees together positions and is often used with two side suspenders to make it more comfortable.

Attachment Four nylon webbing straps are fixed to the sling for attachment to the spreader bar. Each strap has three loops to give flexible adjustment.

Support The sling gives good support to the trunk and legs. After an initial lift the leg supports may need adjusting to remove any creases in the fabric under the thighs.

Toileting and personal cleansing Access is good. Clothing needs adjustment before the sling is fitted, and it is best used in the divided leg position.

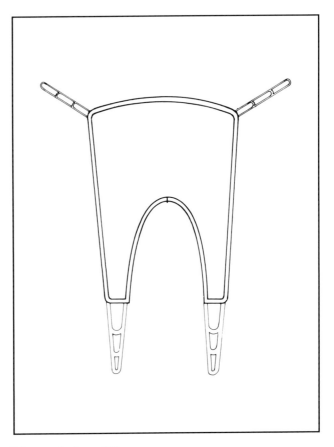

Price guide from £48

❏   PAYNE QUICK-FIT HEAD SUPPORT SLING

This sling is similar to the one-piece basic Quick-fit sling but has head support. It is a divided leg design with an aperture for personal cleansing and is suitable for those who need full body and head support.

Sizes Small, medium and large.

Positioning and removal The sling can be positioned and removed in a bed by rolling the user from one side to the other or to a person sitting in a chair.

Attachment Six nylon webbing straps are fixed to the sling for attachment to the spreader bar. Each strap has three loops for adjustment. In addition two metal side suspenders each 300mm long are available. These allow the user to be lifted in a more reclined position and are useful when lifting a bed-bound person to change the bed clothes or for toileting.

Support The sling gives good support to the trunk and legs. The head is supported from the back but there is no lateral support. After an initial lift the leg supports may need adjusting to remove creasing under the thighs before the lifting is completed.

Toileting and personal cleansing Access is good. Clothing needs adjustment before the sling is fitted.

Support Limited support. Very uncomfortable under the arms if used to aid standing.

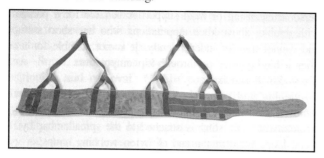

Price guide £60

❑   WESSEX STANDING HARNESS

This harness is a band sling designed to help people stand from a sitting position and is often used as a dressing aid. A person using it must have some weight bearing ability in their legs. It is not suitable for anyone with a chest condition.

Sizes One size only.

Positioning and removal Easy to position on a seated person or to someone lying in bed.

Attachment A metal ring is fitted to each end of the harness band. A webbing strap with a metal ring at each end is passed through both these rings and attached to a central mounting on the spreader bar. As the person is lifted the sling is pulled tight around the chest. During lifting the person must hold on to both ends of the spreader bar to stop it swinging.

Support Limited support. Can be uncomfortable under the arms during lifting.

Price guide £60

Specialised slings/harnesses/frames

❑   BOW SAN SLING

The Bow San Sling can be used with a specially developed hoist, or with any mobile or overhead hoist with a conventional spreader bar, provided the manufacturer has given approval. Trial is strongly recommended before purchasing this sling as it may not suit all individuals.

Material This composite sling is made up of three separate units. The back strap, which is 305mm wide and made from padded black vinyl, is available in a plain standard form or in a reinforced version strengthened to give extra support and prevent creasing. This strap together with two gutter-shaped thigh supports, made from stainless steel with sheepskin covers, makes up the Bow San Sling. Black nylon webbing straps each with two "D" rings are fixed to all the units for attachment to the spreader bar. This gives flexibility for adjustment depending on the user's size.

Size One size only.

Positioning and removal The sling is easy to position to someone sitting in a chair or lying in bed. The back strap is put in place and the thigh supports are rolled under the thighs.

Support The sling gives good support to the back and thighs, but none to the head. For a sling of this type it is comfortable during lifting. As the person is lifted the weight of the body brings the straps together and the metal thigh supports push against each other to give support to the legs and thighs. This is more effective when the sling is used in conjunction with the Bow San hoist as the attachments on the spreader bar are centralised.

There is a danger that a severely disabled person could slip through the sling while being lifted.

Toileting and personal cleansing In common with other slings of this type access for toileting is good. Clothing can be adjusted while the sling is in position.

Cleaning The back strap can be wiped clean and the sheepskin covers on the thigh supports are easily removed for washing.

Instructions for use The sling should be thoroughly demonstrated and tried before purchase. Instructions are provided by the manufacturer and a video on the correct use of the sling is available on request.

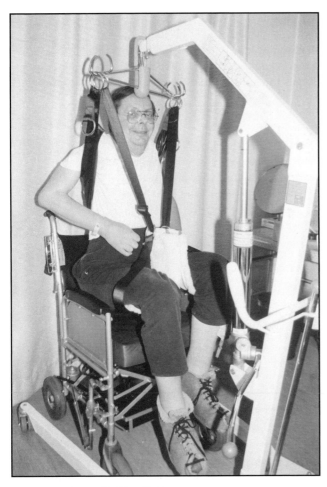

Obtainable from Hoskins Ltd
Price guide Hoist £700   Sling £145
Export available

❏ CHRISTINA GORDON HARNESS AND FRAME

This harness and frame can be used with any overhead or mobile hoist which has a good range of lift. The sling has been designed for independent use by a person who has some upper body mobility and is not mentally impaired, to make transfers between bed, chair, toilet or bath. It is also suited for attendant use and in conjunction with the appropriate hoist can be used for picking a person up from the floor.

Construction The harness is made from blue water resistant cotton drill material with black nylon webbing straps and plastic clip fastenings.

The frame or spreader bar is square and constructed from nylon coated steel. The attachments for the sling are good quality, quick release snap-action clips.

Fitting The harness/sling fastens in the front and fits 32" chest with some scope for adjustment. It is one size and fitting requires no rolling or lifting of the user. To position the harness it is passed over the user's head and the front flap is pulled down to waist level and fastened tightly round the body with a belt secured by a plastic buckle. The thigh supports, which are a continuation of the back flap,

are brought round the side of the body and up under the thighs, as close to the groin as possible, to fasten in front with two clip-in buckles. The support straps are then clipped to the square four-point spreader bar/frame ready for hoisting. If the thigh supports slip down the leg to behind the knee, they give poor support and are uncomfortable during lifting.

When fitting the harness to someone lying in bed it is easier to position the thigh supports correctly if the legs are drawn up into flexion.

Comfort/Support The user is lifted in a good sitting position with adequate support to the trunk and legs, but none to the abdomen and head. There is no support for the head when lifting a person from a bed. The padded area around the neck hollow does offer some support in the initial lift.

The back and buttocks are left clear which makes it easy to remove clothes for toileting.

Safety When properly fitted the harness is very safe for most people, but it is not suitable for those who lack body control or are liable to spasm, as they may slip through.

Optional extras A modified version of the harness is available with 'D'ring fittings which can be used on a standard spreader bar with a two point attachment.

A grab handle which fits onto the centre of the frame and can be used as a lifting aid when not wearing the harness.

Instructions for use Good instructions with clear diagrams are available. Trial is recommended before making a purchase.

Lifting capacity 140kg

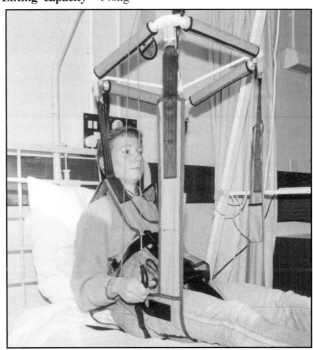

Obtainable from   Christina Hollick
Price guide   Harness and frame £360
              Harness plus 'D'rings without frame £155
              Grab handle £50

Export available

❏ HANDI-MOVE MOBILE UNIT

(Electric version)

Suitable for use in hospitals, residential homes and larger private houses, this unit offers an alternative to the conventional sling hoist for making transfers between chair, bed, toilet and the floor.

Construction The lifting frame is made from stainless steel tubing with moulded foam plastic chest supports and nylon or rubber coated steel leg supports secured to the frame by nylon straps. When tested the lifting frame was mounted on a portable hoist, but it can also be fixed to the floor or fitted to an overhead track system. The unique scissor action of the frame gives automatic adjustment of the supports to fit any size person. As the hoist is lifted the person's weight on the leg supports provides the force needed to grip the chest. The minimal amount of effort needed to position the supports makes it possible for some people to use the hoist independently.

Power supply The hoist is powered by an electric lifting motor. A cheaper version is also available with a hand operated hydraulic pump. Two dry cell rechargeable 12v batteries provide the power.

Controls The lift is operated by a rocker switch on a hand-held pendant control. This is held on the frame by a magnetic back when not in use.

Brakes Acting on the rear wheels they are effective but sometimes difficult to release as they tend to swivel under the frame.

Comfort The positioning of the leg supports is important to ensure that the weight of the patient is taken equally by the chest and legs. It is most comfortable with the leg supports positioned as high up the thigh as possible. When these supports are in a lower position to allow adjustment of clothes for toileting, most of the body weight is taken through the chest and axillae. This is only comfortable for short periods of time.

Manoeuvring Although large the hoist is easily manoeuvred on smooth ground by double castors at the front and rear of the base. Larger castors are available for use on carpeted floors. It passes readily through doorways although care must be taken to lower the hoist. The base is sufficiently adjustable to embrace armchairs.

Safety Care is needed in lowering the hoist as the user could be hit by the support frame. During lifting the gripping action around the thorax makes it almost impossible for the user to fall out of the support frame.

Stability The hoist is stable but the patient may need to be steadied during transit. A fixed joint is available to stop swivelling when using the overhead track.

Storage The mast separates from the base for transport and storage.

Instructions for use Provided by the manufacturer.

Servicing and maintenance Technical back-up is available if necessary from the manufacturer.

Accessories Pads are available for the chest and leg supports.

Dimensions

Maximum height	2410mm
Minimum height	1750mm
Height to top of mast	1730mm
Overall length of chassis	1180mm
Boom length	850mm
Height of chassis	110mm
Range of lift	1260mm
Height of base	110mm
Diameter of wheels	75mm or 125mm
Range of adjustment - base	
Legs open 1150mm, closed 620mm	
Weight	60kg
Lifting capacity	145kg

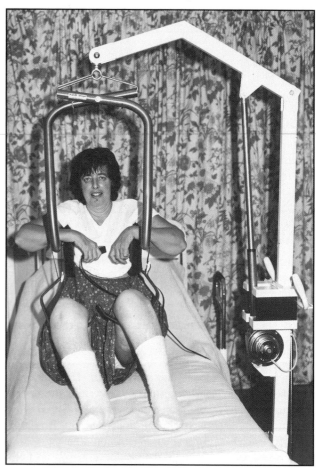

Obtainable from Velmore Ltd
Price guide   Handi-move £473
Handi-move mobile (Electric) £1856
Handi-move mobile (Hydraulic) £1050
Handi-move and overhead track system   from £993 to £1510 for lifting motor.
Track £23 per metre.
Export available

SWIMMING POOL LIFTS

Points to consider

✳   Other transfers may be needed at the pool besides lowering swimmers into the pool so consideration should be given to see if one piece of equipment can solve them all.

✳   If slings are used instead of a seat or stretcher then dog-clips must be used to prevent the sling floating free from the supporting arm while in the water.

❑   ARJO MANUALLY OPERATED POOL LIFT

This manually operated pool lift is most suited for use in specialised pools or hydrotherapy units. It can be permanently mounted on a base plate at the side of the pool or used as a portable hoist which slots into a sunken socket in the pool surround.
   The lift is suitable for bathers with various types of disabilities as it includes a stretcher amongst the options for transfer. Swimmers can enter the water either in a sitting or recumbent position.
Sitting swimmers   A chair and carriage system similar to the Ambulift D model (page 29) is used to transfer swimmers straight from the changing rooms into the water. A pool lift swimchair with large wheels is available as an alternative. This has a permanently fixed chassis and can be wheeled in the water at the shallow end of the pool.
Recumbent swimmers   A stretcher which fits onto a detachable wheeled carriage is used to transfer the person into the water. There is no padding on the main support bracket and care should be taken with people liable to spasm.
Construction   The steel frame of the hoist is heavily protected against corrosion. The boom swings out over the water and the chair or stretcher is lowered into the water on the stainless steel mast.
Controls   The hoist is operated by a simple winding mechanism situated at the top of the support column.
Hoisting action   The lift moves slowly and smoothly and the action is easily controlled by the helper.
Access for user   Good. The boom swings round through 360° to give easy access.
Installation   A base plate or permanent socket are set in the pool surround as appropriate.
Instructions for use   Provided by the manufacturer.
Servicing and maintenance   Minimal servicing required, but a contract can be arranged with the manufacturer.
Dimensions
Range of lift   1270mm
Lifting capacity   160kg

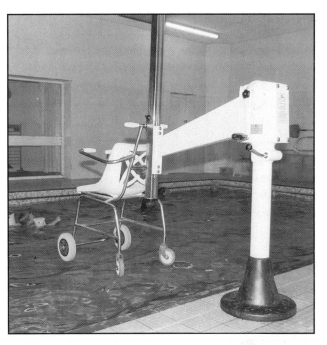

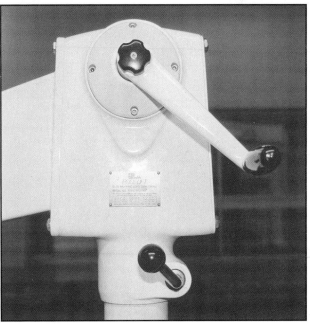

Winding mechanism

Obtainable from Arjo Mecanaids Ltd
Price guide   Socket-mounted with swimchair £5090
Export available

❑   ARJO OTTER POOL LIFT

The Arjo Otter pool lift is designed for use with all sunken pools. It is fully transportable on wheels attached to the back of the base and slots onto two "T" hooks which fit into permanent sockets set in the pool surround. The lift is suitable for those with good head control, trunk control and sitting balance.
Construction   The frame of the hoist is made of stainless steel. The mast projects under the water parallel to the pool edge to give the hoist stability and strength. Two hooks on

the base slot onto the "T" bolts at the pool edge to anchor the hoist. The frame of the chair is made of tubular stainless steel with a white plastic seat and armrests. It travels up and down the mast and swings through an arc of 180º to allow the swimmer to transfer from the pool edge. The chair locks in position by a foot operated safety catch.

Controls   The lift is operated by a simple winding mechanism situated at the top of the mast.

Hoisting action   The lift moves slowly and smoothly and the action is easily controlled by the helper.

Access for user   Good.

Installation   Two permanent sockets are set in the pool surround. These are hardly noticeable when the hoist is not in use.

Instructions for use   Provided by the manufacturer.

Servicing and maintenance   Minimal servicing required, but a contract can be arranged with the manufacturer.

Dimensions

Height of seat (fully raised)   720mm above water level
Range of lift   1530mm
Lifting capacity   160kg

Obtainable from Arjo Mecanaids Ltd
Price guide   £3390
Export available

This pool lift was not evaluated and the report is based solely on the manufacturer's technical literature.

❏   THE OXFORD DIPPER

This hydraulically-operated lift can be used in sunken pools, but raised floor-mounting or wall-mounting may be required for use in hydrotherapy tanks or free-standing pools. It is fully portable and when used in sunken pools slots into a permanent socket set in the pool surround. The lift is suitable for those with good head control, trunk control and sitting balance.

Construction   The frame of the hoist is made of plastic-coated steel which is corrosion proof. It breaks down into four pieces for easy transport and storage. A rigid seat made of white plastic, which can be rotated through 360º, is fixed to the boom of the hoist by a curved arm. A wheeled chassis which slots into the base of the seat for transfer to and from the changing rooms is removed before the swimmer is lowered into the water.

Controls   Operation of the hydraulic pump raises the lift and a controlled release valve, which can be stopped at any point, lowers the swimmer into the water.

Hoisting action   The lift moves slowly and smoothly and the action is easily controlled.

Access for user   This is good as the swimmer is wheeled to the hoist already seated in the chair. Large people may find the chair a little narrow.

Installation   A permanent socket is set in the pool surround.

Instructions for use   Provided by the manufacturer.

Servicing and maintenance   Annual by arrangement with the manufacturer.

Dimensions

Length of boom   1525mm
Range of lift   1865mm
Lifting capacity   140kg

Obtainable from F J Payne (Manufacturing) Ltd
Price guide   From £1851
Export available

❑ THE OXFORD POOLSIDE

This hydraulically-operated lift is used in public swimming pools. It is fully transportable and slots easily into a permanent socket set in the pool surround. The lift is suitable for those with good head control, trunk control and sitting balance.

Construction The frame of the hoist is made from plastic-coated steel which is corrosion proof. The wheeled chair is made of plastic-coated tubular steel with a white plastic seat and foot rest. The swimmer is transferred from the changing rooms to the pool side in the chair. This is then suspended on the spreader bar by nylon webbing straps, and the hoist is raised before the swimmer is lowered into the water in the chair.

Controls Operation of the hydraulic pump raises the lift and a controlled release valve, which can be stopped at any point, lowers the swimmer into the water.

Access for user This is good as the swimmer is wheeled to the hoist already seated in the chair.

Installation A permanent socket is set in the pool surround. This is sealed with a flush fitting plug when the hoist is not in use.

Instructions for use Provided by the manufacturer.

Servicing and maintenance Annual by arrangement with the manufacturer.

Dimensions

Length of boom	1524mm
Range of lift	1803mm
Minimum depth of pool	914mm
Lifting capacity	115kg

Obtainable from F J Payne (Manufacturing) Ltd
Price guide From £985
Export available

❑ MINIVATOR POOL LIFT

Suitable for use with hydro-therapy tanks, free-standing or sunken pools, this pool lift is operated by mains water pressure. It is fully portable and is easily moved into position at the side of the pool on wheels attached to the frame.

It is suitable for use by those with good head control, trunk control and sitting balance.

Construction The frame of the lift is made of tubular stainless steel supported by a stanchion which slots into a permanent socket set in the surround of the pool. When fixed in place one end of the frame rests on the side of the pool to give extra support and stability. The white plastic chair is attached to brackets which move up and down the frame. An arm rest or grab handle is fitted to either the right or left side of the chair. The chair locks in position while the bather transfers and its height can be adjusted to suit the user. A seat belt and head rest are available as optional extras.

Controls A lever fixed to the frame opens the control valve to release the water pressure which lowers the chair into the water.

Power supply The lift is operated by water pressure supplied by a high pressure hose. A booster pump may be required if the mains pressure is inadequate.

Hoisting action The lift moves smoothly but slowly and the action is easily controlled.

Access for user ·As the chair lowers it swivels through 90° to give access to the bather. Transfer from a wheelchair is awkward as the chair is positioned over the water. For an assisted transfer there is little room between the stanchion and the seat for the helper.

Installation A permanent socket 102mm in diameter is set in the pool surround. When not in use the whole hoist unit is removed.

Instructions for use Provided by the manufacturer.

Servicing and maintenance The manufacturer offers a full servicing and maintenance scheme. The lift is guaranteed for one year after installation.

Dimensions

Minimum pool depth	1067mm
Maximum weight	152kg
Range of lift	1067mm
Lifting capacity	146kg

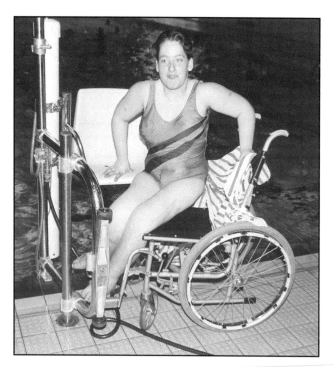

Obtainable from Sunrise Medical Ltd
Price guide   £1495
Booster pump price on application
Export available

CAR HOISTS

Points to consider

✳   Several specifically designed car hoists are available to lift a person in and out of a car.

✳   Prior to purchase the user should make sure that the hoist will fit his particular model of car and that there is good access.

✳   The type of car may limit the choice of hoist. Two-door cars normally have wider doors which open at a greater angle and give more room for manoeuvre.

✳   The position of the parked car in relation to the house and the space available for manoeuvre should be suitable and adequate to make the transfer.

✳   There should be enough space in the car to store a wheelchair either behind the passenger seat, in the boot or using specifically designed equipment. (See *Equipment for the Disabled Outdoor Transport* 6th edition (1987)).

✳   The spreader bar may need padding to prevent damage to the user's head.

✳   The user may need to bend his head forwards and/or sideways when using the hoist.

✳   If a mobile hoist is needed for transfers about the house then it may be possible to use this hoist for car transfers.

✳   If a mobile hoist is used to make car transfers there must be sufficient room in the car to stow it, and a wheelchair, while travelling.

❏   BURVILL CAR-TOP HOIST

This attendant operated car hoist has been specially designed to transfer a person between a wheelchair and a car.
It fits on the car roof using four steel gutter clamps or an alternative method of fixing is available for those cars without gutter channels. No modification to the vehicle is necessary.
   The whole unit is easily removed for storage or transfer to another car.
Construction The main body of the hoist is made of steel and finished in a grey powder coating. The cantilevered boom slides in and out of the housing on nylon rollers. The lifting arm is attached to one end of the boom by a socket which allows it to rotate in a horizontal plane through 110°. The spreader bar, which hooks onto the end of the lifting

arm, has four attachment points for different slings. This gives a good range of movement.

Power supply The boom is operated manually and the lifting is unit is powered by a hydraulic pump with a knob release.

Storage The entire pump unit, spreader bar and support arm are easily removed for storage in the car during transit or while parking. The boom is returned to the housing, locked in place and fastened with a safety chain.

Lifting capacity 90kg
Weight of lift 25kg
Range of lift 380mm vertically.

Installation Easily done by any competent person.

Instructions for use Full instructions with diagrams are supplied by the manufacturer.

Slings

Style A conventional one-piece sling (not quick-fit) or two piece band slings are supplied by the manufacturer.

Material Canvas which is not comfortable for all day sitting.

Fitting It is difficult to fit the standard sling around someone sitting in a chair. The band slings are easier to fit but may not be suitable for all users.

Sizes Standard one size but larger slings are available upon request.

Fastening Chain attachments on the slings allow a good range of adjustment and enable the user to be lifted in a good sitting position.

Support Good to the back and legs but none to the head.

Obtainable from S.Burvill & Son
Price guide £496
Export available

❏ MEYLAND PERSON LIFT

This hoist is new in the design of car lifts. It is intended chiefly for making transfers between wheelchair and car but can also be wall-mounted and used in the home for transfers in the bedroom or bathroom. The hoist is suitable for independent use or with attendant help.

For independent operation of the hoist a person should have good control of his arms and be able to lift his feet into the footwell of the car. Two wheelchair lifting and storage devices are available to help the independent user stow the wheelchair for travelling after transfer (see *Equipment for the Disabled Outdoor Transport* 6th edition (1987)).

It can be fitted to cars with two or four doors although two doors are preferred because they open at a wider angle and there is more space to manoeuvre. The minimum width needed to operate the hoist is 890mm.

Construction The frame is made from coated tubular steel.

The mounting post is fixed permanently on either the right- or left-hand side of the car between the dashboard and floor. The arm and spreader bar fold away parallel to the post and the hoist remains in position during a journey or for parking. The hoist arm which is adjustable to fit different cars, is jointed and pivots on the mounting post allowing a versatile range of movement within the length of the arm.

The user is lifted in a sling attached to the spreader bar. This is close to the person's chest during the lift but does not present a hazard.

Power supply The lift is operated by a 12v motor which is powered by the car battery. Only the lifting is powered, all sideways movements are made manually.

Controls Push buttons are contained in a hand-held box, with a magnetic backing. This is attached to the motor by a coiled wire, allowing extended use.

Storage The hoist is easily removed from the post for storage when not in use.

Lifting capacity 108kg
Weight of lift 13.5kg
Range of lift 390mm

Installation Can be done by a skilled DIY person but is best installed by a motor mechanic.

Instructions for use Supplied by the manufacturer. Demonstrations can be arranged through nationwide agents.

Slings

Style Quick-fit style.
Material Woven nylon with webbing straps.
Fitting Can be fitted by user or helper while sitting in wheelchair.
Sizes Five sizes available.
Fastenings On the spreader bar there are three points of attachment for the slings which are fastened with keyhole fittings that are simple and secure in use.

Support Good support to the trunk and upper thighs but none to the head.

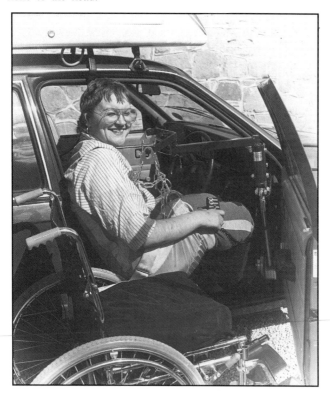

Obtainable from Autochair
Price guide   Hoist £1182 including one sling
              Slings £32
Export available

❑ PARRY MK4B CAR HOIST

This is a well made and effective car hoist which requires attendant help during use. It clamps on the roof of any car using a conventional roof rack fitting. The whole unit can be easily removed especially if the boom is taken out first to lighten the weight. A windshield is fitted in front of the unit to cut down the noise whilst travelling.

It is important to site the hoist correctly on the roof to allow maximum movement in use as the boom has limited front to back movement. It slides in and out of the frame and there is no swivel joint on the support arm to turn the spreader bar. This is 420mm in length and has one good hook at either end.

Construction Steel with nylon bearings.
Power supply The boom is pulled in and out of the housing manually. Its action is not always smooth and it may require an extra push from the attendant. This might cause the person to swing unpleasantly, although it is quite safe.

The lifting action is powered by a hydraulic pump which is operated by a lever and it is important to release this slowly in order to lower the user safely.
Storage After use the spreader bar and pump handle are stored in the car and the hoist jack must be fully lowered. Failure to do this will result in the hydraulic ram rusting.

The boom is pushed into the sleeve and the pump mechanism locked in place on the roof. The whole is then covered for storage while parked or travelling.
Lifting capacity   95kg
Weight of lift   20kg
Range of lift Approx. 330mm
Installation Can be done easily by any competent person.
Instructions for use Full instructions with diagrams are supplied by the manufacturer.

Slings

Style A standard sling, which gives a comfortable lift, is supplied with the hoist. The manufacturer, however, is happy for people to use their own slings if they prefer to do so.
Material Canvas, but not comfortable for all day sitting.
Fitting It is difficult to fit the sling around a person already seated.
Sizes One size only.
Fastening Chain attachments at the top and bottom of the sling give a good range of adjustment and enable the user to assume a good sitting position during hoisting.
Support Good to the trunk and legs but none for the head.

Obtainable from T Parry (Car Hoists)
Price guide £335
Export available to all countries except US and Canada.

LIFTS

Points to consider

Types of lifts
Powered stairlifts
- Seated model
- Standing model
- Wheelchair-carrying model

Powered home lifts
- Partially or fully enclosed cars (through-floor lifts)
- Enclosed model with a shaft

Manually driven balanced personal home lift

The relevant British Standard specifications are as follows:
BS 5776: 1979 Specification for powered stairlifts
BS 5900: 1980 Specification for powered home lifts
BS 5965: 1980 Specification for manually-driven balanced personal home lifts
   These are obtainable from the British Standards Institution (see *Addresses* page 130).

* Those considering the installation of any lift are strongly recommended to read the relevant British Standard and particularly Appendix A: *Guidance to purchaser*. The Standards include sections relating to design consideration, building requirements, technical specifications, testing, inspection and servicing. Appendix A contains points to consider when selecting the type of stairlift: its suitability for the type of disability, the suitability of the stairway or building; the electrical supply; the controls, operating instructions; special considerations for those living alone for long periods; maintenance; breakdowns and change of user.

* When getting up stairs to bedroom, bathroom and WC is a problem or becomes impossible the alternatives are to live downstairs and use a commode or chemical toilet instead of the WC; build a ground floor extension; move to more suitable accommodation elsewhere or install a stair or through-floor lift.

* Installing a lift may be cheaper than building an extension and a preferable solution to moving away from a known area.

* The therapist should check that the disabled person will be able to make full use of the upstairs rooms.

* The installation and use of a lift must be acceptable to the disabled person and his family and they must be involved in the discussions from the outset.

* The availability of assistance, generally, and in an emergency, needs to be considered.

* It is helpful if the user and family can try a similar lift to the one under discussion.

* Both district councils and social services departments are able to help with adaptations in private and public sectors.

* Acoustic insulation may be needed to reduce noise from stairlifts and home lifts in semi-detached or terraced houses; it costs less if fitted at the time of installation. Many lifts now use nylon rollers on aluminium tracks and are powered by much quieter motors than previously.

* The user should notify his insurance company of the installation of the lift whether it is put in private or public sector housing.

* A cordless phone or alarm system is a reassurance to the user and a useful safety measure to summon help for someone living alone.

Assessment for a lift
* The community occupational therapist involved with the recommendation and installation of a lift will liaise with the district council's environmental health officer or housing officer.

* The therapist will assess the person's abilities, the property and their social situation before making a recommendation.

Indemnity and instruction in safe use of the lift
* It is recommended that when an occupational therapist has been involved in giving advice the user should be asked to sign an indemnity form confirming that verbal and written instructions have been given regarding the safe use of the lift.

* If the social services department has assisted with financial arrangements an indemnity form may be used to confirm the agreement reached with the person regarding ownership and maintenance.

Ownership
* District Councils remain the owners of lifts provided in their own properties.

* A lift which is provided by Improvement Grant becomes the property of the grant applicant.

* If the social services department contributed to the cost of the lift it may make an arrangement with the user to take

over the lift when it is no longer required.

Maintenance and service

✳ Responsibility for regular maintenance and servicing of the lift should be clarified before it is installed.

✳ The lift should be examined and serviced at least once a year. Further details for servicing and testing are given in Section 7 of BS 5776: (1979). Lifts in public places should be serviced four times a year.

✳ The Authority makes arrangements for property owned by the District Council.

✳ When the Social Services department has assisted with the financial arrangements and agreement has been reached with the user that the lift can be resited when it is no longer needed, maintenance and servicing can be financed by the social services department.

Further reading

1 *Stairlifts and Home Lifts for Disabled People* (1984) Proceedings of a seminar. Centre on Environment for the Handicapped, London. March 1984. (Obtainable from Centre for Accessible Environments see *Addresses* page 130.)

2 Stowe J. (1988) *Guide to the selection of stairlifts.* Rheumatology and Rehabilitation Research Unit, Leeds, UK.

Stairlifts

General points to consider

✳ Building Regulations approval is not necessary for a stairlift unless it is fitted into a house during construction, or alterations to the staircase are necessary. Charges for permission do not apply to work carried out for disabled people.

✳ A stairlift is wired into a wall socket outlet and powered from the domestic electricity supply. Power through a pre-payment meter is not suitable.

✳ Most stairlifts are designed for straight flights of stairs, but some manufacturers make stairlifts for curved stairways to individual specification. These are more expensive.

✳ Because of the complexity of curved stairlifts and the cost of installation, it may be worthwhile considering a through floor lift.

✳ One or two rails are fitted on the stairway to retain and guide the carriage that supports the chair or platform throughout its travel.

✳ Most stairlifts travel on a single rail which can be fitted on the right or left side of the staircase. Some stairlifts require a rail fitting on each side of the stairway.

✳ Where it is necessary for a rail to project from the stairs several manufacturers supply a hinged rail which is folded up when not in use to avoid a potential hazard.

✳ Some rails are fitted flush to the edge of the stairs which may make carpet cleaning difficult and will require the stairlift and rail to be moved if a new carpet is laid. Others are fitted on vertical supports which makes cleaning easier and new carpets can be laid by cutting holes for the supports or by laying the carpet in the centre of the stairway only.

✳ Some rails flatten out on the top landing and continue parallel to the floor for some distance away from the edge of the stairs giving the user safe access and exit from the seat or platform.

✳ In some models the motor is fitted in the seat of the stairlift unit, in others it is installed separately at the top or bottom of the stairs, on the landing, under the stairs or in an adjacent room. (A stairlift with the motor under the seat should not be chosen if the user is incontinent).

✳ An emergency hand-winding mechanism is incorporated into the motor for use by an attendant in the event of a mains power failure. The purchaser should make sure that it is easy for a helper to reach when the user is seated.

✳ Wall-fixed call/send and emergency stop controls and/ or key switches are fitted as standard by some manufacturers and as optional extras by others.

✳ The height and position of the wall controls are usually fitted to suit the user.

✳ Controls can be fitted for attendant use if necessary.

✳ For safety, controls for direction of travel are fitted with a few seconds delay before any journey commences or is resumed.

✳ **Sensitive edges and surfaces** stop the stairlift when an obstruction is encountered but permit the controls to be operated in the reverse direction so that it can be cleared.

✳ An **alarm** is not usually supplied as a standard feature but may be available as an extra.

✻ The **safe working load** of a stairlift is given on the load plate which is fixed either on the stairlift carriage or at each landing adjacent to the lift. If the user's weight exceeds the safe working load the manufacturer should be consulted before placing an order.

✻ Overspeed governors are fitted on some stairlifts as an extra precaution in case the drive mechanism fails. This allows the lift to descend slowly and safely to the lower floor. All stairlifts have a safety mechanism to bring them safely to the lower floor if the drive system fails.

✻ A 24 hour emergency call-out service is usually provided by the manufacturer.

✻ Individual requirements and adaptations should be discussed with the manufacturer before purchase.

✻ Stairlifts usually require servicing annually though some manufacturers recommend six-monthly.

Specific points to consider

Seated model
✻ A seated model will be necessary if the person cannot travel safely standing.

✻ A seated model comprises a seat with backrest, single or double armrests and a footrest.

✻ On some models seat, footrest and armrests can be folded, separately or together, to save space. Some seat and footrests are interlinked which saves the user from bending. This is particularly useful if the person is likely to become dizzy when bending over at the top of the stairway, or for a person who cannot operate the knob or lever which releases the platform.

✻ Some seats can be swivelled for ease of transfer; they lock automatically in the direction of travel and the stairlift will not move unless they are locked. The user must be able to operate the knob or lever which releases the seat and be able to swivel the chair round by pushing on the wall or use his feet to 'paddle' it round.

✻ If the standard seat design and size are unsuitable the manufacturer should be consulted about possible modification.

✻ Car safety seats for children are fitted to the stairlift by some manufacturers, usually as an extra.

✻ A seat belt is essential for a user with poor balance. It may be fitted as standard or as an optional extra.

✻ On some models the user travels with the seat facing down the stairs, on others facing sideways; those with stiff legs should travel facing downwards but make sure they can dismount at the top.

✻ Most models are available with different sizes of footrest. A person with difficulty in bending his knees will require a large footrest.

Standing model
✻ Standing platforms or perching seats are available for people who have difficulty rising from a sitting position.

✻ A standing model is fitted with a safety rail or harness, hand grips and controls.

✻ On some models, the platform, safety rail and hand grips can be folded away to save space. To do this the person must be able to bend down to reach the platform when it is parked.

✻ The user should make sure that the controls are easily reached and he can operate them satisfactorily.

✻ At the lower landing there may be a small step (under 200mm) up to the platform; it will be necessary to make a shallow well so that the platform stops flush with the floor if the person cannot negotiate the step. At the top landing the platform stops flush with the top step.

✻ Grab rails can be fitted on adjacent walls at the top and bottom of the stairway for safety when transferring.

✻ Walking frames must *not* be carried on a stairlift. A duplicate set should be obtained and one set kept on each floor.

Wheelchair platform
✻ The wheelchair platform is fitted with safety barriers to ensure that the wheelchair is correctly positioned and restrained during travel. Controls are positioned on the side unit and the user should make sure he can reach and operate them. On some models grab handles are fitted.

✻ When not in use some platforms can be folded against the wall to save space.

✻ Access and exit at the lower landing is usually by ramps attached to the platform. Occasionally a shallow well may be necessary so that the platform fits flush with the floor. At the top landing the platform stops flush with the top step.

✻ This lift can be a hazard in private homes where it may block the stairs in an emergency.

Assessment of functional ability of the user

* Is the person mobile with or without a walking aid?
* Can he climb one or more stairs? If so, of what height?
* Could he travel standing?
* Can he sit safely? Can he transfer?
* Is he fully or partially sighted?
* Does he have balance problems or dizziness?
* Does he have involuntary movements or spasm?
* Does he have contractures? Limited range of joint movement? Muscle weakness?
* Does he have pain or discomfort?
* Is sensation lacking?
* Is he prone to pressure sores?
* Is he incontinent?
* Can the person use his hands to operate the controls and to fasten and unfasten a safety belt?
* Is the person in a wheelchair?
* Does the person require constant supervision?
* Is he confused or mentally handicapped?
* Does the person live alone?

Prognosis

* The therapist will need to know whether the person's condition is stable or whether it will deteriorate.

* The therapist must consider whether there is a dependable helper capable of giving assistance, generally and in an emergency, and if the user is at ease operating the lift.

* Safety factors should be considered, particularly if there are small children in the family. A key switch should be fitted to prevent unauthorized use and the possibility of accidents should children play with the lift.

Social assessment

* The assessment will take into account the disabled person's motivation, family relationships, his wishes and those of the family concerning the installation of a lift.

* If the person lives alone or is alone for long periods, an alarm system may be necessary to summon help from outside the house.

Assessment of property

* Electricity must be supplied from the mains and not through a pre-payment meter.

* Is the stairway suitable?

* Is it straight or curved?

* Is there an intermediate landing?

* What is its width and gradient?

* Is there adequate head room?

* Is it sufficiently wide to leave space for others to use the stairs safely?

* Is there space to get on and off the lift?

* Consider the layout in relation to doors and windows, access to the stairway, width of the stairs, space on the landing, circulation areas, access to rooms.

* Will a stairlift obstruct passageways, doorways, access to cupboards? Will it present hazards such as projections or wells?

* Is there adequate light on the stairway and landing at all times?

* If grab rails are necessary make sure that they can be positioned where they will be used.

* It is possible to fit a straight lift to a staircase with a turn at the top if there is room to bridge the gap with a fold down platform, which can be motorised if necessary. This will be much cheaper than installing a curved lift.

* If a folding platform is used at the top of the stairs, there may be a risk of the passenger seated in a side facing chair trapping his toes as he reaches the platform.

Straight or curved stairs

❏   GIMSON STRATUS

The Gimson Stratus stairlift is individually made to fit any curved or straight staircase where the gradient changes, such as on a half landing.

The manufacturer specifies that the lift has been tested and complies with BS 5776:1979.

Construction The 5mm solid steel rail is supported by steel piers bolted to the stairs. The passenger chair is also made of steel and finished with a padded vinyl seat, back and arm rests. The footrest, operated by a handle, folds up against the casing when not in use. The standard chair travels sideways, at a speed of $0.15m^{sec}$ and although the armrests fold up, it does not swivel sideways to allow the passenger easy access. If this is a problem, an extra length of track can be fitted onto the landing. This can be hinged to fold back when not in use. Alternatively a swivel chair is available as an optional extra. In common with other stairlifts of this type, tall people may knock their knees when travelling on a narrow staircase.

Controls The simple up/down controls are incorporated in the end of either armrest together with a panic button. Call/send controls are sited at the top and bottom of the stairs. The handle for manual winding in an emergency is stored in the chair frame. As the chair travels the balance is maintained by a self-levelling device.

A joystick pendant control for passenger or attendant use and key switching for security are also available as optional extras.

Power supply The lift is powered by mains electricity. The drive motor and control unit are housed under the seat of the chair, and the supply flex is controlled by a roller system.

Ride Smooth with gentle stopping and starting.

Safety The bases of the footrest and chair are fitted with sensitive facings. A safety belt is provided for passenger use, and an adult or child restraining harness and ankle restraint can be bought as extras. The lower armrest is of sufficient length to steady an able passenger.

Instructions for use Demonstrated at time of installation and written instructions are given to the user.

Servicing and Maintenance Guaranteed for 12 months after installation.

Breakdown Manufacturer operates a 24 hour call-out service.

Dimensions

Width of rail from wall   200mm
Chair seat   400 x 330mm
Width of footrest from wall   710mm unfolded, 500mm folded
Height from floor to footrest 160mm
Lifting Capacity   115kg

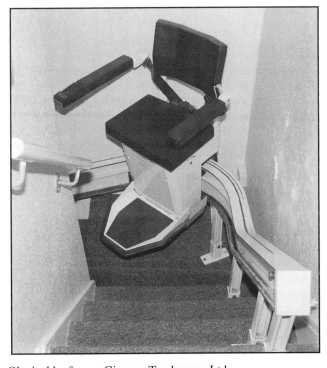

Obtainable from   Gimson Tendercare Ltd
Price on application
Export available

❑   PROJECT AND DESIGN LIBERTY LX

Purpose-built to suit individual stairways, this lift is designed to carry a seated passenger, facing sideways, up a straight or curved flight of stairs.

Another version of this lift, **The Liberty LT lift**, is also available with a higher headrest.

The manufacturer states that the lift complies with BS 5776:1979.

Construction The steel welded track is individually built at the factory after a survey of the stairs. The rail is fixed on the stairtreads at the side of the stairway. The chair travels up and down the rail on a rack and pinion drive. The motor is sited under the chair and incorporates an emergency hand-winding mechanism for use by an attendant. A light is fitted either side of the motor housing. The chair seat, back and armrests are made of moulded plastic with a padded vinyl or fabric finish, and the armrests drop down and rotate to fold round the passenger when travelling. The seat and armrests fold up for storage when the lift is not in use. At the top and bottom of the stairs the seat swivels to make it easier for the passenger to get on and off the chair safely. The footrest is set back under the seat and is finished with a non-slip surface. Some users with stiff knee joints may find it uncomfortable to rest their feet on it. An extended footrest is available as an optional extra.

Controls Call/send buttons and on/off controls are situated at the top and bottom of the stairs to suit the user. The same set of control buttons is fitted at the end of either armrest with a key switch underneath to prevent unauthorised use.

Power supply 240v mains supply

Ride Smooth and feels safe. The seat remains level whatever the gradient of the stairs.

Safety There are no exposed moving parts. The underside of the footrest and the top and bottom entries into the motor housing are fitted with sensitive pads.

A lap safety belt is fitted as standard.

Instructions for use Correct and safe use of the lift are demonstrated when it is installed and the user is given written instructions.

Servicing and maintenance The manufacturer offers a full servicing and maintenance scheme. The lift is guaranteed for one year after installation.

Breakdown Contact the manufacturer.

Dimensions

Chair

Width from wall   (unfolded) 737mm   (folded) 370mm

Height of back rest   355mm

Footrest   250 x 240mm

Seat   380 x 510mm

Lifting capacity   115kg

Obtainable from Project and Design Ltd

Price guide £3125

Export available

❑   STANNAH GOLDEN RAIL

Custom built for individual stairways, this lift is designed to carry a seated passenger, facing sideways, up a straight or curved flight of stairs.

The manufacturer states that the lift complies with BS 5776:1979.

Construction   The rail is fixed to supports on the stairtreads at the side of the stairs. The chair uses a rack and pinion drive to travel up and down the rail. The motor is sited under the chair and incorporates an emergency hand-winding mechanism for use by an attendant. Where access is restricted at the bottom of the stairs a hinged rail may be fitted which folds up when the lift is not in use. This is electrically interlocked for safety and is motorised so that it can be operated from the top of the stairs. If the bottom of the stairs are out of sight when operating the rail, care should be taken that no children or animals are playing in the vicinity, as the hinged joint could be a hazard. The chair seat and backrest have a padded vinyl finish and the armrests are made of moulded plastic. The footrest is finished with a non-slip surface. The seat, foot and armrests fold up when the lift is not in use. If the track is carried on to the level landing at the top of the stairs it is easier for the passenger to get on and off the chair safely and the chair is out of the way when not in use. A swivel

seat is available as an optional extra if space is limited at the top of the stairs.

Controls   Call/send buttons and on/off controls are situated at the top and bottom of the stairs to suit the user. An identical set of control buttons can be fitted at the end of the armrest and a key switch is fixed under either armrest to prevent unauthorised use. Joystick switches are available as optional extras.

Power supply   240v mains supply

Ride   Smooth and feels safe. The seat remains level whatever the gradient of the stairs.

Safety   There are no exposed moving parts. The underside of the footrest and the top and bottom entries into the motor housing are fitted with sensitive pads.

Care should be taken when getting on to the chair to avoid accidently pressing the controls as this will start the chair moving before the passenger is fully seated.

A range of safety belts are available as optional extras.

Instructions for use   Correct and safe use of the lift are demonstrated when it is installed and the user is given written instructions.

Servicing and Maintenance   The manufacturer offers a full servicing and maintenance scheme at a cost of £196 per year.

Breakdown   Contact the manufacturer.

Dimensions

Chair

Width from wall   (unfolded) 700mm   (folded) 520mm

Height of seat from footrest   440mm

Footrest   305 x 215mm

Backrest   380mm

Seat   410 x 400mm

Lifting capacity   120kg

Obtainable from Stannah Stairlifts Ltd

Price guide £3800

Export available

Straight stairs only
Seated/standing

❑ ASGO GLIDE

This stairlift is designed to carry a seated passenger sideways up and down a straight flight of stairs.

The manufacturer states that it conforms to BS 5776:1979.

Construction The track is made of 240mm wide extruded aluminium which is mounted to the steps at the wall side of the stairway. The lift moves up and down the track on a chain drive powered by a motor fitted beneath the chair seat and an overspeed governor is included as standard. An emergency stop button for attendant use is located on the motor housing. The chair is a modern office style design, upholstered in brown fabric, which swivels to allow easy access. The seat, arm and footrests fold up when the lift is not in use.

Controls Call/send switches are located at the top and bottom of the stairs to suit the user. Constant pressure up/down controls are also fitted to the end of the armrest.

Power supply 240v mains supply

Ride Smooth with a three to four second delay before the start.

Safety No moving parts are exposed. The seat is interlocked and must be unfolded before the lift can be called from the top or bottom of the stairs.

The lift will stop if anything is obstructing the track as sensitive edges are fitted to the entry/exit to the motor and to the underside of the footrest.

Instructions for use An instruction manual is supplied by the manufacturer.

Servicing and Maintenance The manufacturer recommends a service once a year. The lift is covered by a warranty for one year after installation.

Breakdown Contact the manufacturer. Breakdown insurance is available on request.

Dimensions

Width from wall (folded)	300mm
Seat width	430mm
Speed of descent	7m per min.
Lifting capacity	115kg

Obtainable from Asgo Ltd
Price guide £1640
Export available

❑ ASGO STAIRGLIDE

This stairlift is designed to carry a passenger in a sitting position up and down a straight flight of stairs. Because the passenger travels facing forwards, this lift is suitable for use on a very narrow flight of stairs. On reaching the top of the stairs the chair swivels round up to 180° to allow the passenger to alight safely. This is not automated so the passenger must be able to do this independently or have help available. Although the track is wider than most other stairlifts of this type, it does not obstruct the stairs.

The manufacturer states that the lift conforms to BS 5776:1979.

Construction The track is 300mm wide and made of extruded aluminium with a wood effect finish. It is fitted flush to the step edges at the side of the stairway. The chair travels up and down the track on a double cable drive and will operate on an incline between 30 and 45°. The motor is fitted beneath the seat of the chair and incorporates an emergency hand-winding device for attendant use. The chair, which looks rather old fashioned, has a brown padded vinyl seat, back and single armrest. A second removable armrest and an extra wide seat are available as optional extras. The footrest does not swivel and is finished with a non-slip surface. When not in use the chair sits at the top or bottom of the stairs.

Controls Call/send buttons are located at the top and bottom of the stairs to suit the user and a lever switch is incorporated in one armrest. An emergency stop switch is located under the seat.

Power supply 240v mains supply or 110v with transformer.

Ride Smooth but no soft start. There is a four second delay and the passenger travels very close to the wall.

Safety There are no exposed moving parts. The track stops just short of the top step and although the chair swivels round to allow the passenger to alight, it would be safer if it extended a little further at this point.

Sensitive edges are included at the back of the seat and underneath the footrest. A seat belt is fitted as standard.

Instructions for use An instruction manual is supplied by the manufacturer.

Servicing and maintenance The manufacturer recommends an annual service.

Breakdown Contact the manufacturer who operates a 24 hour call out service. Breakdown insurance available on request.

Dimensions

Width of chair unit   406mm
Seat width (standard)   380mm, (extra wide) 457mm
Speed of travel   6.7m per min.

Lifting capacity   . 115kg

Obtainable from Asgo Ltd
Price guide £1640
Export available

❑ BROOKS DELUXE STAIRLIFT

This model of the Brooks Deluxe stairlift is due to be superseded by a new version which incorporates the following improvements:
- the drive motor has been resited beneath the chair seat
- the chair now travels on a chain drive
- sensitive pads have been incorporated into the entry and exit of the drive mechanism
- the track design has been altered to finish flush with the top step.

The new version has not been seen so this report is based on an evaluation of the old model.

This stairlift is suitable for carrying a seated passenger, facing downwards, up and down a straight stairway. The manufacturer states that the lift conforms to BS 5776:1979.

Construction The extruded aluminium track is fitted to vertical supports on the right or left hand side of the stairway and projects 250mm at the top of the stairs. The chair travels up and down the stairs on a cable drive, and the motor and winding drum are enclosed and located at the top of the stairs. The motor incorporates an emergency hand-winding mechanism for use by an attendant. The frame of the chair is made of tubular steel and the seat, back and armrests are upholstered in padded vinyl. The chair swivels through 180° to allow the passenger to mount/dismount safely. This is not automated so the passenger must be able to do this independently or have help available. The chair is interlocked so that the lift will only operate when it is facing downstairs. The swivel release lever is fitted under the arm rest and is easy to operate. To fold the chair up it is swung round 90° to face sideways and the seat and armrests which are interlinked are closed together.

Optional extras include a hinged rail at the bottom of the stairs and a manual or motorised platform for "fanned" stairs or sub-landings.

Controls Constant pressure colour-coded push buttons and a key switch to prevent unauthorised use are fitted to either armrest of the chair to suit the user.

Call/send buttons are fitted at the top and bottom of the stairs.

Power supply Standard mains supply.

Ride Feels smooth and safe and stops gently.

Safety Sensitive pads are fitted to the underside of the footrest and at the entry/exit of the drive mechanism. A safety belt is fitted to the chair as standard.

Instructions for use The installer demonstrates the correct and safe use of the lift and gives the user written instructions.

Servicing and maintenance The manufacturer offers a full servicing and maintenance scheme. The lift is guaranteed for one year after installation for parts and labour and for two years parts only.

Breakdown   Contact the manufacturer.
Dimensions
Chair
Width from wall   (folded)   305mm
Seat height   470-559mm   (Adjustable to suit user)
Seat   420 wide x 340mm deep
Height of platform   75mm
Width of track from wall   266mm
Lifting capacity   115kg

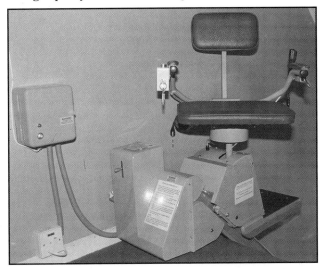

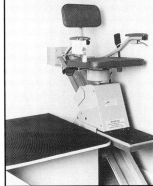

Motorised platform in 'up'   Motorised platform in
position   position

Obtainable from Brooks Stairlifts Ltd
Price guide £1450
Export available

❑   BROOKS SUPREME
This stairlift is designed to carry a seated passenger, facing
sideways, up a straight flight of stairs.
   The manufacturer states that the lift conforms to
BS 5776:1979.
Construction   The aluminium track is fixed to the stair
treads alongside the wall of the stairway and finishes flush
with the top stair. The chair moves up and down the stairs
on a chain drive. The motor is located under the seat and
incorporates a hand-winding mechanism for attendant use
in emergency. The seat, arm and backrests of the chair are
upholstered in padded vinyl and fold up when not in use.
The footrest folds up and has a non-slip finish. There is a
choice of a fixed or swivel chair on the standard model.
   Optional extras include a folding rail at the bottom of the
stairs, a soft start and a pendant control for attendant use.
Controls   Wall mounted call/send buttons are sited at the
top and bottom of the stairs to suit the user. Guarded push
button controls are fitted to either armrest of the chair with
a key switch for security. A toggle switch can be fitted as
an optional extra.
Power supply   Standard mains supply.
Ride   Smooth and quiet.
Safety   A sensitive area covers the under surface of the
footrest and the entry and exit to the drive mechanism. A
safety belt is fitted to the chair in the standard model. A
full harness and a child's seat are available as optional
extras.
Instructions for use   The installer demonstrates the correct
and safe use of the lift and gives the user written
instructions.
Servicing and maintenance   The manufacturer offers a
full servicing and maintenance scheme. The lift is
guaranteed for one year after installation for parts and
labour and for two years for parts only.
Breakdown   Contact the manufacturer.
Dimensions
Chair
Width from wall   (folded) 360mm, (unfolded) 580mm
Height of fixed seat from footrest   419 - 559mm
Height of swivel seat from footrest   470 - 559mm
Height of footrest   50mm
Lifting capacity   115kg

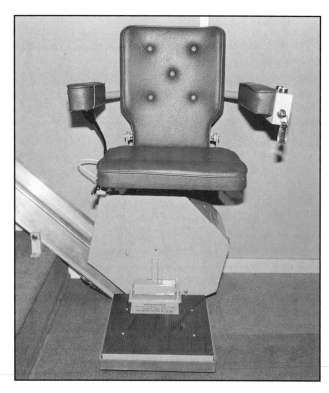

Obtainable from Brooks Stairlifts Ltd
Price guide £1395
Export available

❏ GIMSON NIMBUS

This lift is suitable for installation in a private or residential home to carry a seated passenger, facing sideways, up a straight flight of stairs.

The manufacturer states that the lift complies with BS 5776:1979.

Construction The extruded aluminium rail is bolted to the stairs at the wall side of the staircase and extends 254mm over the top of the stairs. A hinged rail can be fitted at the bottom of the stairs, as an option, if space is limited.
The chair travels on a rack and pinion drive and an overspeed governor is fitted as standard. The motor is situated under the seat of the chair and incorporates a hand-winding mechanism for attendant use in case of emergency. Power is supplied by a cable fitted into the rail.

The steel-framed back, seat and armrests of the chair are covered with moulded plastic and the seat is upholstered in padded vinyl. The platform, seat and armrests fold up neatly when not in use. They are not electrically interlocked on the standard model, but this is available as an optional extra.

Controls A toggle switch is located in the end of either armrest of the chair with an on/off switch fitted beneath. Call/send buttons and on/off switches are fixed at the top and bottom of the stairs. Key switches for security purposes are available as optional extras.

Power supply Standard mains supply.

Ride The lift gives a smooth ride.

Safety There are no exposed parts. A full sensitive panel is fitted to the under side of the platform and to the entry/exits of the drive mechanism.

Care should be taken getting on to the chair to avoid pressing the toggle switch, as this will start the chair moving before the passenger may be fully seated.

A lap belt or full safety harness are available as optional extras.

Instructions Correct and safe use is demonstrated at the time of installation and the user is given written instructions.

Servicing and maintenance Six-monthly servicing is recommended.

Breakdown A 24 hour call-out service is provided by the manufacturer.

Dimensions

Chair Seat	width 540 x depth	330mm
Height of footrest from ground		75mm
Width of chair (unfolded) from wall		600mm
Width of chair (folded)from wall		310mm
Width of track from wall		225mm
Lifting capacity		115kg

Obtainable from Gimson Tendercare Ltd
Price on application
Export available

❑ PROJECT AND DESIGN STAIR-EL MK6

This stairlift is designed to carry a seated passenger, facing sideways, on a straight stairway. A version with a downward facing chair is available if preferred. Adaptations can be made by the manufacturer to accommodate stairs which turn or a small landing with stairs off the main stairway. The maximum angle of climb is 50°.

The manufacturer states that the lift complies with BS 5776:1979

Construction The steel rail is bolted to the stair treads either side of the stairway. The motor is fitted at the top of the track and the chair moves up and down on a chain drive at a speed of 9m/min. A hand-winding mechanism is incorporated in the motor for use by an attendant in an emergency. The frame of the chair is constructed from steel with a large padded vinyl seat, back and single armrest. The seat is either fixed or swivel depending on the user's preference. The seat, armrest and footrest all fold up neatly when not in use. The seat and footrest are linked together to help those who cannot easily bend. These are not electrically interlocked on the standard model but this is available as an optional extra.

Controls Constant pressure buttons and an on/off switch are fitted to the end of the armrest of the chair. Call/send buttons together with an on/off switch are located at the top and bottom of the stairs. Key switches are available as optional extras.

Power supply Standard mains supply.

Ride Feels smooth and safe. Stops gently.

Safety There are no exposed moving parts as the chain runs inside the track. Sensitive edges are fitted on the underside of the platform. A lap safety belt is fitted to the standard model.

Instructions for use The manufacturer demonstrates the correct and safe use of the lift after installation and gives the user written instructions.

Servicing and maintenance Annual servicing recommended.

Breakdown A 24 hour call-out service is provided by the manufacturer.

Dimensions
Chair

Seat	600 x 370mm
Width from wall (seat folded)	200mm
Width (seat unfolded)	500mm
Footrest	320 x 340mm
Lifting capacity	115kg

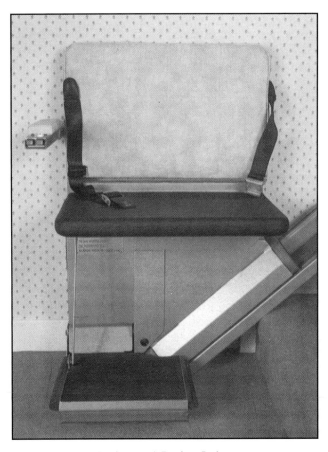

Obtainable from Project and Design Ltd
Price guide £1440
Export available

❑ MINIVATOR 901

The purpose of this stairlift is to carry a standing passenger, or someone seated sideways, up and down a straight flight of stairs.

The manufacturer states that the lift complies with BS 5776:1979.

Construction The aluminium track is fitted flush to the stair treads at the side of the stairway and the track extends 140mm beyond the top of the stairs. A hinged rail is available as an optional extra at the bottom of the stairs. The chair travels on a chain drive and the motor is located under the seat of the chair. It incorporates a hand-winding mechanism for use in emergency. The frame is made from painted tubular steel and the padded seat and backrest are upholstered in fabric. There are no conventional armrests but a tubular safety rail which doubles as an armrest and folds parallel to the backrest when not in use. This is interlocked and the lift can be called when it is either folded or unfolded. The seat is fixed and folds up with the footrest when not in use.

Controls The control unit is attached to the chair by a wander lead. It has a velcro backing and may be fixed to any part of the chair to suit the user. The standard controls are constant pressure push buttons but a joystick is available as an option. Call/send controls are located at the top and bottom of the stairs. An emergency stop button is fitted to the side of the motor housing. Key switches are available as optional extras.

Power supply   Standard mains supply.

Ride   Smooth but there is no soft start.

Safety   Sensitive edges are fitted round the footrest and on its underside, and to the entry and exit of the chain drive. A safety belt or harness are available as optional extras.

Instructions for use   The installer demonstrates the correct and safe use of the lift and gives the user written instructions.

Servicing and maintenance   The manufacturer offers a full servicing and maintenance scheme. The lift is guaranteed for one year after installation.

Breakdown   Contact the manufacturer.

Dimensions

Chair   Standard 575 x 300mm
                    Extended 650 x 300mm
Width from wall   (folded) 300mm, (unfolded) 610mm
Height of seat from footrest   505mm
Seat   450mm wide x 330mm deep
Height of footrest   100mm
Size of footrest   (standard) 360 x 320mm
                    (extended) 360 x 390mm

Lifting capacity   113kg

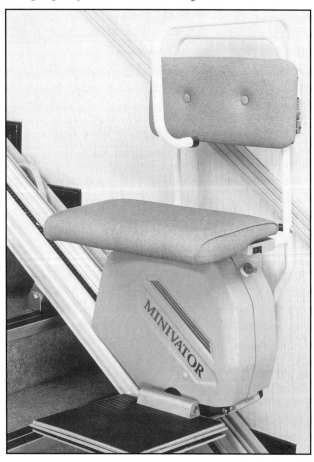

Obtainable from Sunrise Medical Ltd
Price guide £1595
Export available

❑   MINIVATOR 903/904

The purpose of these stairlifts is to carry someone seated sideways, up and down a straight flight of stairs. The two models are the same except that the 903 has a fixed seat which folds up when not in use and the 904 has a swivel seat.

The manufacturer states that the lift complies with BS 5776:1979.

Construction   The aluminium track is fitted flush to the stair treads at the side of the stairway and the track extends 140mm beyond the top of the stairs. A hinged rail is available as an optional extra at the bottom of the stairs. The chair travels on a chain drive and the motor is located under the seat of the chair. It incorporates a hand-winding mechanism for attendant use in emergency. The frame is made from painted tubular steel and the padded seat, backrest and armrests are upholstered in fabric. The seat on the 903 model is fixed and folds up with the foot and armrests when not in use. The 904 model features a swivel seat for ease of access.

Controls   Controls are fitted in the armrests. The standard controls are constant pressure push buttons but a joystick is available as an option. Call/send controls are located at the top and bottom of the stairs. An emergency stop button is fitted to the side of the motor housing. Key switches are available as optional extras.

Power supply   Standard mains supply.

Ride   Smooth and safe with a soft start.

Safety   Sensitive edges are fitted round the footrest and on its underside, and to the entry and exit of the chain drive. The armrests and swivel seat are electronically interlocked. A safety belt or harness are available as optional extras.

Instructions for use   The installer demonstrates the correct and safe use of the lift and gives the user written instructions.

Servicing and maintenance   The manufacturer offers a full servicing and maintenance scheme. The lift is guaranteed for one year after installation.

Breakdown   Contact the manufacturer.

Dimensions

Chair   510 x 320mm
Width from wall   (folded) 300mm, (unfolded) 610mm
Height of seat from footrest   903 - 505mm
                                        904 - 520mm
Seat   450mm wide x 330mm deep
Height of footrest   100mm
Size of footrest   360 x 390mm or 360 x 320mm
Lifting capacity   113kg

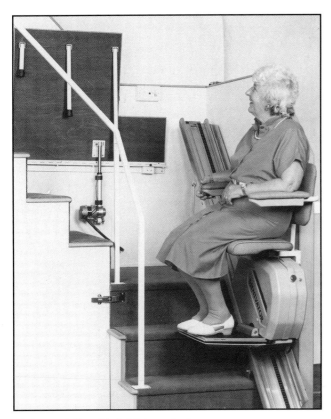

Minivator 903 with bridging platform

Obtainable from Sunrise Medical Ltd
Price guide £1595
Export available

☐ MINIVATOR 907

This stairlift is designed to carry a seated passenger, facing
sideways or downwards, up and down a straight flight of
stairs.

The manufacturer states that the lift complies with
BS 5776:1979.

Construction The aluminium track is fitted flush to the
stair treads at the side of the stairway and the track extends
140mm beyond the top of the stairs. A hinged rail is
available as an optional extra at the bottom of the stairs.
The chair travels on a chain drive and the motor is located
under the seat of the chair. It incorporates a hand-winding
mechanism for attendant use in emergency. The frame of
the chair is made from coated steel and the seat, back and
armrests are upholstered in grey fabric. It swivels through
180° to allow easy access for the passenger. A feature of
the lift is that it has two footrests which fold up when not
in use. The seat and armrests also fold up for storage and
the arms are interlocked. The chair can be called from
either level whatever their position.

Controls Constant pressure push buttons are fitted at the
end of either arm of the chair but, if preferred, a joystick is
available as an option. Call/send controls are located at the
top and bottom of the stairs. An emergency stop button is
fitted on the side of the motor housing. Key switches are

available as optional extras.

Power supply Standard mains supply.

Ride Smooth and safe with a soft start.

Safety Sensitive edges are fitted round the edges and
across the undersides of both foot rests, as well as to the
entry and exit of the chain drive. A lap safety belt or full
harness are available as optional extras.

Instructions for use The installer demonstrates the correct
and safe use of the lift and gives the user written
instructions.

Servicing and maintenance The manufacturer offers a
full servicing and maintenance scheme. The lift is
guaranteed for one year after installation.

Breakdown Contact the manufacturer.

Dimensions

Chair	470 x 320mm
Width from wall	(folded) 450mm, (unfolded) 750mm
Height of seat from footrest	520mm
Seat	450mm wide x 330mm deep
Height of footrest	100mm
Size of footrest	360 x 390mm or 360 x 320mm
Lifting capacity	113kg

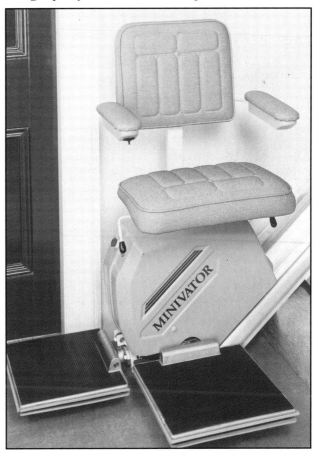

Obtainable from Sunrise Medical Ltd
Price guide £1795
Export available

❏ WESSEX SLIMLINER STAIRSEAT SILVER MEDAL

This lift is designed to carry a seated passenger, facing sideways, up a straight flight of stairs.

The manufacturer states that the lift complies with BS 5776:1979.

Construction The steel track is fitted flush to the wall side of the stairway and the chair travels up and down on a winch drive. The seat, back and armrests are upholstered in padded vinyl. The arms and footrest and seat fold up when the chair is not in use. The footrest is finished with a non-slip surface. The standard seat is fixed but a swivel version is available as an optional extra. This turns on one corner through 60° to give the passenger safer access at the top of the stairs. The drive motor, which incorporates a hand-winding mechanism for use by an attendant, is located under the seat of the chair. Optional extras include an alarm, extended armrests and footrests and a child seat.

Controls Constant pressure push-button controls are fitted on the end of either armrest of the chair. Call/send constant pressure buttons are located on the wall at the top and bottom of the stairs to suit the user, together with an on/off switch which activates an indicator light. Key switching and a joy stick control are available as optional extras.

Power supply Standard mains supply.

Ride A smooth ride after a four second delay.

Safety A full sensitive edge is fitted under the footrest and where the cable enters the motor housing. A lap safety belt is fitted to the chair.

Instructions for use The installer demonstrates the correct and safe use of the lift and gives the user written instructions.

Servicing and maintenance The manufacturer offers a full servicing and maintenance scheme. The lift is guaranteed for one year after installation.

Breakdown Contact the manufacturer.

Dimensions

Chair
Width   (unfolded) 720mm (folded) 430mm
Height of backrest   330mm
Seat   420 wide x 395mm deep
Height of seat from footrest 345-545mm to suit user
Footrest   270 wide x 305mm deep
Lifting capacity   115kg

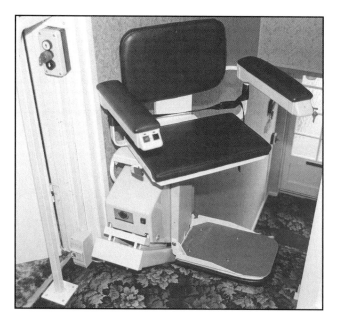

Obtainable from Wessex Medical Equipment Co Ltd
Price guide £1290
Export available

Standing/seated

❏ GRORUD BISON BEDE CLASSIC STAIRLIFT

This lift is suitable for installation in a private or residential home to carry a passenger, standing or seated facing sideways, up and down a straight flight of stairs.

The manufacturer states that the lift complies with BS 5776:1979.

Construction The extruded aluminium track is bolted to the stair treads at the side of the staircase with no overhang at the top of the stairs. A hinged track is available for the bottom of the stairs as an optional extra. This can be interlocked with the movement of the chair if required , if not the user must ensure that it is down before making a descent.

The chair travels up and down the stairs on a steel rack and pinion drive. The motor is sited under the seat and incorporates a hand-winding mechanism for attendant use in case of emergency.

Several different versions of the chair are available to suit the user. All have a steel-framed backrest, seat and armrests which are upholstered in padded vinyl or dralon and available in a range of colours. The standard chair has a fixed or swivel seat. The footrest, seat and armrests fold up neatly when not in use. The armrests are not electrically interlocked on the standard model but this is available as an optional extra. An automatically operated platform can be fitted, as an option, to bridge the gap of a sub-landing up to five steps higher. When the platform is installed two folding safety rails are fitted on the down side of the chair so there is no risk of the person falling down the stairs while making a transfer.

The standing passenger version of the lift includes a

narrow perching seat and, in place of arm rests, two safety rails which are linked and fold up together.

Controls Constant pressure buttons are located in the end of either armrest or fitted to the safety bar together with an on/off key switch. A toggle switch is available as an optional extra if preferred. Call/send buttons and on/off switches are situated at the top and bottom of the staircase.

Power supply Standard mains supply.

Ride The lift gives a smooth ride with a soft start.

Safety There are no exposed moving parts. A full sensitive panel is fixed to the under side and all leading edges of the footrest and sensitive edges are fitted round the entry/exits of the drive motor. A seat belt is fitted as standard but other belts can be made-to-measure as optional extras.

Instructions for use Correct and safe use of the lift is demonstrated at the time of installation and the user is given written instructions.

Servicing and maintenance A two year guarantee is given on parts and labour. A 24 hour call-out service is provided by the manufacturer.

Dimensions

Platform Fits up to 1500mm landings up to a maximum of five steps

Seat height   430 - 500mm

Height of footrest   60mm

Lifting capacity The standard lift is 115kg but a heavy duty model is available to carry up to 225kg.

Perching/Standing version

Manual hinged rail

Motorised bridging platform   Seated version - top of stairs

Obtainable from Grorud Bison Bede Ltd.

Price guide £1340

Export available

❑   STANNAH SILVER RAIL

This stairlift is designed primarily for home use to carry a seated passenger, facing sideways, up a straight flight of stairs. A stand-on version of this lift is available for those who prefer to travel this way.

The manufacturer states that the lift has been tested and complies with BS 5776:1979.

Construction The rail is made of extruded aluminium and is fixed flush to the step edges at the side of the stairway. Where access is restricted at the bottom of the stairs a hinged rail may be fitted which folds away when the lift is not in use. This is electrically interlocked so that the lift will not operate when the rail is folded up. A chamfered rail is an optional extra for the top of the stairs.

The chair moves up and down on a chain drive and the motor is fitted under the seat of the chair. It incorporates a hand-winding mechanism for use by a helper in an emergency. The back, seat and single armrest of the chair are upholstered in beige vinyl. The seat is normally fixed but a swivel version is available as an option. Double armrests can be requested and the chair controls can be placed on either armrest. The seat and footrest are linked together and fold up in one movement, which is helpful if the user finds it difficult to bend down.

Controls Constant pressure call/send buttons and on/off rocker switches are located at the top and bottom of the stairs to suit the user. Call/send constant pressure push button controls are incorporated in the end of the downside armrest of the chair. A key switch on the underside of the arm is used to turn the lift on and off.

Power supply 240v mains supply

Ride Smooth with a soft start. There is no initial delay before the lift starts, so the key should be off while the user is alighting in case the switches are accidently touched.

Safety There are no exposed moving parts and the cable supplying the power is laid inside the track.

The under surface of the foot platform is a sensitive area. At present the footrest stops just short of the top stair, leaving a small gap which could be a hazard for some people, but the manufacturer is working to rectify this. Several different safety belts are available as optional extras.

Instructions for use Correct and safe use of the lift are demonstrated when it is installed and the user is given written instructions.

Servicing and maintenance The manufacturer offers a full servicing and maintenance scheme at a cost of £196 per year.

Breakdown Contact the manufacturer.

Dimensions
Chair
Width from wall
(fixed seat)   (unfolded) 585mm, (folded) 296mm
(with swivel seat) (unfolded) 630mm, (folded) 340mm
Height of seat from footrest   430mm
Footrest   370 x 370mm
Backrest   380mm
Seat   585 x 400mm
Lifting capacity   120kg

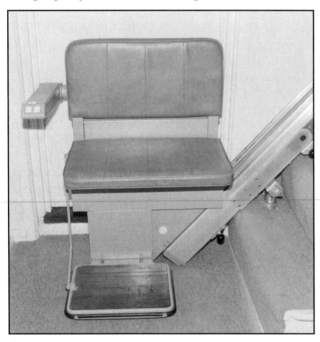

Obtainable from Stannah Stairlifts Ltd
Price guide £1600
Export available

Wheelchair passengers

❑ BHP CARNABY LIFT

The Carnaby wheelchair stairlift is suitable for installation
on straight staircases in public buildings or private houses.
   The manufacturer states that the lift conforms to BS
5776:1979
Construction The lift is simple in construction and is
powered by a small motor housed in a pit at the bottom of
the stairs, normally 457mm deep but for very steep stairs it
is up to 584mm deep. The neat, slim platform travels up
and down chains contained in two tracks bolted to the sides
of the stairs. Chrome finished bars on two sides of the
platform protect the user but leave one side of the platform
free for wheelchair access, and allow other people to walk
up and down stairs when the platform is parked at the
bottom of the stairs.
   The manufacturer will provide a safety gate if required.

The floor of the platform can have either a non-slip ribbed
rubber finish or carpet to match the surroundings.
Controls Constant pressure buttons are sited on the
platform and at the top and bottom of the staircase.
Power supply The motor runs off the domestic 240v
supply. The power cable is carried in a plastic casing
above the track on the side of the stairs.
Safety The leading edge and the whole of the under
surface of the platform are pressure sensitive areas.
The lift moves smoothly and there are no moving parts
exposed. In an emergency the system of lowering the
platform is complicated and would be difficult to operate in
the dark during a power cut. The carers should familiarise
themselves with the system in readiness for such an
occasion, since the platform could block the stairs unless
parked at the bottom, causing a hazard to other members of
the house.
   To operate the emergency system the brake access plates
must first be removed before unlocking a padlock to
operate the winding handle.
Servicing and maintenance Free servicing for twelve
months after which maintenance contracts are available
from the manufacturer. Guaranteed for 12 months for parts
and labour.
Dimensions
Platform 950 x 620mm (narrow) to as wide as stair width
permits
Lifting capacity 127kg

Obtainable from Bright Home Products
Price guide £4500
Export available

❏ GIMSON SPIRALIFT

Designed primarily for use in public buildings, the Spiralift is also suitable for some private houses. Each installation is specially made to fit the stairway with the lifting rail fitting discreetly in a steel tube which doubles as the bannister rail (see photo).

Three models are available, one to carry a wheelchair, one a seated passenger and a combination model. These are all suitable for straight or curved stairs, in or out of doors.

The manufacturer states that the lift complies with the safety requirements of BS 5776:1979.

Construction

Wheelchair platform: Two standard platforms are supplied by the manufacturer. Each platform has an anti-slip surface and is spring-balanced so that it can be raised or lowered one-handed. The ramps are operated by levers at each side of the back panel and form an integral part of the platform at both ends and act as safety barriers. Only the appropriate ramp will open at the designated landing. Additional safety devices are mounted on the access flaps and underneath the platform. These stop the lift if travel is in any way obstructed. A safety barrier at body level is not provided. When not in use the platform is parked in the vertical position and cannot be "called" unless in this position. Another safety device prevents lift operation during wheelchair transfer.

Chair: The seat and armrests fold down from the back and the passenger travels sideways. A lap safety belt is supplied.

Controls The lift is operated by constant pressure controls. For wheelchair users a toggle switch is situated on the back of the platform or an attendant wander lead control can be plugged into a socket on the platform. The attendant must walk with the passenger when using this control, as it does not operate from a distance. Chair controls are fitted on either arm rest to suit the user. Call/send buttons are situated on each terminal landing together with an emergency stop button, which is the type that needs resetting after use. This can be difficult if a user is on a different level in a wheelchair waiting for the lift. Key switches are fitted to restrict use of the lift to authorised persons.

Power supply The lift is powered by a single 240v 50Hz electric motor driven by the mains supply and incorporates a hand-winding mechanism for use in a breakdown. The drive unit can be sited in any suitable position, but the most effective place is at the top of the stairs.

Ride Smooth and stops gently but some users may feel a little insecure without a safety bar

Instructions for use The correct and safe use of the lift is demonstrated after installation and the user is given written instructions.

Servicing and maintenance Six-monthly. Contract servicing available from the manufacturer.

Breakdown A 24 hour call-out service is provided by the manufacturer

Dimensions

Wheelchair platform 750 x 700mm, folded width 260mm.
Chair Width 685mm, folded width 305mm
Backrest height 370mm
Footrest width 520mm, depth 510mm
Height of seat from footrest specify when ordering

Lifting capacity Wheelchair model 150kg
Chair model 130kg
Combined model 150kg

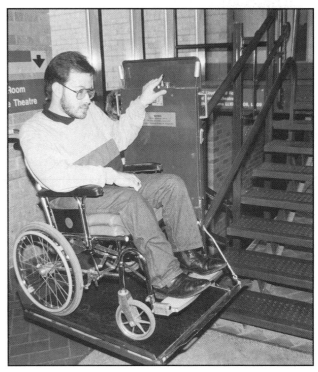

Platform stored at bottom of stairs

Obtainable from Gimson Tendercare
Price on application
Export available

❑   GIMSON WHEELCHAIR LIFT GCL MARK III
This wheelchair lift is designed for use on a straight flight
of stairs in public and private buildings.

The manufacturer states that the stairlift complies with
BS 5776:1979.

Construction The steel passenger platform carries
handrail guards, and may be fixed or folding. Access to the
fixed platform is via shallow ramps and hinged flaps or by
the platform fitting flush to the floor in a 75mm pit. The
hinged ramps fold up to form a safety barrier when the lift
is in action. When not in use the fixed platform is parked at
ground level. Access to the folding platform is by hinged
access ramps only and when not in use it is stored folded
up.

The platform moves along aluminium tracking fitted either
to a load bearing wall or support stanchions. The lift is
powered by a motor which can be installed under the stairs,
on the landing or in the loft. It incorporates a hand-winding
mechanism for attendant use in an emergency.

Controls A constant pressure toggle switch on the
platform controls up/down movement. A hand-held
pendant control for operation by an attendant walking with
the lift is available if required.

Call/send buttons are situated at the top and bottom of the
stairway to suit the user.

Keyswitch isolation is available to prevent unauthorised
use.

Power supply Standard 240v mains supply

Safety The access flaps are operated by the handrail and
are interlocked so that the lift only moves when they are
folded up correctly. The flaps and underneath of the
platform are fitted with sensitive safety devices.

Instructions for use The correct and safe use of the lift is
demonstrated at the time of installation and the user
receives written instructions.

Servicing and maintenance Six-monthly recommended
by the manufacturer. A 24 hour call-out service is
provided.

Dimensions Standard platform (fixed or folding) 1000 x
610mm. This can be varied to suit individual users.

Lifting capacity 150kg

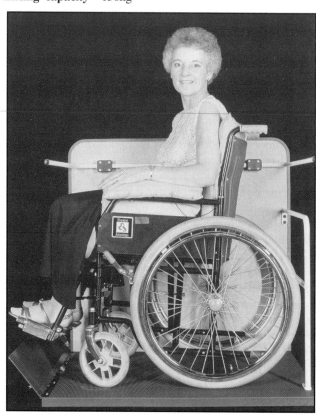

Obtainable from Gimson Tendercare
Price guide £4920
Export available

❏ FREEDOM FOUR STAIRLIFT

This lift is designed to carry a wheelchair user up and down a straight flight of stairs. It is suitable for installation in public and private buildings.

The manufacturer states that the stairlift complies with BS 5776:1979.

Construction The lift is mounted on tracks fixed to the left or right side walls of the stairway. An electric motor operates a winch, which may be fitted above or below the stairs. A hand-winding mechanism is incorporated in the motor for use in an emergency.

Hinged guard rails and ramps are fitted at each end of the platform. These are interlocked so that the lift cannot move when the ramps are down. On reaching the top of the stairs the leading ramp bridges the gap between platform and landing. The platform has an anti-slip surface.

On reaching the ground the lift stops automatically 75mm above the surface unless a shallow pit is provided to bring the platform flush with the floor.

Controls Constant pressure push-buttons, a lock-in emergency stop which needs resetting after use and a key switch are fitted to the side of the platform. Alternatively a pendant control can be provided.

Call/send constant pressure push-buttons and a lock-in emergency stop button are fitted at the top and bottom of the stairs

Power supply 240v mains supply

Safety The ramps and under surface of the platform are fitted with sensitive devices.

Instructions for use Correct and safe use are demonstrated at the time of installation and the user is given written instructions.

Servicing and maintenance Six-monthly servicing is required.

Breakdown A 24 hour call-out service is provided by the manufacturer in the event of breakdown.

Dimensions The size of the platform is governed by the space available. If the width across the stairs is less than 835mm, then the maximum width of the platform will be the measurement across the stairway minus 150mm.
Standard platform   915 x 685mm
A space of about 1500mm beyond the bottom step is required.

Lifting capacity   150kg

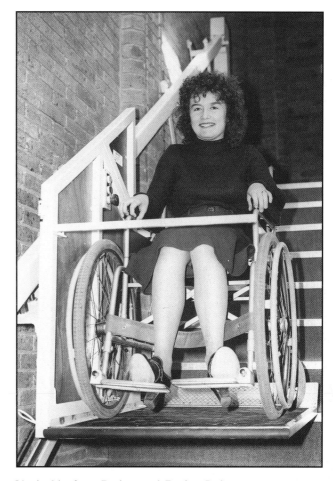

Obtainable from Project and Design Ltd
Price guide £4500
Export available

❏ STANNAH ACCESS WHEELCHAIR LIFT

This wheelchair lift is designed for use on straight stairways primarily in public buildings, but it can also be fitted in private houses if the width of the stairway is more than 1115mm.

Two versions are available, fully or partially automatic, the only difference being that in the partially automatic model the counterbalanced travelling platform and barrier arms have to be operated manually.

The manufacturer states that the safety features of the lift are in accordance with BS 5776:1979.

Construction The rail is mounted on the left or right side wall of the stairway or on a floor-mounted support. The motor is situated in the side unit and has an emergency hand-winding mechanism for use by an attendant.

During transit the wheelchair is held in place by the ramps which fold up at the sides of the platform, and the passenger is protected by the barrier arms which lock round him. The lift will not operate until the barriers are locked, and raising the arm automatically lowers the ramp.

Controls A constant pressure toggle switch and a key security switch are sited on the carriage together with an on/off switch. If this has been switched off it is impossible

to reach it to turn it on when sitting in a wheelchair. Call/
send and emergency stop buttons are located at the top and
bottom of the stairs.

Safety   Along with other lifts of this type, the carriage
locks onto the rail if the drive fails.

Instructions for use   The correct and safe use of the lift is
demonstrated at the time of installation and an instruction
manual provided.

Servicing and maintenance   Six-monthly in a private
house and three-monthly in a public building. A free
service is carried out six weeks after installation. A 24 hour
call-out service is provided by the manufacturer in the
event of breakdown. The instruction manual lists points to
check before calling the engineer.

Dimensions

Platform (standard)   1000 x 800mm
　　　　　(large)　　1200 x 800mm
Lifting capacity　　　　　225kg

Obtainable from Stannah Lifts (Domestic Products) Ltd
Price guide   Semi-automatic from   £6500
　　　　　　Fully automatic from £7200
Export available

Mobile stairlifts

❑   GIMSON STAIRMATE

The Stairmate is designed primarily for use on straight
stairs in public buildings or institutions. Turns in the
stairway can be negotiated if the landing platform is
sufficiently wide. It has a limited application in a domestic
setting since it can only safely negotiate stairs up to 35°
pitch and many stairs are steeper. The rubber tracks
normally grip well even on wet, outdoor steps but carpeted
stairs should not be attempted. It is essential that the

assistant is mentally alert, has good balance, co-ordination
and reasonable strength. The effort of moving a wheelchair
occupant up stairs is considerably reduced when the
assistant keeps the Stairmate on its balance point. When
positioning the chair at the first step the assistant's back is
bent but does not take an excessive load.

Construction   The carrier will accept a range of standard
adult wheelchairs (minimum width between wheels
420mm) which have sufficient clearance for the power unit
and tracks. A comfortable head cushion, adjustable in
height, supports the head in a reclined position. The wheels
have caterpillar tracks. If the carrier back is tipped slightly,
it can be pushed along on level ground on its four small
wheels with solid tyres. The carrier is not designed for
uneven ground but can climb a step of over 125mm high.

The operating capacity of the battery is up to 400m or 60
minutes with a maximum load. The Stairmate travels
upstairs at 6.5m per minute and down at 7.7m per minute.
The stability is satisfactory and the carrier will fit through a
Wheelchair Housing Standard width doorway with direct
access. It is not easy to manoeuvre in a restricted space.

Controls   On/off key and a foot-operated mechanism
reclines the chair. The brakes are automatic and fail-safe.

Power supply   12v non-spill, gel battery. The power point
to charge the battery is located low down on the end of the
battery pack.

Storage/transport   The carrier can be dismantled; it is
heavy to lift but can be ramp-loaded into a large car boot or
a hatchback.

Optional Extras   Spare battery, seat, car-loading ladder.

Servicing and maintenance   Servicing and repairs can be
arranged with the manufacturer. The carrier has a one year
warranty.

Dimensions

Height　　　　　910mm
Length　　　　　1420mm
Width　　　　　660mm
Weight　　　　　47kg
Lifting capacity   130kg

Obtainable from Gimson Tendercare Ltd
Price guide £2350
Export not available

❑   STAIRMATIC MK 4

The Stairmatic is designed to carry a person up and down straight, angled or spiral stairs; straight stairs only were attempted during evaluation. The manufacturer claims that stairs of almost any pitch can be negotiated. Carpeted stairs are no problem, but it is advisable to check that any covering has been securely fitted to the stairs. The assistant must be mentally alert, have good balance, coordination and reasonable strength. Full training in the techniques of handling the Stairmatic must be given to all attendants who will use the chair.

When descending a slope the attendant should be walking backwards with the chair facing up the slope. He should keep the Stairmatic in the upright position allowing it to roll backwards on its wheels. The small wheels on the chains can be used to brake the machine to give the attendant a rest.

The Stairmatic can climb steps up to 220mm high and can travel up 500 steps on a fully charged battery, at a speed of 5.5 seconds per step.

The stability of the Stairmatic is dependent on the ability of the attendant to keep it and the occupant balanced. It will pass through narrow doorways and is easy to manoeuvre in a restricted space, and will even pass down an aircraft aisle.

The effort of assisting a disabled person up stairs is considerably reduced when the assistant has learnt how to keep the Stairmatic on the correct balance point. The Stairmatic can be useful in situations where several changes of level have to be negotiated, as it involves one transfer instead of many if separate lifts were fitted. A similar model is available to carry a range of standard wheelchairs up and down stairs.

Construction   The seat is comfortably padded and upholstered in vinyl, and the lift-up armrests allow for sideways transfer. The footplate can be lifted so that the tubular support legs rest on the floor to hold the Stairmatic in position during transfer. The wheels are 160mm diameter with solid rubber tyres for use on level ground. A series of small wheels are attached to a drive chain and propel the Stairmatic up the steps. This mechanism is safely guarded. An automatic fail-safe device prevents the Stairmatic from rolling off steps.

Controls   On/off toggle switch. When the power is switched on the speed remains constant. A rocker switch at the top of the backrest, marked with directional arrows, is used to move the chair up and down and the directions are indicated by arrows on top of the switch.

Power supply   The motor is powered by a 12v maintenance-free, sealed battery. This together with a battery charger are fitted in a closed unit under the seat. It is recommended that the battery is charged at least once a week.

Storage/transport   The Stairmatic is heavy to lift. It can be carried in a hatchback if the frame is detached from the power unit, or an estate car without dismantling.

Instructions for use are stuck on the back of the head rest as a useful reminder of training.

Servicing and maintenance   The manufacturer gives a one year warranty on parts, with labour extra. Arrangements for servicing and repairs can be made with the suppliers.

Dimensions

Height	1580mm
Width	500mm
Weight	54kg
Seat	
Height from floor	580mm
Width	430mm
Depth	430mm
Backrest Height	700mm
Lifting capacity	120kg

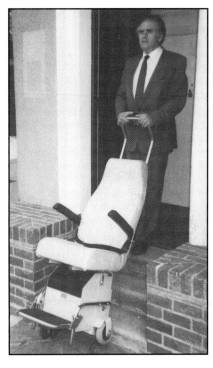

Manufactured by Sageka
Obtainable from Baronmead International Ltd
Price guide £2550 with charger and battery
Export available

Home lifts

Points to consider

✳   Three types of home lift are available:
  - through-floor home lifts
  - enclosed with a shaft,
  - manually-driven balanced personal home lifts

The relevant British Standard specifications are as follows:
  BS 5900: (1980) Specification for powered home lifts
  BS 5965: (1980)Specification for manually-driven balanced personal home lift
  These are obtainable from the British Standards Institution (see *Addresses* page 130).

✳   A home lift may be fully enclosed in a shaft or open to the room. The carriage of an open lift may be fully or partially enclosed. Most carriages run on guide rails attached to a supporting wall.

✳   Planning permission may be required if the shaft of an enclosed home lift is constructed on the outside of the property.

✳   Charges for planning permission do not apply to work carried out for disabled people.

✳   Home lifts are wired into a socket outlet from the mains electricity supply.

✳   The motor can be installed in a separate motor room in the loft, or above the lift shaft. It must be easily accessible as it incorporates the emergency hand-winding mechanism for use by an attendant in a power failure; the therapist should make sure that the attendant can operate it.

✳   Doors on totally or partially enclosed home lifts are electrically interlocked so that they cannot be opened when the lift is moving and the lift will not move if the doors are open.

✳   Call/send controls, emergency stop and/or isolating key switches are fitted on the upper and lower levels and in the carriage as standard by some manufacturers and as optional extras by others. All lift carriages are fitted with direction of travel or floor selection controls as standard.

✳   If it is difficult for the user to operate the standard wall-mounted controls different types are available.

✳   The height and position of the wall-mounted controls should be assessed for the individual user.

✳   An alarm or telephone is not usually fitted as a standard item but may be available as an extra.

✳   A competent person will be needed to assist with transferring and operating the home lift if the user cannot manage independently.

✳   The therapist should make sure that the user can tolerate being confined in a totally enclosed lift carriage and is entirely happy with use and operation of the lift.

✳   The safe working load of the home lift (i.e. the maximum number of passengers and/or wheelchairs to be carried) is stated on the load plate in the lift carriage. If the user's weight is greater than this the manufacturer should be consulted.

✳   The manufacturer will recommend whether the home lift requires three monthly, six-monthly or annual servicing.

✳   A 24 hour emergency call-out service is usually provided by the manufacturer.

✳   Individual requirements and any special adaptations should be discussed with the manufacturer.

Through-floor home lifts

✳   The carriage is fully or partially enclosed. It runs on guide rails attached to the wall, which may or may not be enclosed. Different sizes of carriage carry one standing or seated passenger or a wheelchair passenger with or without an attendant.

✳   Some carriages have seats which adjust in height and slide in and out of the carriage for ease of transfer. The user should make sure that he can operate the sliding mechanism.

✳   Enclosed carriages and some partially enclosed carriages have internal lighting, usually controlled from a switch inside the carriage; other partially enclosed carriages are lit from the rooms they serve. Some models have battery-operated emergency lighting for use in a power failure.

✳   Fully enclosed carriages have folding, sliding or hinged doors and a vision panel can be fitted.

✳   Partially enclosed carriages have a door at the same height as the carriage walls which is opened by simply pulling or pushing or using a handle. A vision panel is not necessary.

✳   Sensitive surfaces and edges stop the lift when an obstruction is encountered but allow it to be reversed so that the obstruction can be removed.

✳   Some models automatically raise a ceiling trap door as the carriage ascends and re-position it during descent. Others have a protective half-wall and door on the upper floor.

✳   Where the ceiling trap is automatically picked up and dropped back by the descending lift there is a potential trapping hazard to someone upstairs.

✳   At the upper landing the lift will stop flush with the floor. If the user cannot negotiate a small step or ramp a shallow well must be installed at the bottom landing so that the carriage door fits flush with the floor.

Enclosed home lift

✳   The lift carriage is enclosed in a shaft. Carriages of different size and capacity are available to carry between one and four standing passengers or a wheelchair passenger and an attendant.

✳   Landing doors are always fitted to guard the shaft. Some carriages are fitted with a door which may be folding, sliding or hinged. A vision panel can be fitted if required.

✳   The floor of the lift carriage always stops flush with the top landing and no step or ramp is required. At ground level a ramp or a well (up to 200mm deep) will be necessary to allow the door to fit flush with the floor.

✳   On some models handrails are fitted as standard, on others they are an optional extra.

Through floor home lifts

❑   AMP HOME ELEVATOR
This through floor lift is suitable for use in private houses as an alternative to a stairlift. Two versions are available, one to carry a seated passenger, and the other a wheelchair with passenger.

The lift is chain driven and runs on two tracks fitted to a load bearing wall. It can be side or end mounted.

As the lift descends there is no panel to close the opening in the ceiling, and the lift is usually parked upstairs when not in use. At first floor level a closed-in lobby is constructed round the ceiling opening with an electrically interlocked door.

The manufacturer states that the lift complies with BS 5900:1980.

Construction   The frame and carriage of the lift are made from epoxy-coated steel. The carriage is box-like in shape with half solid and perspex side panels. Access for the user is up a 450mm long ramp which acts as a safety barrier. It is electrically interlocked but operated manually by a double handle which is easily managed from a wheelchair. An automatic ramp is available as an optional extra. The drive motor is located in the upper storey at the top of the track.

In the seated model the carriage is fitted with a padded vinyl seat. This slides forward to the edge of the door for easy transfer, and slides back and locks during transit. A fixed seat is also available.

Controls   Call/send buttons are situated at the upper and lower levels and on the side of the carriage. A red stop button is also fitted in the carriage.

Power supply   Standard mains supply.

Safety   Sensitive surfaces are fitted to all leading edges of the carriage, and a full sensitive panel is fitted to the under surface of the platform.

Servicing and maintenance   Can be arranged with the manufacturer. Full cover is given in case of emergency.

Installation   Carried out by the manufacturer. Building work necessary will be done by the manufacturer if required.

Dimensions
Seated model
Carriage (internal)   Length   735mm, Width 610mm
Wheelchair model
Carriage (internal)   Length 1170mm, Width 790mm
Height of ramp   70mm
Lifting capacity   180kg

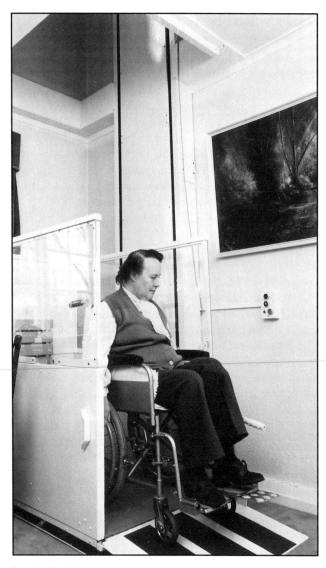

Obtainable from AMP Engineers Ltd
Price guide £3971
Export available

❏ AMP 2000 HOME ELEVATOR

This through floor lift is intended to provide transport for a wheelchair user between the ground and first floors of a house.

Unlike other lifts in the AMP range, the 2000 has an automatic ceiling trap which closes the opening when the lift is on the ground level.

The manufacturer states that the lift conforms to BS 5900:1980.

Construction The track is wall-mounted and the carriage moves up and down between floors on two steel ropes. Power is provided by an electric motor fixed at the top of the track and a hand-winding mechanism is incorporated for use in emergency. The box-like carriage is made of steel with solid side panels. As the unit rises between the floor levels it automatically lifts the trap which seals the opening in the ceiling while it is on the lower level.

To enter the carriage the user reverses up a ramp and through a door. These are both electrically interlocked and function automatically.

Controls Call/send and stop push-button controls are situated in the carriage and at each floor level to suit the user. A switch to operate the door is fitted in the carriage and a key switch is fixed on the upper or lower level.

Power supply Standard mains supply

Safety Weight sensors are incorporated in the ceiling trap to prevent the lift rising if someone is standing on it at the upper level. A sensitive panel is fixed to the base of the carriage, and the top edges of the sides and door are also sensitive.

Servicing and maintenance Can be arranged with the manufacturer.

Installation Carried out by the manufacturer.

Dimensions

Carriage	Length	1170mm
	Width	800mm
Ramp		200mm
Height of ramp		200mm
Lifting capacity		180kg

Obtainable from AMP Engineers Ltd
Price guide £3300
Export available

This lift was not seen or evaluated and the report is based entirely on the manufacturer's technical literature.

❑ GIMSON PERSONAL VERTICAL LIFT

This through floor lift is designed to carry one seated passenger between two floors and it is an alternative to consider before installing a stair lift in a private house. It is not suitable for wheelchair users.

The manufacturer states that the lift complies with BS 5900: 1980.

Construction The box-like carriage is made from steel with solid sides painted beige. It runs up and down a double track which is fixed to a load bearing wall. Panels enclose the steel wire lifting ropes and the drive unit is fitted at the top of the track. A hand-winding mechanism is incorporated in the motor for use in an emergency. As the lift ascends it automatically picks up a ceiling trap which is replaced as the lift descends.

The seat is covered with padded vinyl and slides forward to the edge of the door for easy transfer. It slides back and locks during transit. A perching seat can be fitted if preferred. A seat belt is fitted as standard.

The user enters the carriage through a solid door up a small step. Grab rails are fitted inside the carriage for the passenger's comfort and safety and to facilitate opening and closing the door.

Controls Call/send push-buttons with guards are situated on the top and bottom floors and on a side panel of the carriage to suit the user. Key switches are available as an optional extra.

Power supply Standard mains supply

Safety Sensitive surfaces are fitted to the underside and all leading edges of the carriage.

Servicing and Maintenance Can be arranged with the manufacturer.

Installation Carried out by the manufacturer.

Dimensions
Carriage Width 620mm
         Length 690mm
Lifting capacity 115kg

Obtainable from Gimson Tendercare
Price guide £4340
Export available

❑ FREEDOM LIFT

The Freedom Vertical through floor lift is for use in private houses as an alternative to a stairlift. Two versions are available, one to carry a seated passenger, and the other to carry a wheelchair with passenger.

The lift is cable driven and runs on two tracks fitted to a load bearing wall. When the lift is on the upper floor, the base closes flush with the ceiling to provide a smoke proof screen. In the event of a fire a smoke detector located in the motor housing automatically calls the lift to the upper level to seal the floor and prevent the fire spreading. An alternative means of escape must be made for the lift user. When the lift is on the ground floor the hole in the ceiling is closed automatically by a trap door mounted on the support rails. A sensor located at the edge of this trap door detects anyone standing on it and prevents the lift rising.

The manufacturer states that the lift complies with BS 5900:1980

Construction The frame and carriage of the lift are made from epoxy-coated steel. The carriage is box-like with a solid door and side panels, and access for the user is up a 30mm high ramp through a door at the front. The door is controlled by a push button on the top, which is interlocked for safety. Grab handles are fixed to the inside of the door. The drive motor is in the upper storey at the top of the lift and incorporates a hand-winding mechanism for use in emergency. A headrest,light and mirror are fitted inside the carriage.

In the seated passenger model the carriage is fitted with a padded vinyl seat. This slides forward to the edge of the door for easy transfer, and slides back and locks during transit. Seat belts are fitted as standard and the seat height can be altered to suit the user.

The seat is removed to use the carriage with a wheelchair.

Controls　Call/send buttons are situated at the upper and lower levels and on the door of the carriage. A red stop button is also fitted in the carriage.

Power supply　Standard mains supply.

Safety　Sensitive surfaces are fitted to the top edges and across the underside of the carriage.

Servicing and Maintenance　Can be arranged with the manufacturer. Full cover is given in case of emergency.

Installation　Carried out by the manufacturer. Normally completed in two days.

Dimensions

Seated model

Carriage　Length　952mm　Width　705mm

Wheelchair model

Carriage　Length　1260mm　Width　730mm

Lifting capacity　　250kg

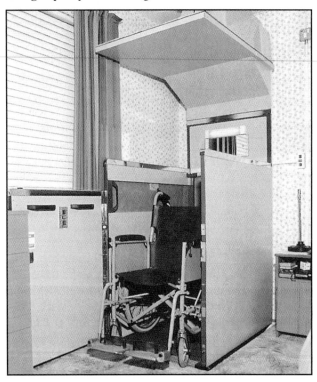

Manufactured by John Pollock Designs Ltd

Obtainable from

John Pollock Designs Ltd

Brooks Stairlifts Ltd

Price guide £3950

Export available

❑　GEMINI 3000

This through floor lift has been designed for use by unattended wheelchair users and gives a maximum lift of 3500mm between floors. The lift is mounted on self supporting track, so installation is not dependent on the presence of a load bearing wall, as the weight of the lift is taken through the floor.

Construction　The carriage is made from coated aluminium walls topped by clear perspex panels which give it a futuristic look. Access to the carriage is gained by reversing up a ramp through the single door at one end. The ramp automatically folds up as the door is manually closed. The floor panel in the upper storey opens and shuts automatically as the lift moves between floors.

Controls　Four control buttons to move the lift up and down, open the door and stop the lift in an emergency are sited on the safety bar across the door, where they are within easy reach of the passenger. Call/send controls are fitted on both floors. Internal and external levers to lower the lift in an emergency are fitted to the carriage.

Power supply　The lift is operated by a hydraulic pump unit which can be sited away from the lift, for example, in the garage or under the stairs. This means noise during use is kept to a minimum.

Safety　Sensitive edges are fitted to the under side of the carriage and to the edges of the door and canopy.

Accessories　Interior light.

Instructions for use　A comprehensive manual is supplied by the manufacturer.

Servicing and maintenance　Free service in first 12 months. The manufacturer provides a 24 hour phone number for contact in emergency.

Installation　Building work and power point not included in price.

Dimensions

Floor aperture　1380mm long x 930mm wide

Capsule　　1250 x 850 x 1530mm high

Ramp　　400mm long x 50mm high

Lifting capacity　　　159kg

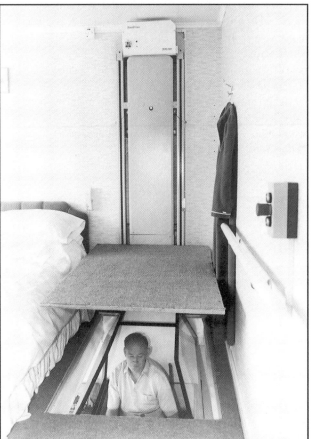

Obtainable from Ratcliff Care Ltd
Price guide   £3450
Interior light £50
Export available

❏   MINIVATOR EAGLE 800

The Minivator 800 through floor lift is designed for use in private houses as an alternative to a stairlift, to carry a wheelchair or standing passenger between two floors.

The lift is cable driven and runs on two tracks fitted to a load bearing wall.

When the lift is on the ground floor the hole in the ceiling is closed automatically by a trap door which is mounted on the support rails. A sensor located at the edge of this trap door detects anyone standing on it and prevents the lift rising.

The manufacturer states that the lift complies with BS 5900:1980.

Construction   The frame and carriage of the lift are made from fire retardant plastic mouldings and coated steel. The carriage is box-like in shape with a half-door and solid side panels. The access ramp folds up to form the lower half of the door. The door and ramp are electrically interlocked and are operated manually by a handle in the carriage. If required this operation can be automated as an optional extra. An emergency key is provided to unlock the carriage door in the event of a power failure. The drive motor is located in the upper storey at the top of the lift and incorporates a hand-winding mechanism for attendant use in case of emergency. A battery powered light and a mirror are fitted inside the carriage.

Controls   Call/send buttons are situated at the upper and lower levels and on the side of the carriage. A red stop button is also fitted in the carriage.

Power supply   Standard mains supply.

Safety   Sensitive surfaces are fitted to all leading edges of the carriage and to the base.

Servicing and Maintenance   Can be arranged with the manufacturer or local agent.

Installation   Carried out by the manufacturer.

Dimensions

Carriage	Width	820mm
	Length	1250mm
Lifting capacity		146kg

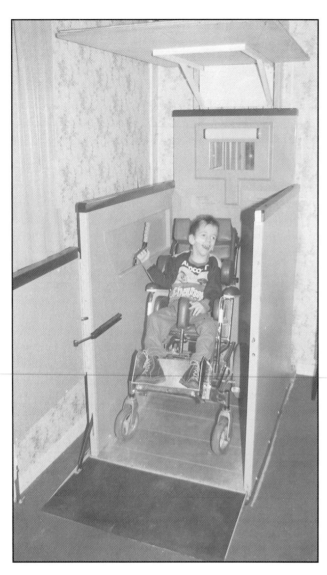

Obtainable from Sunrise Medical Ltd
Price guide £4500
Export not available

☐   MINIVATOR EAGLE 520

The Minivator 520 through floor lift is a smaller version of the Minivator 800. It can be used in a private house as an alternative to a stairlift to carry either a seated or standing passenger between floors. The lift is cable driven and runs on two tracks fitted to a load bearing wall.

When the lift is on the ground floor the hole in the ceiling is closed automatically by a trap door mounted on the support rails. A sensor located at the edge of this trap door detects anyone standing on it and prevents the lift rising.

The manufacturer states that the lift complies with BS 5900:1980.

Construction   The frame and carriage of the lift are made from epoxy-coated steel. The carriage is box-like in shape with a solid door and side panels. Access for the passenger is up a 70mm high step. The door is electrically interlocked and is operated by a push button on top of the door. An emergency key is provided to unlock the carriage door should there be a power failure.

The carriage is fitted with a vinyl padded seat. This slides forward to the edge of the door for easy transfer, and slides back and locks during transit. The seat height can be altered to suit the user and seat belts are fitted as standard on this model. The seat is removed when using the lift for a standing passenger.

The drive motor is located in the upper storey at the top of the lift and incorporates a hand-winding mechanism for use in emergency. A battery powered light and a mirror are fitted inside the carriage.

Controls   Call/send buttons are situated at the upper and lower levels and on the side of the carriage. A red stop button is also fitted in the carriage.

Power supply   Standard mains supply.

Safety   Sensitive surfaces are fixed to all leading edges of the carriage and to the base.

Servicing and maintenance   Can be arranged with the manufacturer or local agent.

Installation   Carried out by the manufacturer.

Dimensions (Internal)

Carriage   Width   560mm

                Length   755mm

Lifting capacity   146kg

Obtainable from Sunrise Medical Ltd
Price guide £4000
Export not available

❑   TERRY HARMONY

The Terry Harmony through floor lift is for use in private
houses as an alternative to a stairlift. Two versions are
available to carry either a seated passenger or wheelchair
user.

The manufacturer states that the lift complies with
BS 5900:1980.

Construction   The pale grey carriage is box-like with
sloping solid sides and vision panels. The door is
electrically interlocked and the carriage is fitted with an
alarm system and a light as standard. It runs on two tracks
fitted to a load bearing wall. The lift is driven by a
hydraulic ram powered by a separate electric pump unit,
which may be sited at a convenient distance from the lift to
cut down the noise. When the carriage is on the upper
floor, the base closes flush with the ceiling to provide a
smoke-proof screen. A steel lining is fitted in the floor
aperture to give a good seal. When the carriage is on the
ground floor the hole in the ceiling is closed automatically

by a trap door which is mounted on the support rails. A
sensor located at the edge of this trap door detects anyone
obstructing the aperture or standing on it to prevent the lift
rising.

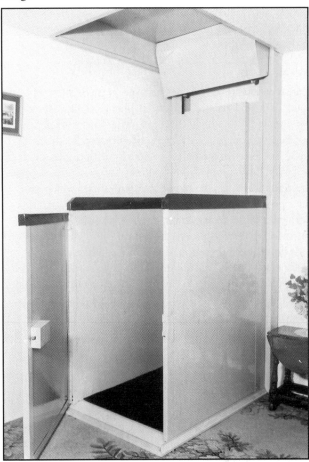

Obtainable from Terry Lifts Ltd
Price guide £4200
Export available

This lift was not evaluated and the report is based on the
manufacturer's literature.

❑   WESSEX VERTICAL SEAT LIFT

The Wessex through floor lift provides an alternative method of transport to the stairlift for carrying a person between the ground and first floors of a private house. Two models are available, one for a seated passenger and the other for a person in a wheelchair, which are either cable or hydraulically driven.

The manufacturer states that the lift complies with BS 5900:1980

Construction   The box-like carriage is made of steel with solid sides and painted beige. An interior light is fitted in the carriage. The whole unit runs on a double track which is fixed end-on or alternatively side-on to a load-bearing wall. The electric motor is covered by a fibre glass casing and fitted at the top of the track. As the unit rises between the floor levels it automatically lifts the trap which seals the opening in the ceiling against draughts and heat loss when the lift is on the lower level. A sensor will stop the lift rising if there is an obstruction on top of the trap door.

Access for the user is up a 50mm step, through an electrically interlocked door, which is manually operated. The switch on top of the door is difficult to operate from a wheelchair. Since this lift was evaluated the wheelchair model has been modified to include as standard an automatic door and ramp operated by a push-button inside the carriage.

The carriage of the seated model is smaller and fitted with a padded vinyl seat. This slides forward to the edge of the door for easy transfer, and slides back and locks during transit.

Controls   Call/send push buttons with guards are situated on the top and bottom floors and on one side panel of the carriage to suit the user.

Power supply   Standard mains supply.

Safety   Sensitive surfaces are fitted to all leading edges and the underside of the carriage.

Servicing and maintenance   Can be arranged with the manufacturer.

Installation   Carried out by the manufacturer.

Dimensions
Seated model
Carriage   Width   559mm
                Length   762mm
Wheelchair model
Carriage   Width   686mm
                Length   1118mm
Lifting capacity Cable   115kg
                Hydraulic 160kg

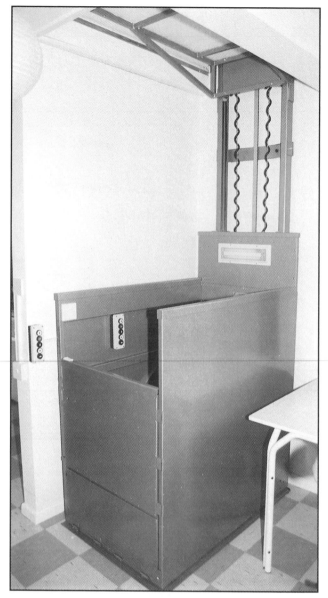

Obtainable from The Wessex Medical Equipment Co Ltd
Price guide   Seated model   £4500
                    Wheelchair model £5000
Export available

Home lifts enclosed in shaft

The following companies make home lifts with shafts for use in nursing homes, residential homes and guest houses.

The lifts all comply with BS 5655:1979. Part 1: safety regulations. They have a minimum capacity of 300kg or four persons. The minimum door width of 800mm is sufficient for wheelchair access, but its worth noting that the minimum size recommended for a wheelchair in a passenger lift is an eight person lift.

More details can be found in BS 5810:1979 "The Code of Practice for Access for the Disabled to Buildings".

Atlantic Medical Ltd
    Hydraulic lifts for four to eight people.

Bell Ltd
    Classic Home lift for four or five people with larger units to order.

British Elevators Ltd
    Lifts for five or eight people.

Gough & Co (Hanley) Ltd
    Home Eight electro-hydraulic passenger lifts for eight or thirteen people.

Hammond & Champness Ltd
    Warden 11 and 111 for six, eight, ten or thirteen people.

Lift & Hoist Co Ltd
    Premier passenger lift for five people.

Manor Lifts Ltd
    TR5 P/O Model lift for five people.

Stannah Stairlifts Ltd
    Piccolo Major for three to eight people.

Wessex Medical Equipment Co Ltd
    Wessex Mountbatten for five and eight people.

The Wessex Attendant Lift and the Wessex Home Lift are reported in detail.

❑   WESSEX ATTENDANT LIFT

The lift, enclosed in a shaft, is designed to carry two standing passengers, or a wheelchair passenger and one standing passenger between two floor levels. The motor, which incorporates an emergency hand-winding mechanism, is installed at the top of the shaft.

The manufacturer states that the lift complies with BS 5900:1980.

Construction   The floor and lower section of the carriage walls are made of non-slip aluminium checker-plate to protect against damage by wheelchair footrests.

The carriage has a sliding door which is electrically-operated by constant-pressure push-buttons, colour-coded and arrowed for direction. No handle is fitted, but the door can be opened manually from either side by releasing a catch and pushing it sideways. It can only be opened only when the lift is in the correct position for the user to enter or leave.

The landing doors are hinged and are electrically interlocked when the lift is in use to close the shaft. A vision panel, and a door handle are fitted. The doors fit flush with the floor and no ramp is necessary for access to the carriage.

The diffused light is operated by pull-cord and push-button controls, easily distinguishable from the lift controls.

Controls   Call/send and stop buttons are fitted on each landing to suit the user. Colour-coded one-touch push-buttons for direction of travel are fixed on the side wall of the lift carriage. Different types and sitings available on request.

Instructions for use   The installer demonstrates the correct and safe use of the lift and gives verbal instructions. The manufacturer states that written instructions are in preparation.

Servicing and maintenance   Six-monthly. A 24 hour call-out service is provided.

Dimensions

Car door width	835mm
Floor area of carriage	1117 x 864mm
Lifting capacity	230kg

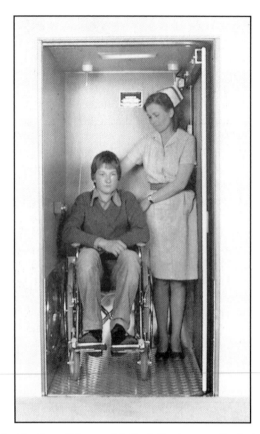

Obtainable from Wessex Medical Equipment Co Ltd
Price guide £7600-8000 including installation
Export available

❑ WESSEX HOME LIFT

The lift, enclosed in a shaft, is designed to carry a standing
or wheelchair passenger between two floor levels. The
motor, which incorporates an emergency hand-winding
mechanism, is installed at the top of the shaft.

The manufacturer states that the lift complies with BS
5900:1980

Construction The floor of the carriage if fitted with a non-
slip aluminium checker-plate.

The carriage door is sliding and can be operated manually
or electrically by constant-pressure push-buttons which are
colour-coded and arrowed for direction. The door can be
opened only when the lift is in the correct position for the
user to enter or leave.

The hinged landing doors are locked with an electrical
interlock when the lift is in use to close the shaft. A vision
panel, and door handle are fitted. The doors fit flush with
the floor and no ramp is necessary for access to the
carriage.

The lighting is diffused and operated by pull-cord and
push-button controls which are easily distinguishable from
the lift controls.

Controls Call/send and stop buttons are located on the
landings to suit the user. Colour-coded one-touch push-
buttons for direction of travel are fitted on the side wall of
the lift carriage. Different types and sitings available on
request.

Instructions The installer demonstrates the correct and
safe use of the lift and gives verbal instructions. Written
instructions are provided by the manufacturer.

Service and maintenance Six-monthly. A 24 hour call-
out service is provided by the manufacturer.

Dimensions
Car door width	800mm
Floor area of carriage	1080 x 800mm

Lifting capacity Standard lift 115kg
Uprated lift 190kg

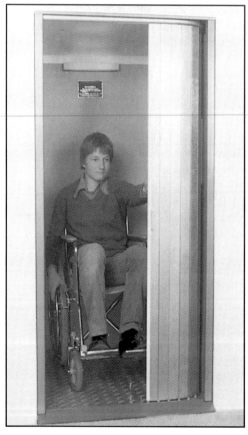

Obtainable from Wessex Medical Equipment Co Ltd
Price guide With manually-operated doors £4500
With electrically-operated doors   Standard model £5000
Uprated model £6000

Installation £500
Export available

Manually-driven balanced personal homelift

❏ TERRY PERSONAL LIFT

This through-floor lift provides a simple means of transport between two or more levels and is a cheap alternative to electric lifts. It works on the principle of counterbalancing the load with weights as the platform moves between two support columns. This means that the lift can be hand-operated with very little effort and its function is unaffected by power cuts. The counterweight is set to suit the combined weight of the user and chair. Extra weights are supplied so that a different person can use the lift. Because of this weight specificity the lift is only suitable for a private home with one disabled user.

Two versions of the lift are available, one for wheelchair users and one for standing passengers. An optional extra is a low power electric motor.

The manufacturer states that the lift complies with BS 5965:1980.

Construction The frame is made of white finished pressed steel uprights which contain the counterweights. The suspension pulleys are located at the top of this frame on the first floor. The polyester suspension ropes run inside the uprights and the winch is fitted to the frame carrying the platform. The chain is exposed, but is not a hazard although it is greased. The wheelchair platform has an interlocking ramp at one end and the standing platform is flat. The platform is secured in the uprights by carriage guide rollers mounted on a small frame to which is fixed the winding handle.

The user is protected during transit by a safety belt. The opening in the upper floor is enclosed by a 1200mm high wall with an interlocking door for access.

Controls The lift is easily operated by the disabled user or attendant pulling down a release cord and winding a handle situated on the lifting platform. Similar controls are situated on the upper floor for operation by an attendant.

Brakes An automatic system locks the lift carriage when the drive handle is released, so preventing any unintentional movement of the lift. It also prevents an uncontrolled descent if the ropes fail.

Lift Smooth and quiet in operation.

Servicing and maintenance Little required but can be arranged with the manufacturer.

Installation Normally completed in one day.

Dimensions

Wheelchair platform   1010 x 660mm

Standing platform   610 x 660mm

Lifting capacity   Standard 150kg; Special 200kg

Obtainable from Terry Lifts Ltd

Price guide £1625

Export available

LIFTING PLATFORMS/ SHORT RISE LIFTS

Points to consider

Types of lifting platforms/short rise lifts
- fixed
- portable

The relevant British Standard is:
   BS 6440:1983 Code of Practice for powered lifting
   platforms for use by disabled persons.
This is obtainable from the British Standards Institution
(see *Addresses*   page 130).
   The Code covers lifting platforms intended solely to carry
a disabled person, either standing, sitting or in a
wheelchair, and accompanied by an attendant if necessary,
between fixed levels where the maximum height of the
platform above the lowest level does not exceed 1.98m.
Appendix A gives guidance to help in the selection of a
suitable powered lifting platform and it is recommended
that potential purchasers should read it.

✷   A powered lifting platform can be installed outside or
inside a public building or private house to overcome the
difference in floor levels, or where there is insufficient
space for a ramp.

✷   In a public building, where there are different users,
duplicate controls may need fitting on different sides of the
platform to cater for one-handed users.

✷   An on/off key switch prevents the possibility of
unauthorised use of the lifting platform.

✷   Clear, concise operating instructions should be
displayed in a prominent position.

✷   Lifts incorporating a hydraulic lifting system have a
simple release valve operated by an attendant for
emergency lowering.

✷   In a private house the correct and safe use of the lifting
platform should be demonstrated at installation and written
instructions provided. These should be kept in a safe place
with the emergency service telephone number.

✷   In a public building the correct and safe use of a lifting
platform should be demonstrated to the purchaser's
representative and those nominated to assist users at the
time of installation. Written instructions covering normal
operation and breakdown should be supplied and kept in a
safe place near the lifting platform.

✷   A technically competent person should carry out
maintenance in accordance with the manufacturer's
instructions.

✷   Short rise lifts usually only move vertically so to
negotiate steps a bridge may have to be built between the
top step and the extended platform.

✷   Often the lift supplied by a firm is installed by separate
contractor. It is important that they liaise to ensure that all
the necessary safety precautions are carried out during the
installation and that the lift conforms to the relevant safety
standards and is safe for the user.

Fixed

❑   ACCESS SOLUTIONS ULTRA LIFT
The Ultra Lift is designed to give wheelchair users access
to public buildings with short flights of stairs or changes in
floor levels. It is driven by a hydraulic ram and the power
unit can be housed up to five metres from the lift. Suitable
for use in or out of doors the lift can be either free-
standing or wall-mounted.
   The manufacturer states that the lift meets the
requirements of BS 6440:1983 and the appropriate
international standards.
Construction It is made from epoxy- coated steel
consisting of a lifting platform and side panels with an
integral top gate. Access to the platform is up a ramp
which folds down/up automatically on use and acts as a
barrier when the lift is travelling. The gate at the top which
is operated manually, is spring loaded. It is fully
interlocking and must be properly closed or the lift will not
operate from the bottom. The lift travels at a speed of
0.8m^{sec}.
Controls Push buttons for up/down and stop are fitted to
the lift and at each level served.
Power supply Standard mains supply.
Safety A sensitive edge is fitted to the complete underside
of the lifting platform and to the leading edge of the
carriage. The ramp is also fitted with sensitive edges and
the lift will not operate if it is obstructed. The lifting
platform has an anti-slip floor covering. In the event of a
power failure the lift can be lowered manually by an
attendant using a simple hydraulic release valve in the
control box.
Servicing and maintenance Full UK service and
breakdown cover available from the manufacturer.
Dimensions
Platform   1254 x 872mm
Range of lift   1980mm
Lifting capacity   230kg

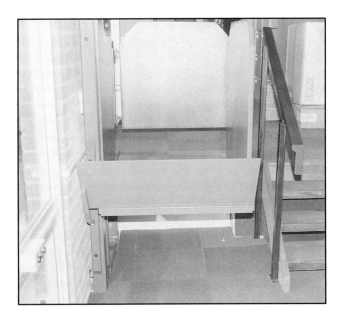

Obtainable from Access Solutions Ltd, a division of Llewellyn-SML Health Care Services, part of the Nesbit Evans Group.
Price guide £4500 including installation
Export available

☐ AMP STEPMASTER

This free-standing, short rise lifting platform is suitable for use in or out of doors in situations where one, two or three steps, up to a maximum height of 700mm, present a barrier to an ambulant disabled person or a wheelchair user.
When not in use the platform is left at ground level and this allows pedestrians to use the steps unhindered.

The unit is fitted to the base of the bottom step and the platform is operated by a hydraulic ram which actuates a scissor lift. The platform is enclosed with automatic doors and side panels which remain at ground level as the lift rises to protect the operating mechanism. The motor is fitted in a side panel and powered by mains electricity. The lift can be lowered in an emergency by opening a hydraulic release valve in the side panel.

At the lower level the platform is 60mm above the ground and access for the user is via a 500mm long fixed ramp. A shallow pit with suitable drainage can be provided to make the platform flush to the ground.

Controls Call/send buttons are situated at the top and bottom levels and in the carriage to suit the user.
Power supply Standard mains supply.
Servicing and maintenance A servicing contact can be arranged with the manufacturer who also provides full emergency cover.
Installation Carried out by the manufacturer.

Dimensions
Carriage   750 wide x 1200mm long
Range of lift   700mm
Lifting capacity   140kg

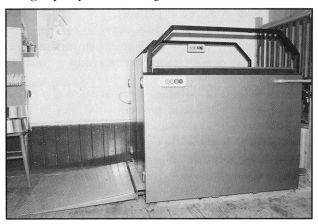

Obtainable from AMP Engineers Ltd
Price guide £2662
Export available

☐ AMP LIFTMASTER

The AMP Liftmaster is a larger version of the Stepmaster with the power to cover heights of up to 1100mm. It cannot be used to bridge steps so is only suitable for use against a vertical surface.
Dimensions
Platform   750 x 1500mm
Lifting capacity   140kg

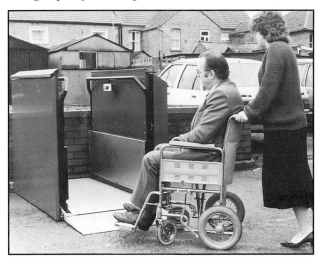

Obtainable from AMP Engineers Ltd
Price guide £2770
Export available

❑ AMP STEP-LIFT

This short rise vertical lift is suitable for installation where space is limited. The passenger is able to mount the platform either from the side or the end allowing the best use to be made of the space available.

It can be fitted in or out of doors and several platform sizes and a number of different ranges of lift are available. A bridging attachment to span up to three steps is another optional extra.

The lift is operated hydraulically by an electrically driven pump powered by the mains supply.

The lift moves up and down a track and the push button control panel is fitted into the top of this unit. A set of controls is also located on the upper level.

The platform is finished with a non-slip surface. A flap which folds up automatically to provide a safety barrier when the lift is moving is also available as an optional extra.

Servicing and maintenance Servicing can be arranged with the manufacturer who also provides full emergency cover.

Range of lift   1200mm

Lifting capacity   140kg

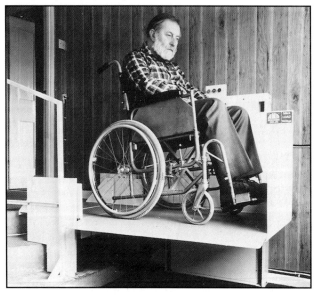

Obtainable from AMP Engineers Ltd

Price £1774

Export available

This is necessarily a brief report as the Step-lift was not seen or evaluated and the report is based on technical literature from the manufacturer.

❑ ASGO PORCH LIFT

This free-standing, short rise lifting platform is suitable for installation, in or out of doors, in a public or residential building, where steps present a barrier to the wheelchair user.

Four versions of the lift are available:

1) PL-LS   Standard version described here.

2) PL-LD   Light duty. Up to 1220mm lift. The ramp folds up automatically to act as a safety barrier.

3) PL-TG   Toe guard model. A telescopic wall rises with the lift to prevent a person or animal entering the space beneath the platform.

4) PL-EN   Fully enclosed model with shaft.

The lift is powered by a screw-drive system contained in the side panel and the motor incorporates a hand-winding mechanism for emergency use.

Construction The steel carriage is box-like with solid sides and door. The enamel finish is corrosion proof. The door is electrically interlocked on all models except the PL-LD. Access is up a ramp which can either be permanently fixed to the floor or fold up automatically as part of the platform when the lift is in use.

At the upper level the platform stops flush with the upper floor so no ramp is required. A step bridge is available as an extra if required.

The manufacturer states that the lift complies with BS 6440:1983.

Controls Call/send buttons are fitted at the top and bottom levels. Constant pressure toggle switches control the lift on the platform with a three second delay. Key switches are provided to prevent unauthorised use.

Power supply Standard mains supply.

Safety The under side of the platform is fitted with a sensitive panel.

Instructions for use The correct and safe use is demonstrated at the time of installation and written instructions are given to the purchaser.

Servicing and maintenance Can be arranged with the manufacturer who also provides a 24 hour breakdown service. Breakdown insurance is available on request.

Dimensions

Platform	Length	1070mm
	Width	900mm
Lifting capacity		225kg

Obtainable from ASGO Ltd
Price guide £2695
Export available

❏ GIMSON VERTIVATOR MODEL 401

This free-standing, short rise lifting platform is suitable for installation, in or out of doors, in a public or residential building, where steps prevent access for a wheelchair user.

Construction
The lift is powered by a screw-drive system contained in the side panel and the motor incorporates a hand-winding mechanism for emergency use.

At the lower level access is up a permanently fixed ramp, or as an alternative, a shallow pit can be constructed so that the platform sits flush with the ground.

At the upper level the platform stops flush with the upper floor so no ramp is required. A simple safety barrier rises and lowers automatically when the platform is in use. Two models are available to span different heights.

Controls Call/send buttons are fitted at the top and bottom levels. Constant pressure toggle switches control the lift on the platform and key switches are provided to prevent unauthorised use.

Power supply Standard mains supply.

Safety The under side of the platform is fitted with a sensitive panel. Simple safety barrier bars operate automatically at either side of the platform to protect the passenger when the lift is in use.

Instructions for use The correct and safe use is demonstrated at the time of installation and written instructions are given to the purchaser.

Servicing and maintenance Can be arranged with the manufacturer. A 24 hour breakdown service is provided.

Dimensions
Platform Length 1400mm
         Width 1000mm
Range of lift 401/130 1300mm
               401/180 1800mm
Lifting capacity 200kg

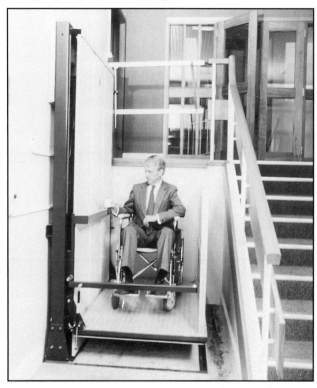

Obtainable from Gimson Tendercare Ltd.
Price guide   401/130 £7200
              401/180 £7400
Export available
This lift was not seen or evaluated and the report is based on the manufacturer's technical literature.

❏ HYMO HANDILIFT

The Hymo Handilift is for use in public buildings where short flights of stairs obstruct access for disabled people. The lift is free standing and powered by a hydraulic ram. Access to the platform at the lower level is through two sets of doors which open automatically after pressing a control button. This sequence is vulnerable to forcing by an impatient user and open to vandalism. Glass panels topped by handrails secure the user at each side of the platform. On reaching the upper landing a single gate opens automatically.

Before descending in the lift, the user should check the position of the wheelchair on the platform to prevent the danger of sitting straddled across the gap between landing and platform.

The platform has no ramp as the lift is installed with a pit so that on the ground it is flat with the floor.

The lift conforms to BS 5323:1980 regulations only.

Construction Made from epoxy coated steel the unit can be finished in a variety of colours to suit the surroundings. The platform has a ribbed rubber floor covering.

Controls Easy to operate push button controls are sited in a box on one of the side panels, and at each level with the option of key controls for security if required.

Servicing and maintenance Little maintenance is required. The hydraulic oil should be checked and replaced every two years. All bearings are lubrication free. A 24 hour call-out service is available from the manufacturer.

Installation Completed by the manufacturer in one day. Any basic building work should be done beforehand.

Range of lift Two options are available:

HX8-8 800mm and HXX8-15 1500mm

Lifting capacity   300kg

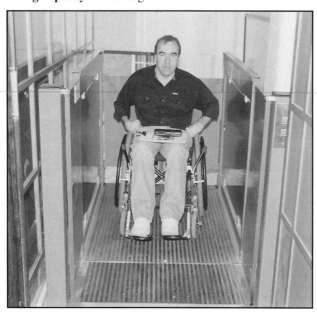

Obtainable from Hymo-Lift Ltd
Price on application
Export available

❑   HANDI PORCH LIFT

The Handi porch lift is for use in public or private buildings to enable wheelchair users to negotiate short flights of stairs, or changes in level up to 1830mm.

The lift is suitable for use in or out of doors and the installation can either be a free standing unit or fixed to a supporting wall. Two models are available to lift to different heights.

Construction The lift is made from galvanised steel. The motor and lifting mechanism are contained in the side panel. The carriage has solid walls and access is via an integral ramp which operates automatically and doubles as a safety barrier. Landing gates are available as optional extras.

Controls A constant pressure paddle switch which can be easily operated by the elbow is situated in the carriage.

Call stations are sited at each level. Key switches are fitted to prevent unauthorised use.

Power supply Standard mains supply.

Instructions for use Demonstrated at the time of installation.

Servicing and maintenance Regular servicing is advised and can be carried out by the manufacturer.

Dimensions

Carriage

Platform   1131 x 813mm

Height of side panels   1070mm

Height of ramp   60mm

Length of ramp   457mm

Range of lift Two models are available:

Up to 1220mm, Up to 1830mm

Lifting capacity   300kg

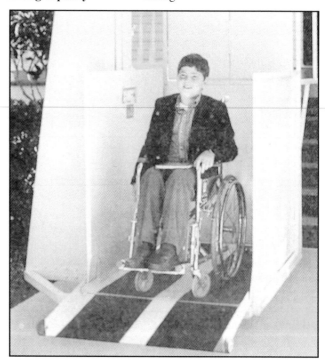

Obtainable from Project and Design Ltd
Price guide £2970
Export available

❑   TERRY MELODY

This lifting platform is primarily for use in or out of doors in public buildings where stairs impede access for the ambulant disabled or wheelchair user.

The lift is carried up and down by two actuator units adjacent to the end of the platform on the upper level served by the lift.

The manufacturer states that the lift complies with BS 6440:1983

Construction The frame of the lift is made from steel and the platform and ramps are aluminium with a non-slip finish. The sides of the carriage are tubular steel and the user is protected during lifting by safety bars at the side and a gate at the rear. This is operated by a release button on the frame. A second gate closes the upper access when the lift is at the lower level. Both these gates are electrically interlocked, but are manually operated.

Controls Call/send buttons are located on the upper and lower landings and on the carriage. Key switching for security purposes is available as an optional extra.

Power supply A constantly charged battery pack which enables the lift to operate normally during a power cut.

Safety The step at the upper level has a sensitive edge to prevent the lift descending with the wheelchair not squarely on the platform. The under surface of the platform is also fitted with a full sensitive surface.

Servicing and maintenance Can be arranged with the manufacturer.

Installation Carried out by the manufacturer.

Dimensions

Platform (internal)   730 x 1410mm
Range of lift   Up to 1800mm
Lifting capacity   225kg

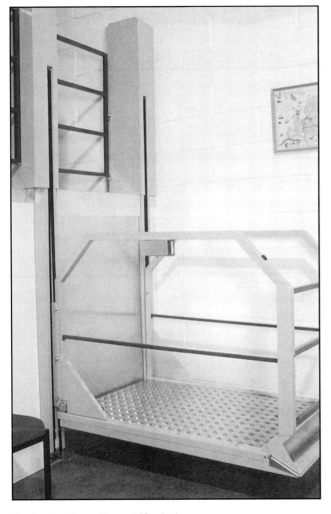

Obtainable from Terry Lifts Ltd
Price guide £4200
Export available

❑   TERRY MAXI-LIFT

Suitable for installation in or out of doors, the Terry Maxi-Lift provides access for disabled people to public buildings where a short flight of stairs is a barrier.

The manufacturer states that the lift conforms to BS 6440:1983.

Construction The lift comprises an aluminium platform with a chequer board non-slip finish and a handrail at each side. A ramp which functions automatically provides access to the platform, and doubles as a safety barrier when the lift is in motion. An optional barrier arm raises automatically when the lift reaches the upper level, and must close again before the lift can return to the lower level. If the barrier encounters any obstruction on lowering it stops until this is cleared. When not in use the platform should be returned to ground level. This happens automatically after three minutes if the lift has not been sent down manually.

The lifting force is provided by large bellows under the platform which are blown up by air from a small compressor unit. During lifting the platform is stabilised by scissor-arms fixed underneath it on either side. Blue vinyl roller blinds extend to cover and protect the lifting mechanism as the platform rises.

Controls Three single action push buttons, up, down and stop, are sited in a box fixed to one handrail of the carriage and at the top and bottom levels.

Power supply The compressor is powered by a small 650 watt motor, run from the mains supply, which can be housed in the barrier arm pedestal or conveniently close by. In the event of a power failure the platform can be lowered by an attendant using a valve sited on the platform.

Safety As the lift rises a small bar closes at the ramp end to stop a wheelchair rolling back.

Servicing and maintenance Carried out by the manufacturer.

Installation A concrete base is required.

Dimensions

Platform   1450 x 1020mm
Range of lift   900mm
Lifting capacity   225kg

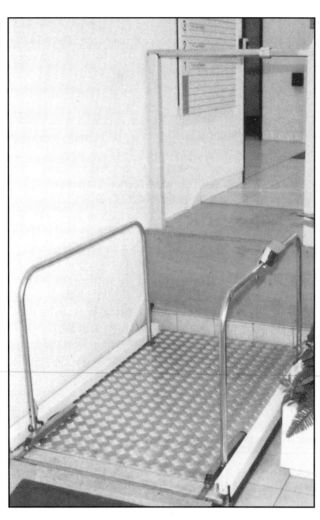

Obtainable from Terry Lifts Ltd
Price guide £1850
Export available

❏ TERRY STEP LIFT

Almost identical to the Terry Maxi Lift this variation is for use in doorways to bridge a height of up to three steps for a wheelchair user.

The original steps are removed during installation and replaced by special treads. As the platform rises it picks up these stair treads which make a solid platform to span the gap.

When not in use the platform is kept at ground level so that an ambulant person can use the stairs as normal.

Safety As the lift rises a small bar closes at the ramp end of the platform to stop the wheelchair rolling back.

Servicing and maintenance Can be arranged with the manufacturer.

Installation A concrete base is required.

Dimensions

Platform   1200 x 915mm
Range of lift   720mm

Obtainable from Terry Lifts Ltd
Price guide £1580
Export available

❏ WESSEX LIBERTY LIFT

The Liberty lift is primarily for use in public buildings to enable wheelchair users to negotiate short changes in level. The lift is suitable for use in or out of doors and the installation can either be a free standing unit or fixed to a supporting wall.

The manufacturer states that the lift complies with BS 6440:1983.

Construction The lift is made from steel with an polyester powder finish. The platform has half solid side panels topped with handrails and incorporates an automatic ramp which acts as a safety barrier when the lift is in use.

The hydraulic rams and tracks are built-in to the side panel and the pump motor can be sited up to three metres away from the lift.

The door at the top level is mechanically and electrically interlocked. When not in use the lift should be returned to the lower level. This option is available as an extra in some models.

Controls Push button controls are situated on the carriage with call stations at each level. Key switches can also be fitted to prevent unauthorised use. A lever on the control box opens the hydraulic valve in case of emergency.

Power supply Standard mains supply.

Installation A level base is required to site the lift.

Instructions for use Demonstrated at the time of installation. Written instruction are given to the user.

Servicing and maintenance Regular servicing is advised and can be managed by the manufacturer.

Dimensions   1700 x 1055mm

Total width from wall   1150mm
Height of ramp   60mm

Range of lift   1980mm subject to approval this height can be exceeded.
Lifting capacity   230kg

Obtainable from Wessex Medical Equipment Co Ltd
Price guide Basic model £4900
Export available

Portable

❏ BROOKS PORTALIFT

The Portalift is designed to help people who have difficulty in getting up and down caravan steps or could be used as a temporary step lift in some situations. It is powered by a 12v battery and the constant pressure toggle control is mounted on the handgrip. It is easily dismantled without tools and may be stored in a car boot. The base of the lift is flat and some method will have to be found to level it on uneven ground. Adjustable top and bottom limit switches are provided enabling the lift to stop at the required step height every time. The non-slip lifting platform tends to tilt backwards slightly under load but remains stable even at its full height.

Dimensions

Platform width	480mm
Platform length	350mm
Height of handle above platform	910mm
Total weight of lift excluding battery	28kg
Weight of heaviest component	16kg
Range of lift	20 - 610mm
Lifting capacity	115kg

Obtainable from Brooks Stairlifts Ltd
Price guide £790 (battery not included)
Export available

❏ QUIKLIFT

The Quiklift is a portable aid for transferring wheelchair passengers in and out of vehicles which are not fitted with a permanent wheelchair lift. It provides an alternative to pushing wheelchairs up steep ramps and requires little effort to fold-up for storage in the vehicle. The Quiklift is simply lifted from the vehicle and manoeuvred into position on its integral wheels ready for use. As the lift rises in an arc rather than vertically it is advisable to try it out empty for the first time to find out the best position to site it. It is essential that the lift comes to a stop over and slightly above the edge of the vehicle floor, allowing for some depression as the wheelchair is pushed on or off the platform.

The Quiklift is best used on flat level ground; on uneven ground it will be necessary to wedge the stabilizer supports to balance the lift. For loading at the side of heavily cambered roads the lift may become unstable at its maximum height.

Construction The lift is a hydraulic jack controlled by a foot-operated release valve. Two ramps are provided for access which also double as a safety feature to stop the wheelchair rolling back during lifting.

Optional extras Centre platform and handrail for lifting ambulant persons.

Dimensions
Folded   Length 1140mm, Width 310mm, Height 300mm
Overall weight   24kg
Lifting capacity   200kg
Maximum lift of tracks from ground   630mm (680mm to order)
Height of tracks from ground when lowered   120mm

Obtainable from   C N Unwin Ltd
Price guide   £466
Centre platform £59
Handrail £24
Export available

CARRYING CHAIRS

❏   TRANS-SIT SEAT

When two helpers are available it may sometimes be quicker and easier to transfer a person from a wheelchair in a carry seat or sling. Examples are on stairs, over rough ground, in public transport and public places, and in homes where corridors or doorways are narrow.

Construction   The Trans-sit seat, which is made of washable, synthetic fabric, has a reinforced and padded backrest and seat and is fitted with strap handles encased in polythene tubes to make them comfortable to the carriers. An easily managed safety belt is supplied. The helpers, preferably of similar height, should walk one on each side of the person. Webbing straps are incorporated into the backrest so that helpers can walk in line through a doorway.

Optional extras   Include shoulder straps, easily attached to 'D' rings on the seat, and worn diagonally across the helpers' bodies during long or heavy lifts. A nylon cover is also available. The seat can be folded flat for storage.

Instructions for use   Are provided by the manufacturer.

Dimensions
Large   470 x 380 x 380mm
Small   390 x 330 x 330mm
Folded size   100 x 460mm
Weight   0.9kg
Maximum load capacity   108kg

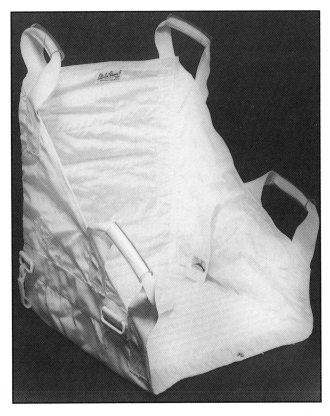

Obtainable from Ellis Son + Paramore
Price guide £37
Export available

❏ COMPACT CARRYING CHAIR

Primarily designed for ambulance work the Compact Carrying Chair can be used as a transit chair or for evacuation in an emergency. Two people will be needed if stairs have to be negotiated.

Construction The chair is made of a tubular steel with a bright nickle plate finish. It runs on two 178mm wheels with nylon strips under the footrest. The carrying handles are an integral part of the frame. The seat and backrest are made from one-piece of flame resistant vinyl-coated nylon material which can be replaced when necessary. The chair is fitted with a black nylon webbing safety belt and an ankle strap to stop the feet falling back when the chair is tipped up.

Transport and storage The chair folds flat in one easy movement and packs into a PVC carrying bag with wall hooks.

Dimensions

Chair folded Length   780mm
              Width   410mm
              Depth   260mm
Diameter of wheels   175mm
Weight   8kg
Maximum load   114kg

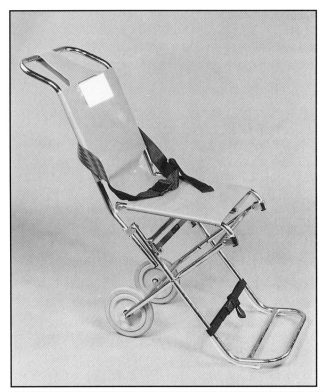

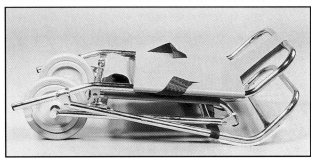

Obtainable from FW Equipment Co Ltd
Price guide £120
Export available

❏ MOBYLE CARRYING CHAIR MK4

Primarily designed for ambulance work the Mobyle MK4 can be used as a transit chair or for evacuation in an emergency. Two people will be needed if stairs have to be negotiated.

Construction The chair is made of tubular steel, with a cream epoxy finish. It runs on four wheels, and the footrest and carrying handles are an integral part of the frame. The seat and backrest are made of flame resistant vinyl-coated nylon material which can be replaced when necessary. The chair is fitted with a black nylon webbing safety belt.

Transport and storage The whole chair folds flat.

Dimensions

Chair folded Length   1230mm
              Width   400mm
              Depth   190mm

Diameter of wheels   125mm
Weight   10.5kg
Maximum load   114g

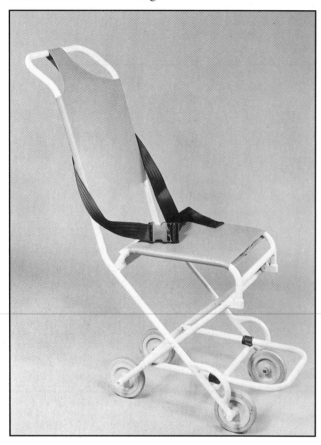

Obtainable from FW Equipment Co Ltd
Price guide £75
Export available

❏   GIMSON CARRYDOWN

The Gimson Carrydown is intended specifically for the
emergency evacuation of disabled people from the upper
floors of a building. It is easily controlled from behind by
one person and it is recommended that potential users
should practise to become familiar with its use.

Construction It is solidly built of red coated tubular steel
with a blue canvas seat incorporating chest and leg
restraining belts and a foldaway footrest, which gives extra
reassurance to the passenger while travelling downstairs.

Brakes The chair includes a dual braking system. The
handbrake is permanently on until released by a handle on
the push bar, so the chair is safe if unattended. As the chair
moves down the stairs on two heavy duty rubber tracks an
integral centripetal braking system controls the speed of
descent to 60m^{min} which is adequate for evacuation.

Manoeuvrability On smooth ground the chair is
manoeuvred by two sets of castors on each side of the
tracks. These are spring-linked and pivoted and there is a
danger that they might flip over while travelling down the
stairs, and not be in the right position to move when
reaching the flat ground at the bottom of the stairs. In an
emergency this may cause an obstruction for other people
evacuating the building.

The chair will travel safely on stairs up to 55° but as the
two tracks are permanently linked by the axles it is not
suitable for curved or carpeted stairways, and the overall
length of the chair makes it difficult to negotiate corners on
narrow stairs. It would be difficult to carry it upstairs to
retrieve a second person during an evacuation.

Storage The chair folds flat for storage and is easily
opened in one manoeuvre. It is very heavy and an awkward
shape so it should be stored ready for use close to where it
may be needed.

Dimensions

Overall length   1450mm
Width   450mm
Seat height   400mm
Knee to footrest 450mm

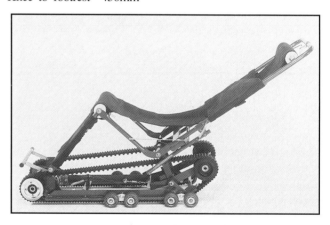

Obtainable from   Gimson Tendercare Ltd
Price guide £875
Export available

❑ EVAC + CHAIR 300

The Paraid Evac chair is made specifically for evacuation from a building in an emergency. It is easy to use once the technique has been mastered, and training in this should be given as a regular part of all fire drills.

The chair slides downstairs on two continuous loop friction V-shaped belts. This action automatically slows the descent of the passenger down to a reasonable pace regardless of his weight. Once on smooth ground the chair is easy to manoeuvre.

The chair is not suitable for curved stairs or those steeper than 38°, but is fine on narrow stairs.

Since the chair does not travel upstairs it is not really suitable for evacuations from basements or split level premises. To use this chair in such situations two people are needed to lift it, using the grab rail which is supplied as an optional extra, and physically carry the person up the stairs.

Two simple 152mm diameter polythene wheels are fitted to the base of the frame so the chair can be pushed across a flat surface.

Construction The chair is light and simple in construction and folds up neatly for storage on a wall at the top of the stairs. The frame is made from 25mm aluminium tubing with a cupped-shaped flame resistant vinyl-coated nylon seat. A 25mm webbed nylon lap safety belt and head/torso restraint are supplied with the chair. Alternatively two other 50mm belts are available as optional extras.

Optional extras

A kickstand to steady the chair while making a transfer.

A seat depth adjuster to alter the angle of the seat for those users finding the cup-shape uncomfortable.

Although supplied as extras these items are needed to make the chair fully versatile in all situations.

Alternative friction belts are available and will be specified for each stairway by a Paraid Representative.

Other optional extras include: 50mm safety harness, cushion wheels for use on uneven surfaces and a dust cover.

Dimensions

Size of folded chair 965mm high x 521mm wide x 203mm thick

Weight of chair	6.5kg
Maximum load	140kg

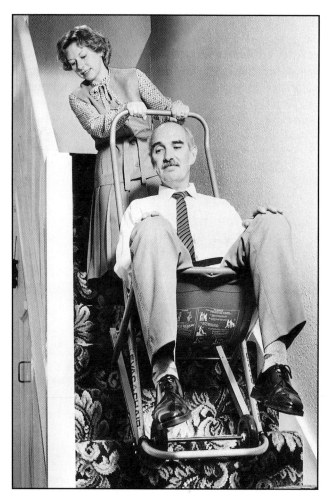

Obtainable from Paraid
Price guide Standard chair £385
50mm harness £26
Dust cover £45 (F/R grade)
Grab handle £27
Cushion wheels £28
Kick stand £44
Seat depth adjuster £20
Maintenance, retraining and service Annual contract with the manufacturer; £64 per chair
Export available

❏   SCOTTISH WAR BLINDED CARRY CHAIR

The tubular steel frame with heavy quality Lionide seat and back fits into a standard wheelchair and provides firm support during transfer. The chair can be carried by two people walking on either side, or by two people walking in line, the front person using the special handles, when mounting a staircase or boarding a plane. Special sizes can be made to order at extra cost.

Obtainable from Scottish War Blinded
Price guide £17
Export available

SELECT BIBLIOGRAPHY

Anon (1984) *Lifting patients.* The Chartered Society of Physiotherapy, London. UK.

Bell R. (1984) *Patient lifting devices in hospitals.* Croom Helm. Beckenham, Kent, UK.

Bell F. (1987) Ergonomic aspects of equipment. *International Journal of Nursing Studies.* **24** (4) 331-337.

Department of Health and Social Security (1984) *Guidelines for the lifting of patients in the Health Service.* HMSO, London. UK.

Farmer P. (1987) Mechanical aids. *Nursing Times*; **82**: (28): 36-37.

Finlay P.A. (1988) *Applications for advanced robotics in medicine and health care.* Fulmer Research Ltd, Slough, UK.

Green W. & McCay G. (1990) *Training package for prevention of back injury.* Oxfordshire Health Authority. Oxford. UK.

Harris C. & Mayfield W. (1983) *Selecting easy chairs for elderly and disabled people.* Institute for Consumer Ergonomics. London. UK.

Health Services Advisory Committee (1984) *The lifting of patients in the Health Service.* DHSS, HMSO, London. UK. pp9.

Health and Safety Commission (1989) Report. *Handling loads at work: Proposals for regulations and guidance.* Health and Safety Commission. London. UK. pp40.

Hearn V. (1988) Safe lifting and moving for nurse and patient. *Nursing* **3** (30) 9-12.

Hollis M. (1985) *Safer lifting for patient care.* 2nd ed. Blackwells Scientific Publications, Oxford. UK.

Leskinen T.P.J., Stahlhammar H.R., Kuorinka T.A.A. & Troup J.D.G. (1983) A dynamic analysis of spinal compression with different lifting techniques. *Ergonomics* **26** (6): 595-604.

Lloyd P. (1986) Handle with care. *Nursing Times* November 19, pp 33-35.

Lloyd P., Osborne C., Tarling C. & Troup. (1987) *The handling of patients: A guide for nurse managers.* 2nd ed. Back Pain Association in collaboration with Royal College of Nursing, London. UK.

Pheasant S. (1987) Some anthropmetric aspects of workstation design. *International Journal Nursing Studies* **24** (4) 291-298

Ransome H. (1981) Keeping the elderly moving in old people's homes: *C.P.A. Homes advice broadsheet 7.* Centre for Policy on Ageing. London. UK.

Royal College of Nursing Advisory Panel on Back Pain in Nurses. (1987) *Guidance on the handling of patients in hospital and the community.* 2nd ed. Royal College of Nursing of the United Kingdom. London. UK.

Royal College of Nursing (1988) *An instructor's syllabus for handling and moving patients.* The Royal College of Nursing Advisory Panel on Back Pain in Nurses. London. UK.

Saywell R.M., Woods J.R., Holmes G.L., Sechrist M.E and Nyhuis A.W. (1987) Reducing the cost of patient transfers. *JONA* **17** (7&8) 11-19.

Skarplik C. (1988) Patient handling in the community. *Nursing* **3** (30) 13-16.

Stowe J. (1988) *Guide to the selection of stairlifts.* Rheumatism and Rehabilitation Research Unit, Leeds. UK. (Obtainable from Mrs J Stowe see *Addresses.*)

Stubbs D.A., Buckle P.W., Hudson M.P., Rivers P.M. & Worrington C.J. (1983) Back pain in the nursing profession. Part 1 Epidemiology and pilot methodology. *Ergonomics;* **26**: 755-765.

Tarling C. (1980) *Hoists and their use.* William Heinemann Medical Books. London. UK. pp. 318.

Troup J.G.D. and Edwards F.C. (1985) Review: *Manual handling and lifting.* Part 1. Health and Safety Executive. HMSO. London. UK. pp1-10.

Troup J.D.G., Leskinen T.P.J., Stahlhammar H.R. & Kuominka T.A.A. (1983) A comparison of intraabdominal pressure increases, hip and lumbar vertebral compression in different lifting techniques. *Human Factors* **25** (5): 517-525.

Waters K. (1988) Every day aids and appliances. Hoists. *British Medical Journal* **296** 1114-1117.

Wood B.D. (1986) *Final report on Domestic Stairlifts.* Consumer Protection Department, South Yorkshire County Council, Sheffield, UK. March 1986.

Videman T., Ranhala H., Asp S., Linstrom K., Cedercrentz G., Kamppi M. & Troup J.D.G. (1989) Patient-handling skill, Back injuries and back pain. A intervention study in nursing. *Spine* **14** (2).

Films/Videos

Multiple Sclerosis Society. *Moving and lifting the disabled person.* Woodhead Faulkner Ltd. MS Society, 25 Effie Rd, London SW6 1EE. UK.

Central Independent Television (1989) *Link on lifting: Techniques for lifting and moving disabled people.* Distributed by R Nathanson, MRS, 8 Morocco St, London SE1 3HB. UK.

ADDRESSES

A

AMP Engineers Ltd   **105, 106, 117, 118**
Unit 2B, Portland Industrial Estate, Arlesey, Beds
SG15 6SG
Tel. 0462 730443

AMP Services   **37**
34a Vale Rd, Portslade, Brighton BN4 1GG
Tel. 0273 418918

Access Solutions Ltd   **44, 116**
4 Davenport Gate, West Portway Industrial Estate,
Andover, Hants SP10 3SQ
Tel. 0264 334434   Fax. 0264 334330

Agility Sports Products Ltd   **3, 5, 6**
112 Banstead Rd, Carshalton Beeches, Surrey SM5 3NH
Tel. 081-642 7683/8948

Arjo Mecanaids Ltd   **21, 22, 29, 33, 37, 47, 50, 51, 53, 59,
60, 61, 77**
St Catherine St, Gloucester GL1 2SL
Tel. 0452 500200   Fax. 0452 25207

Asgo Ltd   **89, 118**
22b Hawthorne Rd, Lottbridge Drive, Eastbourne,
Sussex BN23 6PZ
Tel. 0323 38228   Fax. 0323 38241

Atlantic Medical Ltd   **113**
Winchmore House, 12-15 Fetter Lane, Loncon
EC4A 1BR
Tel. 071-583 9481

Autochair   **81**
Millford Lane, Bakewell, Derbys DE4 1DX
Tel. 0629 813493

B

Baronmead International Ltd   **103**
Bank Building, 39 Elmer Rd, Middleton-on-Sea, West
Sussex PO22 6DZ
Tel. 0243 586692   Fax. 0243 585065

Bell, FM, Ltd   **55, 113**
Tuley St, Manchester M11 2DY
Tel. 061-223 9144

Bright Home Products   **98**
7 Lancaster Rd, Carnaby Industrial Estate, Bridlington
YO15 3QY
Tel. 0262 606376/675564

British Elevators Ltd   **113**
Unit 13, Roman Industrial Estate, Tait Rd, Croydon,
Surrey CR0 2DT
Tel. 081-665 6555   Fax. 081-684 5647

Brooks Stairlifts Ltd   **90, 91, 107, 123**
Westminster Industrial Estate, Station Rd, North
Hykeham, Lincoln LN6 3QY
Tel. 0522 500288   Fax. 0522 500448

Burvill, S, & Son   **80**
Primrose Rd, Hersham, Surrey KT12 5JD
Tel. 0932 221124/227454

Buttboard   **16**
33 Leighton St, West Croydon, Surrey CR0 3SB
Tel. 081-688 7322

C

Carters, (J & A), Ltd   **9, 23, 33, 41, 42, 62, 63**
White Horse Business Park, North Bradley, Trowbridge,
Wilts BA14 0XA
Tel. 0225 751901   Fax. 0225 751629

Chattanooga UK Ltd   **4, 5, 7**
Goods Rd, Belper, Derbys DE5 1UU
Tel. 0773 826993   Fax. 0773 820396

Centre for Accessible Environments   **84**
35 Great Smith St, London SW1P 3BJ
Tel. 071-222 7980

Chiltern Medical Developments (Equipment) Ltd   **42, 43,
48, 64, 65**
Chiltern House, Wedgewood Rd, Bicester, Oxon OX6
7UL
Tel. 0869 246470   Fax. 0869 252866

D

Daws, Mrs J V   **1**
Co-ordinator of Continuing Education, Nurse Education
Centre, Kent and Canterbury Hospital, Canterbury, Kent
CT1 3NG

DIAL UK   **viii**
Park Lodge, St Catherine's Hospital, Tickhill Rd, Balby,
Doncaster, South Yorks DN4 8QN
Tel. 0302 310123

Disability Alliance ERA   **ix**
25 Denmark St, London WC2H 8NJ
Tel. 071-240 0806

Disability Scotland   **viii**
Princes House, 5 Shandwick Place, Edinburgh EH2 4RG
Tel. 031-229 8632

Disabled Living Centres   **viii**
Belfast
Disabled Living Centre, Regional Disablement Services,
Musgrave Park Hospital, Stockman's Lane,
Belfast BT9 7JB
Tel. 0232 669501 ext 565
Birmingham
Disabled Living Centre, 260 Broad St, Birmingham
B1 2HF
Tel. 021-643 0980

Caerphilly
Resources (Aids & Equipment) Centre, Wales Council
for the Disabled, 'Llys Ifor', Crescent Rd, Caerphilly,
Mid Glam CF8 3SL
Tel. 0222 887325/6/7

Cardiff
The Demonstration Aids Centre, The Lodge, Rookwood
Hospital, Llandaff, Cardiff, South Glam CS5 2YN
Tel. 0222 566281 ext 5166

Edinburgh
Disabled Living Centre, Astley Ainslie Hospital, Grange
Loan, Edinburgh EH9 2HL
Tel. 031-447 6271

Exeter
Independent Living Centre, St Loye's School of
Occupational Therapy, Millbrook House, Topsham Rd,
Exeter EX2 6ES
Tel. 0392 59260

Leeds
The William Merritt Disabled Living Centre, St Mary's
Hospital, Greenhill Rd, Leeds SL12 3QE
Tel. 0532 793140

Leicester
Disabled Living Centre, Medical Aids Department, 76
Clarendon Park Rd, Leicester LE2 3AD
Tel. 0533 700747

Liverpool
Merseyside Centre for Independent Living, Youens
Way, East Prescott Rd, Liverpool L14 2EP
Tel. 051-228 9221

London
Disabled Living Foundation, Equipment Centre, 380/
384 Harrow Rd, London W9 2HU
Tel. 071-289 6111

Manchester
Disabled Living Centre, Disabled Living Services,
Redbank House, 4 St Chad's St, Cheetham, Manchester
M8 8QA
Tel. 061-832 3678

Newcastle upon Tyne
Council for the Disabled, The Dene Centre, Castles
Farm Rd, Newcastle upon Tyne NE3 1PH
Tel. 091-284 0480

Nottingham
Resource Centre for the Disabled, Lenton Business
Centre, Lenton Boulevard, Nottingham NG7 2BY
Tel. 0602 420391

Southampton
Aid and Equipment Centre, Southampton General
Hospital, Tremona Rd, Southampton SO9 4XY
Tel. 0703 777222 ext 3414

Stockport
Disabled Living Centre, Stockport Area Health
Authority, St Thomas' Hospital, Shawheath, Stockport
SK3 8BL
Tel. 061-419 4476

Swindon
Centre for Disabled Living, The Hawthorn Centre,
Cricklade Rd, Swindon, Wilts SN2 1AF
Tel. 0793 643966

Aberdeen
Hillylands Disabled Living Centre, Croft Rd, Mastrick,
Aberdeen AB2 6RB
Tel. 0224 685247

Aylesbury
Stoke Mandeville Independent Living Exhibition, Stoke
Mandeville Hospital, Mandeville Rd, Aylesbury, Bucks
HP21 8AL
Tel. 0296 84111 ext 3114

Blackpool
Disabled Living Centre, 8 Queen St, Blackpool, Lancs
FY1 1PD
Tel. 0253 21084 ext 1 or 4

Bodelwyddan
North Wales Resource Centre for Disabled People, Glan
Clywd Hospital, Bodelwyddan, Clwyd LL18 5UJ
Tel. 0745 583910

Braintree
Independent Living Advice Centre, Black Notley
Hospital, Braintree, Essex CN7 8NF
Tel. 0376 21068

Colchester
Disabled Living Centre, Occupational Therapy Dept.,
Colchester General Hospital, Colchester, Essex CO4 5JL
Tel. 0206 853535 ext 1 or 4

Dudley
Disabled Living Centre, 1 St Giles' St, Netherton,
Dudley, West Midlands DY2 OPR
Tel. 0384 237034

Huddersfield
Disabled Living Centre, Kirkless Social Services, Unit 6
Silvercourt Trading Estate, Silver St, Huddersfield, West
Yorks HD5 9HE
Tel. 0484 518809

Hull
St Hilda House, National Demosntration Centre,
Kingston General Hospital, Beverley Rd, Hull HU3 1UR
Tel. 0482 28631 ext 332

Inverness
Disabled Living Centre, Raigmore Hospital, Inverness
IV2 2UJ
Tel. 0463 234151 ext 293

Macclesfield
Centre for Disabled Living, Macclesfield District
General Hospital, Macclesfield, Cheshire SK10 3BL
Tel. 0625 21000

Middlesbrough
Department of Rehabilitation, Middlesbrough General
Hospital, Ayresome Green Lane, Middlesbrough,
Cleveland TS5 5AZ
Tel. 0642 850222 ext 158

Newcastle-Under-Lyme
Independent Living Centre, (The Arts Centre),
Brampton Park, Newcastle-Under-Lyme, Staffs ST5
0QP
Tel. 0782 634949

Paisley
Disability Centre for Independent Living, Community
Services Centre, Queen St, Paisley PA1 2TU
Tel. 041-887 0597

Portsmouth
Disabled Living Centre, The Frank Sorrell Centre,
Prince Albert Rd, Eastney, Portsmouth PO4 9HR
Tel. 0705 737174

Swansea
Disabled Living Association Centre, St John's Rd,
Manselton, Swansea SA5 8PC
Tel. 0792 580161

Welwyn Garden City
The Woodside Centre, The Commons, Welwyn Garden
City, Herts AL7 4DD
Tel. 0707 324581

Disabled Living Centres Council   **ix**
380/384 Harrow Rd, London W9 2HU
Tel. 071-266 2059

Disabled Living Foundation   **iii,viii**
380/384 Harrow Rd, London W9 2HU
Tel. 071-289 6111

E

Egerton Hospital Equipment Ltd   **19**
Farwig Lane, Bromley, Kent BR1 3TU
Tel. 081-460 9878   Fax. 081-464 3266

Ellis Son + Paramore   **124**
Spring St Works, Sheffield, South Yorks S3 8PB
Tel. 0742 738921   Fax. 0742 754864

F

FW Equipment Co Ltd   **125**
Hanworth Rd, Low Moor, Bradford, Yorks BD12 0SG
Tel. 0274 601121   0274 600389

G

Gimson Tendercare Ltd   **86, 92, 99, 100, 102, 107, 119, 126**
62 Boston Rd, Beaumont Leys, Leicester LE4 1AZ
Tel. 0533 366779   Fax. 0533 366198

Gough & Company (Hanley) Ltd   **113**
Clough St, Hanley, Stoke on Trent, Staffs ST1 4AP
Tel. 0782 208708   Fax. 0782 202452

Grorud Bison Bede Ltd   **96**
Castleside Industrial Estate, Consett, Co Durham
DH8 8JB
Tel. 0207 590149/508308   Fax. 0207 503097

H

Hammond & Champness Ltd   **113**
159/173 St John St, London EC1V 4JQ
Tel. 071-253 2044

Health and Comfort Ltd   **18**
PO Box 15, Westbury, Wilts BA13 4LS
Tel. 0373 822394   Fax. 0373 858478

Holborn Surgical Instrument Company   **31**
Dolphin Works, Margate Rd, Broadstairs, Kent
CT10 2QQ
Tel. 0843 296666

Hollick, Christina   **75**
Top of the Hill, Shantock Lane, Bovingdon,
Herts HP3 0NG
Tel. 0442 832264

Homecraft Supplies Ltd   **7, 16, 19**
Low Moor Estate, Kirkby-in-Ashfield, Notts NG17 7JZ
Tel. 0623 754047   Fax. 0623 755585

Hoskins Ltd   **74**
Upper Trinity St, Birmingham B9 4EQ
Tel. 021-766 7404   Fax. 021-766 8166

Hymo-Lift Ltd   **119**
Scaldwell Rd, Brixworth, Northants NN6 9EN
Tel. 0604 880724   Fax. 0604 881314

J

Jarvis Manufacturing Co   **3**
116 Seaside, Eastbourne, East Sussex BN22 7QP
Tel. 0323 411993

L

Langham Products   **14, 16**
Unit 26, Bennetts Field Trading Estate, Wincanton,
Somerset BA9 9DT
Tel. 0963 33869   Fax. 0963 34651

Lift and Hoist Co Ltd   **113**
1 Queens Row, Southwark, London SE17 2PX
Tel. 071-703 8383   Fax. 071-708 5230

Llewellyn-SML Health Care Services   **10, 11, 24, 25, 53, 56, 65, 66, 67**
1 Regent Rd, City, Liverpool L3 7BX
Tel. 051-236 5311   Fax. 051-236 4698

M

Manor Lifts Ltd   **113**
22a Sefton St, Litherland, Liverpool L21 7LB
Tel. 051-928 9222

Masterpeace Products Ltd   **10**
Tormen House, Booth Hill Lane, Oldham, Lancs
OL1 2PH
Tel. 061-624 2041   Fax. 061-627 0464

Medeci Rehab Ltd   **12**
  The Research Unit, Warley Hospital, Brentwood, Essex
  CM14 5HQ
  Tel. 0277 212637
MEDesign Ltd   **3, 8**
  Clock Tower Works, Railway St, Southport, Merseyside
  PR8 5BB
  Tel. 0704 542373   Fax. 0704 545214

N

Nesbit Evans, J, & Co Ltd   **6, 26, 27, 67**
  Unit 8, Woods Bank Trading Estate, Woden Rd West,
  Wednesbury, West Midlands WS10 7BL
  Tel. 021-556 1511   Fax. 021-502 2092
Nopac Healthcare Services Ltd   **28**
  74 Ongar Rd, Brentwood, Essex CM15 9AX
  Tel. 0277 373209
Northern Ireland Council on Disability   **viii**
  2 Annadale Avenue, Belfast BT7 3JR
  Tel. 0232 491011
Nottingham Rehab Ltd   **7, 9, 18**
  Ludlow Hill Rd, West Bridgford, Nottingham NG2 6HD
  Tel. 0602 452345   Fax. 0602 452124

P

Paraid   **127**
  Weston Lane, Greet, Birmingham B11 3RS
  Tel. 021-706 6744   Fax. 021-706 6746
Parker Bath Developments Ltd   **39, 51**
  Queensway, Stem Lane, New Milton, Hants BH25 5NN
  Tel. 0425 622287   Fax. 0425 621959
Parry, T, (Car Hoists)   **82**
  Church Avenue, Bangor-Is-y-Coed, Wrexham, Clwyd
  LL13 0AF
  Tel. 0978 780279
Payne, FJ, (Manufacturing) Ltd   **28, 29, 32, 36, 53, 55, 68,
  69, 70, 78, 79**
  Stanton Harcourt Rd, Eynsham, Oxford OX8 1JT
  Tel. 0865 881881   Fax. 0865 882878
Pear Associates Ltd   **4, 6, 16**
  Iroko House, Bridge St, Derby DE1 3LB
  Tel. 0332 291851
Pollock, J   **107**
  Designs for the Disabled Ltd, 8A Kilroot Park, Carrick
  Fergus, Co Antrim, Northern Ireland BT38 7PR
Power-Tech (UK) Ltd   **38**
  Unit 8C, Ford Airfield Industrial Estate, Arundel, West
  Sussex BN18 0HY
  Tel. 0903 713227   Fax. 0903 731010
Project & Design Ltd   **87, 93, 101, 120**
  72 Jay Avenue, Teesside Industrial Estate, Thornaby,
  Stockton-on-Tees, Cleveland TS17 9LZ
  Tel. 0642 750707   Fax. 0642 750709

R

Ratcliffe Care Ltd   **108**
  Barn Way, Lodge Farm Industrial Estate, Harlestone Rd,
  Northampton NN5 7UW
  Tel. 0604 582528   Fax. 0604 587597
Rehabilitation Engineering Unit   **16**
  Chailey Heritage, North Chailey, Nr Lewes, East Sussex
  BN8 4EF
  Tel. 081-572 2112
REMAP (Technical Equipment for Disabled People)   **ix**
  25 Mortimer St, London W1N 8AB
  Tel. 071-637 5400
Roma Medical Aids Ltd   **11**
  Llandow Industrial Estate, Nr Cowbridge, South Glam
  CF7 7PB
  Tel. 0446 774519
Royal Association for Disability and Rehabilitation
  (RADAR)   **ix**
  25 Mortimer St, London W1N 8AB
  Tel. 071-637 5400

S

Sageka   **103**
  12 avenue des Pres, 78180 Montigny-Le-Bretonneux,
  France
Samson Products (Dorset) Ltd   **34**
  19 Willis Way, Fleet Industrial Estate, Poole, Dorset
  BH12 4AP
  Tel. 0202 666055
Scottish War Blinded   **128**
  Linburn, Wilkieston, Kirknewton, Midlothian, Scotland
  EH27 8DU
  Tel. 031-333 1369
Southern Lift Co Ltd   **45, 56, 70, 71**
  Units 1-6, 362B Spring Rd, Sholing, Southampton,
  Hants SO2 7PB
  Tel. 0703 685727   Fax. 0703 685761
Spencer, James, & Co Ltd   **11, 12**
  Moor Rd Works, Leeds LS6 4BH
  Tel. 0532 785837   Fax. 0532 743956
Stannah Stairlifts Ltd   **88, 97, 101, 113**
  Watt Close, East Portway, Andover, Hants SP10 3SD
  Tel. 0264 332244   Fax. 0264 53943
Stowe J, Mrs   **129**
  Head Research Occupational Therapist, Rheumatology
  and Rehabilitation Research Unit, School of Medicine,
  36 Clarendon Rd, Leeds LS2 9PJ
Sunrise Medical Ltd   **79, 93, 94, 95, 109, 110**
  Fens Pool Avenue, Brierley Hill, West Midlands
  DY5 1QA
  Tel. 0384 480480   Fax. 0384 480345

T

Terry Lifts Ltd **111, 115, 120, 121, 122**
Unit 6, Wolfe Close, Parkgate Industrial Estate,
Knutsford, Cheshire WA16 8XJ
Tel. 0565 50376/7 or 3211   Fax. 0565 55062

U

Unit Installations **16**
Unit 6, Horseley Fields Trading Estate, Horseley Fields,
Wolverhampton
Tel. 0902 351041

Unwin, CN, Ltd **123**
Lufton, Yeovil, Somerset BA22 8SZ
Tel. 0935 75359   Fax. 0935 31229

V

Velmore Ltd **76**
55 Swandene, Pagham, West Wussex PO21 4UR
Tel. 0243 267424

W

Wales Council for the Disabled **viii**
'Llys Ifor', Crescent Rd, Caerphilly CF8 1XL
Tel. 0222 887325

Wessex Medical Equipment Co Ltd **46, 47, 57, 71, 72, 73,
74, 96, 112, 113, 114, 122**
Budds Lane, Romsey, Hants SO51 0HA
Tel. 0794 830303   Fax. 0794 512621

INDEX

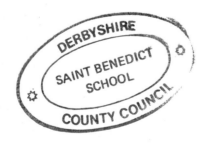